LUNACY

JOHN KRUTH

LUNACY

THE CURIOUS PHENOMENON
OF PINK FLOYD'S
DARK SIDE OF THE MOON,
50 YEARS ON

Backbeat
Books

Published by Backbeat Books
An imprint of Globe Pequot, the trade division of
The Rowman & Littlefield Publishing Group, Inc.
4501 Forbes Blvd., Ste. 200
Lanham, MD 20706
www.rowman.com

Distributed by NATIONAL BOOK NETWORK

Cover design by Sally Rinehart
Book design by Tom Seabrook

Library of Congress Cataloging-in-Publication Data:
Names: Kruth, John, author.
Title: Lunacy : the curious phenomenon of Pink Floyd's
Dark side of the moon, 50 years on / John Kruth.
Description: Essex, Connecticut : Backbeat, 2023. |
Includes bibliographical references and index.
Identifiers: LCCN 2022044297 (print) | LCCN 2022044298 (ebook) |
ISBN 9781493067169 (paperback) | ISBN 9781493067176 (ebook)
Subjects: LCSH: Pink Floyd (Musical group). Dark side of the
moon. | Rock music--1971-1980--History and criticism.
Classification: LCC ML421.P6 K58 2023 (print) | LCC ML421.
P6 (ebook) | DDC 782.42166092/2--dc23/eng/20220913
LC record available at https://lccn.loc.gov/2022044297
LC ebook record available at https://lccn.loc.gov/2022044298

☉™ The paper used in this publication meets the minimum requirements
of American National Standard for Information Sciences—Permanence
of Paper for Printed Library Materials, ANSI/NISO Z39.48-1992

For Maya
My devoted co-pilot

And all my friends
"Lost in the Stars"

*"Follow your inner moonlight,
don't hide the madness."*
ALLEN GINSBERG

CONTENTS

FOREWORD

BY STEVE WYNN OF
THE DREAM SYNDICATE

Back in the early 1980s, most of my Paisley Underground buddies worshipped at the altar of Syd Barrett. In fact, two of the bands who were part of the LA scene, Salvation Army and True West, actually covered "Lucifer Sam." And don't get me wrong, I owned my copy of *Piper at the Gates of Dawn* and played it often, especially grooving on "Interstellar Overdrive" and "Astronomy Domine," the trippier, lengthier, and maybe eviller and less whimsical tracks on the album.

But much of that early Pink Floyd material felt like something experienced at a distance. It was passive and intellectualized. To put it simply, it didn't blow my mind. Maybe it's because I was a child of the '70s before I was a student of the '60s, but I was always more influenced and transfixed by their breakthrough hit records, *Dark Side of the Moon* and *Wish You Were Here*. They came out when I was thirteen and fifteen years old, respectively, and those are heavy years for a music fan and for life in general.

I was living those records in real time, and the themes of mental aberrations, societal rejection, need for both isolation and connection, escape and transcendence—those are the things that spoke to me in my teenage bedroom as I stared at the blue glow of my Marantz receiver.

There was so much space in the music, such simplicity in the lyrics, almost to the point of feeling like shorthand, and both of those tendencies for understatement allowed the listener to fill in the sonic and narrative gaps. If the early Syd Barrett records allowed a front-row study of a genius mind in the state of unraveling, these records let the listener have a chance to feel what it might be like to be the lunatic on the grass.

A few years later, punk rock hit me, once again, right at the perfect age— seventeen years old, living away from home with a car that could take me to any live show or independent record store. The exploration moved outside my head and into a more visceral world. At that point, I had no room for the decidedly "uncool" sounds of Pink Floyd. But in later years, as a member of the Dream Syndicate, I found myself rediscovering those favorite teenage records, and, once again, it was the '70s records that spoke to me. You can hear a hell of a lot more of *Dark Side of the Moon* than *A Saucerful of Secrets* in the Dream Syndicate (especially on our more recent records).

The funny thing is that, as a musician, *Dark Side of the Moon* seems more approachable now than when I was a young teen. At that time, I heard it as nothing but mystery. I had already been playing guitar for four years when it came out and had even been in a few bands. But I didn't hear the record as a collection of parts and performances. It was just *Dark Side of the Moon*!

Now, decades later, when I listen to the record, I hear very simple sounds and parts and bass lines and drum patterns and solos and understand how it all was done. And, in a way, that makes it even more exciting. It makes the music even more of a magic trick—"Look, nothing up my sleeve, examine the deck and ... presto! *Dark Side of the Moon*!" I could do it ... but I didn't.

I've only covered a Pink Floyd song once, during the sessions for the Dream Syndicate's *Out of the Grey* back in 1985. We were having fun, goofing around on covers, most of which we didn't really know. During the session, we asked the engineer, Jim Hill, to keep the two-track machine rolling whenever we played, so we'd have the results of our silliness for fun listening later on. We gamely attempted "Brain Damage" at one point, succeeding to some extent in remembering the chords and words and landing squarely and nervously between irony and tribute.

In retrospect, I can see that we were reaching for the sound and message that would have been right for us, had we followed the lead, a psychedelic band that had done our best to shed the paisley tag and grow into something of our own. We might have been well served to have remembered the mental trips of our youth and to dive back into our minds, into our subconscious. The answer was right there all along. It just took us a few more decades to recognize and remember the message. We were both too old and too young to explore the dark side of the moon, where all the most mysterious nooks and crannies laid—but that time would come when we were ready.

PROLOGUE

THE LASTING ECHO OF
COUSIN DEBBIE'S ROOM

Frank Zappa had a problem with "Debbie." On April 5, 1984, the preeminent Mother of Invention delivered an outrageous speech to the American Society of University Composers (ASUC), complaining about how "Debbie," who represented the "taste" of teenage girls, has dictated "the size, shape, and color of all music broadcast and sold in the United States during the latter part of the twentieth century."

Before beginning his tirade, Frank reminded those assembled that he too was a composer. Detesting schools and teachers, Zappa had taught himself composition "by going to the library and listening to records. . . . If that weren't bad enough," he goaded, "I earn a living by playing the *electric guitar*."

"Some of you don't know about Debbie, since you don't have to deal with radio stations and record companies the way the people from *the real world* do, but you ought to find out about her," he warned. "Debbie is thirteen years old. Her parents like to think of themselves as *average, God-fearing American white folk*. . . . Debbie is *incredibly stupid*. She has been raised to respect the values and traditions which her parents hold sacred. Sometimes she dreams about being kissed by a lifeguard."

While she sounds rather harmless, Debbie, in the eyes of the major record companies, was the "*ultimate arbiter of musical taste for the entire nation*. Everything musical in this country would have to be modified to conform to *what they computed to be her needs and desires*," Frank implored. "Debbie prefers only short songs with lyrics about boy-girl relationships, sung by persons of indeterminate sex, wearing S&M clothing."

"*Large money*" is at stake, Frank warned. "Now, as a serious American composer, should Debbie really concern you? I think so."

Zappa's attitude, although he'd never cop to it, was most likely due to jealousy. With his big nose, wonky voice, and gross sense of humor, Zappa knew he was never going to get any of "Debbie's" babysitting money. Frank's music was never too popular with women, especially those he offended with songs like "Catholic Girls" and "Dinah-Moe Humm." But while Zappa's inclination to shock and provoke cost him more than his fair share of female fans, feminist Germaine Greer has requested that his "G-Spot Tornado" be played at her funeral.

Pink Floyd's music hasn't fared much better with the gals. Conducted in 2009, the "Big Pink Floyd Survey," a study comprised of 2,130 participants from the UK and the United States, presented what it considered "a pretty accurate representation of the typical Pink Floyd fan." Its findings revealed that only eleven percent of the band's audience was women.

Smarmy as Zappa was, he was brutally honest and a harsh yet good judge of people—particularly politicians—and the sorry state of our world. Grace Slick once called him "the most intelligent asshole" she'd ever met.

My cousin Debbie concurs. Although she has the same name, she shared none of the attributes of the "Debbie" that Frank so callously disparaged.

One Thanksgiving in the early '70s, I was up in my cousin Debbie's room, checking out her cool record collection. Debbie's room was everything I imagined a bohemian garret might be. She burned candles and incense and had a bright, swirling, paisley Indian bedspread. But on the wall, rather than the typical posters of Snoopy or rock stars, or a print of Lorraine Schneider's iconic "War Is Not Healthy for Children and Other Living Things" (which graced the walls of thousands of teenage girls' rooms at the time), she hung her own painting of a big hand . . . with six fingers. There was also a wicker peacock chair, like the kind Morticia Addams used to perch in, except she hung it upside-down from the ceiling, along with a handful of flowery teacups and an old coffee percolator. It was all very *Alice in Wonderland*.

A few years my senior, Debbie fingerpicked classical guitar and turned me on to tons of great music, from Andrés Segovia to Robert Johnson, the Incredible String Band, Tim Buckley, and Morton Subotnick's electronic opus *Silver Apples of the Moon*.

We were sitting on the carpet, spacing out to the celestial shimmer of "Echoes," from Pink Floyd's newest album, *Meddle*, rippling from her speakers, when her dad, my uncle Bobby, suddenly appeared and announced that dinner was served. Standing in the doorway for a moment, he listened curiously with his head cocked, looking slightly bemused. "We used to make those kinds of pinging sounds back when I was in the navy," he said, referring to Rick Wright's minimalist keyboard note that punctuated the piece.

During World War II, Uncle Bobby (the future egg-headed nuclear physicist who spent his life splitting atoms at the local cyclotron) sat on the bottom of the Pacific Ocean in a submarine for long months at a time, doing reconnaissance work. Living in cramped quarters with just a few distractions provided by books, card games, chess and checkers, and tinkering with small instruments like ukuleles, harmonicas, or kazoos, he and the other members of the already restless crew soon became bored. Eventually, some of them began exploring the sonic possibilities of the sonar equipment.

Designed for navigation, sonar employs acoustic waves to locate objects in the ocean by sending out a sonic pulse from a transducer and then precisely measures the time it takes for the pulse to be reflected back. "We used to make up songs by bouncing soundwaves off of whatever was out there," Uncle Bobby explained, between mouthfuls of turkey and stuffing. "We'd take two modular generators and sync them up at one hundred cycles, then move one ever so slightly until we got beep tones. Then we'd clip that waveform by sending out another, and by the time it returned it was a new waveform."

Wow! Uncle Bobby might have been a science nerd, but he was much hipper than I ever knew. A pioneer of electronic sound, he was making beats from sonar beeps back in the 1940s!

●

"The opening theme is simply a repeated piano note with echoes added, twisted further by the spinning Doppler effect from the Leslie speaker," imparts Brian Kehew, author, producer, engineer, and occasional keyboardist for the Who and the Moog Cookbook. "Like the experimental avant-garde artists, it's a fine example of seeking new tones using traditional instruments with experimental processing. It starts as a sound effect but evolves into a more standard piano part, always wobbling but more tonal as each minute passes."

Comprising the entire B-side of Pink Floyd's 1971 album *Meddle*, "Echoes," as David Gilmour later claimed, is where the band "found its focus" after losing legendary front man Syd Barrett. Strung together from song fragments, melodies, and rhythms with original working titles like "Nothing" and "Son of Nothing," the twenty-three-minute "Echoes" was something of a sonic sausage. Pink Floyd's long, sometimes painstaking songwriting process, which relied heavily on intuition and editing, was at its creative peak here.

Anyone involved in making an album, shooting a movie, or writing a book will inevitably tell you, "Nothing is ever finished." For those who loyally serve their muse, Ralph Waldo Emerson's axiom, "It's not the destination, it's the journey," resounds in the cathedral of their souls like the "tolling of the iron bell."

Taking the listener on a mesmerizing sonic odyssey, "Echoes" was arguably Pink Floyd's finest work since their debut album, *Piper at the Gates of Dawn*. In the wake of charismatic leader Syd Barrett's departure, the band's direction seemed as ambiguous as the abstract portrait of an ear under water that graced *Meddle*'s cover.

Allegedly a pun inspired by the rising popularity of "metal," the album's title might have come about after Pink Floyd were chastised for endlessly fooling about in the recording studio. In search of new sounds, they were sternly reprimanded by an in-house recording engineer that "artists weren't allowed to meddle," as David Gilmour later told the BBC.

Like Brian Wilson's "Good Vibrations" and the Beatles' "Strawberry Fields Forever" (with which John Lennon claimed he was never satisfied), some consider "Echoes" a first-rate piece of visionary art. Yet for Roger Waters, the side-length suite represented the end of "all the airy-fairy mystical bollocks of the '60s." But it would take another two years, with a brief detour to Château d'Hérouville, outside of Paris (where Elton John recorded *Honky Chateau*) to record their third and final soundtrack album, *Obscured by Clouds*, before Pink Floyd forged their "masterpiece."

By the time their eighth album was released in the States on March 1, 1973 (March 24 in the UK), the Floyd had reached their do-or-die moment. That April, *Melody Maker* exclaimed that the album "took nine months to make at Abbey Road and is worth every second of studio time."

"*Dark Side* was incredibly well recorded," engineer/guitarist Robert Musso concurs. Best known for his work with Bill Laswell's Axiom label, Musso's credits include Stevie Wonder, Bob Dylan, and David Bowie, to name-drop a few. "They were in one of the best studios on the planet at the time and had a gigantically enormous budget, and they recorded that album over the course of a year. So, if you add that all up, between money, time, and talent, hopefully you'll come out with a great album, which they did! But that's not always the case!"

The story of *Dark Side of the Moon* is inseparable from rock's transformation from the counterculture's cherished soundtrack to mainstream media's played-to-death theme song. Following a devastating trainwreck of deaths of '60s rock icons that included Brian Jones, Jim Morrison, Jimi Hendrix, and Janis Joplin—compounded by the breakup of the Beatles and the closing of Bill Graham's Fillmore concert halls (New York's "East" on June 27, 1971, followed by San Francisco's "West" on July 4)—an entire generation couldn't help but wonder if the music had indeed not died.

Concerts had suddenly become big business. Ticket prices soared as private jets chauffeured bands like the Stones and the Who to sold-out capacity crowds at sprawling sports arenas. Only a few years earlier, most American bands could be found playing high-school gyms, auditoriums, and local zoos, with the occasional more dignified ballroom or theater date. (Not that both the groups and fans didn't deserve better venues with better sound quality, but a certain level of intimacy and immediacy was irrevocably lost; a feeling that only punk rock managed to bring back for a few years in the late '70s.)

The times were a-changin'—fast! On May 5, 1972, Led Zeppelin broke the Beatles' record for the largest ever concert audience in the United States, with 56,800 attending their concert at Tampa Stadium in Florida.

Whether one considers the pinnacle of rock to be 1966...or 1971, 1973 still had plenty of fire, kicking off with *Greetings from Asbury Park*, the passionately verbose debut of Bruce Springsteen, the latest in a long line of "New Dylans" that included Loudon Wainwright, John Prine, and many others. In April, the Wailers' *Catch a Fire* spread the infectious reggae rhythm and Rastafarian creed worldwide with Bob Marley's righteous message music.

June saw the long-awaited return of Sly and the Family Stone with their funky, foot-foolin' *Fresh*, while Harry Nilsson torched a set of standards on *A Little Touch of Schmilsson in the Night*, unwittingly triggering a trend among rockers (from Rod Stewart to Bryan Ferry, Linda Ronstadt, and, in recent years, Bob Dylan) to look to the past for inspiration rather than the future for innovation.*

Other milestones of 1973 included the Who's second monumental rock opera, *Quadrophenia*; Herbie Hancock's electronic cauldron of jazz/funk fusion, *Headhunters*; and Elton John's *Goodbye Yellow Brick Road*... but *Dark Side of the Moon* arguably remains the benchmark of the bunch (certainly in terms of sales and cultural impact).

Beyond its status as "a classic rock album," *Dark Side* has become ingrained in Western culture, a global phenomenon whose presence and influence continues to stretch beyond the time it was created. The infamous record sleeve, depicting a prism refracting a thin beam of white light into a multilayered rainbow, stands as a universal symbol—a metaphor for human diversity that shows that, beyond our differences, we all spring from the same source. Whether printed on posters or T-shirts, painted on walls, embroidered on jeans, or tattooed into every shade of skin, this iconic image has become as familiar as the cross or the Star of David.

"That, to me, is one of the best album covers—ever!" enthuses Marijke Koger-Dunham, who, with her then-partner, Simon Posthuma, comprised the Dutch design collective known as the Fool. Their bright colors and flowing lines exemplified the '60s visual esthetic. Everyone from the Beatles to the Hollies, the Move, and Procul Harum all donned their psychedelic garb. They painted Eric Clapton's guitar (which he in turn nicknamed "The Fool"), John Lennon's piano, George Harrison's Mini Cooper, and, most famously, the mural outside the Beatles' doomed boutique, Apple. Their colorful graphics adorned the stunning album jacket of the Incredible String Band's psychedelic-folk opus *The 5000 Spirits or the Layers of the Onion*, and they created the dazzling sets for Joe Massot's obscure 1968 film *Wonderwall*.†

---

* Released three years previously, in March 1970, Ringo Starr's debut solo album, *Sentimental Journey*, paved the way for a generation of longhairs to embrace the Great American Songbook. But despite the efforts of legendary arrangers George Martin, Quincy Jones, Elmer Bernstein, and Oliver Nelson, the record was deemed "a grievous faux pas" by the *NME*, and, worse, "an embarrassment" by Starr's old pal John Lennon.

† Harrison's soundtrack to *Wonderwall* would ultimately outshine the low-budget film that inspired it. With its mesmerizing Indian music and a guest appearance by Eric Clapton, *Wonderwall* was the first solo album by a Beatle, released on their own label, Apple Records, in November 1968.

On a grander scale, *Dark Side of the Moon* would transcend all boundaries of age and society while breaking all previous existing sales records—selling approximately forty-five million copies and counting—and topping the *Billboard* charts, where it stubbornly squatted in the Top 100 for the next seven years. The band's bassist, Roger Waters, who composed much of the album's music and all its lyrics, once groused that Pink Floyd would "always be remembered for the number of weeks *Dark Side* remained on the *Billboard* charts, and not for anything we did."

But beyond (or despite) its overwhelming success, *Dark Side* continues to speak to people around the world, whether through the simple truth of its lyrics or through a brilliant confluence of musical styles that seamlessly melds blues, country, gospel, and rock with elements of electronic sound and the dynamics of a symphony orchestra.

As their one-time producer, Joe Boyd, observed, "None of us imagined that, decades later, you could go to the remotest part of the globe and find cassettes of *Dark Side of the Moon* rattling around in the glove compartments of third world taxis."

In his understated way, David Gilmour viewed Pink Floyd's tremendous success as one of those "strange inequalities that happen through chance."

1

A LOOSE AND
HALLUCINATING
CANNON

After nearly two decades of postwar gloom, the fog had finally lifted over the rain-grey, dirty old town that *Time* magazine dubbed "Swinging London" in April 1966. With food and clothing rationing finally ending in 1949, a new generation of teenagers, yearning to forge their own identity, sought something edgier than the insipid pop music regularly served up by the BBC. Much to their parents' chagrin, they began falling under the spell of the wild, exotic sounds of American blues, country, and rock 'n' roll.

The social mores of Victorian England had finally begun to lose their grip as young Brits passionately embraced all aspects of American culture, from movies to cars, fast food, and music. Meanwhile, back in the "Land of the Free," white church groups pressured advertisers to boycott radio stations that played "Negro records" and launched fear campaigns in a desperate and feeble attempt to save American youth from the evils of "race music."

"London had suffered during World War II," Shel Talmy, producer of early hits by the Kinks and the Who, recalls.

> There was still rationing going on into the late 1950s. When I landed in London in 1962, it seemed like everyone and everything was about to explode. I had been a recording engineer in LA in my early twenties at the time, and I worked with a guy at a studio who kept extolling the virtues of London. So, before life passed me by,

I flew to England to check out what was happening. I'd been good friends with Nick Venet [the producer responsible for signing the Beach Boys] at Capitol Records. He told me to take his acetates with me and say I made them. So, I went to see Dick Rowe [the A&R man who notoriously turned down the Beatles] at Decca Records and played him Lou Rawls' "Music in the Air" and the Beach Boys' "Surfin' Safari," and he said, "You start today!" The second record I made with Decca was a hit called "Charmaine" by the Bachelors. From that point on, I had a whole bunch of hits and stayed for seventeen years.

When I got to London, I moved to Kings Road in Chelsea. I was in the right place at the right time. The scene consisted of probably four hundred people who knew each other, who more or less traveled around in one huge rat pack. If there was a party, all of us would turn up. We would sit around late into the night, talking about what we were gonna do, and then the whole damn thing exploded—everything from photography to modeling, acting, and music. It was all happening at the same time.

The first "ambassador" of Black American roots music had arrived on England's shores back in 1951, just as jazz and blues records began to capture the ears and imaginations of thousands of young Brits. Neglected in his hometown of Chicago, Big Bill Broonzy was working as a janitor in Iowa City when he was unexpectedly invited to play a handful of concerts in England. With his husky, soulful voice and virtuosic guitar skills, Broonzy was greeted with standing ovations wherever he performed, and in turn he inspired a new generation of aspiring British musicians to dive headfirst into Black roots music.

"I was too young to see him, but some people I knew had," says poet Pete Brown, who famously wrote the lyrics to Cream's "Sunshine of Your Love" and "White Room" with bassist/vocalist Jack Bruce. "Big Bill was very, very important indeed. His early records were electric and revealed the beginnings of R&B. But when came over here, he reinvented himself as a folksinger and played acoustic guitar because people considered that 'authentic.' My old friend Davy Graham was the guy who really brought Bill Broonzy's music into the British scene, and then everybody else listened to him, including Bert Jansch and John Renbourn [of Pentangle]."*

While British acoustic "purists" initially snubbed the high-voltage rhythms of Chuck Berry and Bo Diddley, a cultural revolution would soon explode with the arrival of a pack of duck-tailed rebel-rockers that included Eddie Cochran, Gene Vincent, and Jerry Lee Lewis (who was literally run out of the UK after the press discovered his polygamous relationship with his thirteen-year-old cousin Myra). Oddly, Elvis Presley never performed "across the pond" (except for his fellow troops in Friedberg, Germany), due to the fact that his shady cigar-chomping manager, Colonel Tom Parker, lacked a passport. But for better and worse, Presley's movies—along with *Blackboard Jungle*, *Untamed Youth*, *The Wild One*, and *Rebel Without a Cause*—would help stoke the fires of discontent and rebellion among teenagers from LA to London.

The first rumblings of what soon became known as "The British Blues Explosion" began with Muddy Waters' arrival in 1958. With the commanding presence of an African king, the Mississippi-born bluesman plugged in his electric guitar and pulverized crowds of young blues fanatics comprised of Alexis Korner, Cyril Davies, John Mayall, and Graham Bond, who quickly formed bands that became workshops for a slew of fledgling musicians who would find international fame as members of the Rolling Stones, Fleetwood Mac, Cream, and Led Zeppelin.

According to British Invasion singer/songwriter Ian Whitcomb, best known for his 1965 hit "You Turn Me On," it was trombonist and bandleader Chris Barber "who started the British Blues and R&B movement." Barber's band played everything from jug band music to electric urban blues and served as a finishing school for up-and-coming musicians, from singer and guitarist Lonnie Donegan to guitarist Alexis Korner and blues harpist Cyril Davies, who formed Blues Incorporated in 1961 with Jack Bruce on bass and Charlie Watts on drums. Watts would be replaced by a bloke known as Peter "Ginger" Baker after jumping ship to join the Rolling Stones.

●

---

* So too did George Harrison, who later namechecked Broonzy in his 1987 song "Wreck of the Hesperus."

For Syd Barrett—still known by his birth name, Roger, among his family and friends in the idyllic university town of Cambridge, located fifty-five miles north of London—the discovery of this new, exotic music, which he dialed in every night from Radio Luxembourg, would help fill the aching void left after his father, Max, a police pathologist, died of cancer on December 11, 1961. Just sixteen at the time, Barrett would spend countless hours with his pal (future Pink Floyd guitarist) Dave Gilmour, spinning records by American musicians from Pete Seeger to Bill Haley and the Comets. While Gilmour learned to strum a borrowed Spanish guitar, Barrett picked the banjo bequeathed to him by his dad. But the banjo had already become a relic of Britain's short-lived trad. jazz craze, and Syd would soon get his hands on a Number 12 Hofner acoustic guitar instead. A year later, Barrett bought his first electric guitar: a red Hofner Futurama (basically a knockoff of a Fender Stratocaster) complete with a whammy bar. Syd immediately learned Hank Marvin's reverb-drenched riff from the Shadows' single "Apache." Along with Dave, he pounded out Bo Diddley's funky, chugging boogaloo "Road Runner," which Pink Floyd covered in their early days.

At the same time, their future bandmate Roger Waters, who claimed to detest rock 'n' roll, fell under the spell of sultry blues singers like Bessie Smith, Billie Holiday, and the legendary Lead Belly, whose "Rock Island Line" had topped the charts in May 1956 in a revved-up rendition by the "King of Skiffle," Lonnie Donegan.

Waters and Barrett had known each other since childhood. Roger W. was eight when he met five-year-old Roger B. when they both took art lessons at the nearby Homerton teacher-training college.

"I'm very glad I went to [school in] Cambridge because it let me meet some very interesting people," filmmaker Anthony Stern recalled to Sophia Satchell-Baeza, in an interview with the Italian webzine *La Furia Umana*. "You're very cut off in Cambridge. Yet there were benefits to a small town."

Beyond the future members of Pink Floyd, Stern befriended filmmaker Peter Whitehead (and eventually worked as his assistant) as well as graphics wizard Storm Thorgerson and other Cambridge "leading lights," including director Nigel Lesmoir-Gordon, who was responsible for various Pink Floyd–related films, notably the short, blurry, and oddly curious *Syd Barrett's First Trip* (1966).

"There must be something about the water in Cambridge," Stern joked. "It would be great to start selling it. 'Eau de Cam'!"

Describing the dynamics of postwar Cambridge, he continued:

> We were all children of people who had fought in the First World War. They were always rebelling against that, and they were also rebelling against us, actually! They rebelled against their children, [and] you can understand why. They risked both life and limb to produce this culture where you can be free in the 1950s and 1960s and here we were, pissing it up the wall. We weren't worthy of it. But define "worthy," that's the problem. My parents were very authoritarian. This group of people had this in common in a way. Our parents were either dead or they were damaged. You either survived or you didn't survive. I only did by turning my back on all that, on academia, and carving my own identity.

Other Cantabrigians who were busy carving out their own identities at the time included Aubrey "Po" Powell, who, along with his partner Storm Thorgerson, formed Hipgnosis in 1967, becoming famous for designing striking album covers for Pink Floyd, Led Zeppelin, Paul McCartney, and the Pretty Things. He recalled his close friend Syd Barrett in a 2015 interview with Craig Bailey for *Floydian Slip*, a radio program devoted to the band:

> In those early days [in Cambridge], Syd was this kind of elfin-like character. He was very skinny. He walked on the balls of his feet. He was very creative, very artistic . . . very popular with the girls, [and] beautiful looking.
>
> In Cambridge, before Pink Floyd even started, [Syd] was playing in all sorts of little bands, the Hollering Blues and other local bands, really sort of cutting his chops. He used to play with David Gilmour a lot. They used to teach each other guitar and stuff like that. I mean nobody could have foreseen that, later on, Syd would disappear from Pink Floyd and David would be his replacement.

Escaping the sedate suburbs of Cambridge, Roger Waters, Nick Mason, and Rick Wright first crossed paths in 1962, while attending London Polytechnic on Regent Street. Quickly growing bored with their architectural studies and sharing a passion for music, they formed a combo they dubbed Sigma 6 in the autumn of '63, with Mason on drums, Waters on guitar, and Rick Wright juggling rhythm guitar, keyboards, and horns. Along with Wright's girlfriend Juliette Gale, who occasionally added vocals, and a variety of bassists, Sigma 6 (sometimes written as σ6) worked up a repertoire of R&B covers and rocked the Poly's basement tearoom, much to the delight of their colleagues.

Sigma 6 soon morphed into the Abdabs—or, better yet, the Screaming Abdabs (slang for an uncontrollable fit)—and appeared in a low-budget independent film shot at the Marquee Club. In the early months of 1964, an article appeared in *West One*, the Polytechnic's student paper, with the headline reading "Architectural Abdabs." It was written by Barbara Walters (no, not her ...), who interviewed Roger Waters, perhaps mistaking him for a distant relative when she referred to him as "Walters," and quoted the fledgling musician's somewhat naïve theories. "It is easier to express yourself rhythmically in Blues-style," he espoused. "It doesn't need practice, just basic understanding. ... Rock is just beat without expression, though admittedly Rhythm and Blues forms the basis of original rock."

Before becoming a fully fledged musician, Roger Waters used to stop by Syd's Cambridge house to observe the occasional jam session taking place. Once he was enrolled at London's Camberwell School of Art in the autumn of '64, Barrett reconnected with Waters. Syd, along with his friend, guitarist/singer Bob Klose, would join forces with Mason, Wright, and Waters (who then switched to bass) of Sigma 6. Renamed the Spectrum Five, the band began "doing the pub scene," as Barrett later recalled. At one point, they changed their name again to the Tea Set and recorded a menacing garage-rocker written by Barrett, "Lucy Leave," along with a throbbing cover of Slim Harpo's "King Bee," one year after the Rolling Stones had their way with the tune.

In their pre-psychedelic days, before anyone had discovered Aldous Huxley's *The Doors of Perception* or dosed their English Breakfast, the Tea Set's brand of blues was rather tepid and tenuous—nowhere as raw and aggressive as the adolescent anthems unleashed by the Who, the Kinks, or the Pretty Things. But before Bob Klose had a chance to don the paisley, his father made certain his son was clad in pinstripes and off to a proper job. With Bob conscripted into the "real world," the Tea Set changed their moniker, once more, to the Pink Floyd Blues Band.

While Brian Jones (a.k.a. "Elmo Lewis"), the aspiring slide guitarist from the sedate suburbs of Cheltenham, named his fledgling blues group in honor of Muddy Waters' song "Rollin' Stone," Syd Barrett, as usual, took the road less traveled. A young art student with a passion for wordplay, abstract painting, and African American roots music, Barrett christened his cats "Pink" and "Floyd" in honor of two obscure bluesmen, Pink Anderson and Floyd Council, long before his band became world famous bearing the curious moniker. Syd initially discovered Council and Anderson while reading the liner notes to *Country Blues 1935–1940*, the 1962 album by Blind Boy Fuller, released twenty-one years after the legendary guitarist (known to his mother as Fulton Allen) died in his mid-thirties from kidney failure.

Born "in the sticks" of Laurens, South Carolina, on February 12, 1900, Pinkney "Pink" Anderson ran away from home at age fourteen to join Dr. W. R. Kerr's Indian Remedy Show. For the next thirty years, he traveled the Southeastern United States, singing and hawking snake oil to gullible crowds. He first learned the rudiments of country-blues guitar from "Blind Simmie" Dooley, and together they played blues, rags, and hokum numbers for tips on street corners and parties, until eventually cutting four tracks for Columbia Records on April 14, 1928. With respectable sales for their two singles, "Papa's About to Get Mad" and "Every Day in the Week Blues," Anderson was offered another chance to record, but he declined when his mentor was not invited along to the session.

While Anderson sang of the many hardships faced by Black Carolinians, he did not scream, shout, or moan the blues, as was common across the Deep South. His delivery, while weary, possessed a warm and friendly resonance.

Floyd "Dipper Boy" Council, the man with whom Anderson would be eternally linked in the annals of popular culture, first recorded in 1937, touting himself (much to Fulton Allen's chagrin) as "Blind Boy Fuller's Buddy." Informed by ragtime piano players and the quick, clean picking of string bands, the Piedmont style of guitar he played revealed a lighter, more bluegrassy feel than the harder, cutting-edge blues commonly played from the Delta to Chicago.

In 1956, Pink Anderson gained a little notoriety with the release of *American Street Songs*, an album he shared with the blind guitar virtuoso Reverend Gary Davis, who was also from Laurens, South Carolina. But there is little doubt that Andersen and Council would have been designated to the dustbin of obscurity had it not been for Syd Barrett's passion for American roots music.

"I finally tracked down Pink Anderson in Spartanburg, South Carolina, around 1968, '69," folk/blues singer and guitarist Roy Book Binder recalls.

> He had this little house, a tiny shack, on the "wrong side of the tracks." He'd written his name, Pink Anderson, with a stick in the concrete in front of his house, and there was a padlock on the door. I asked somebody if he was dead, and they said, "No, he just don't like people lookin' at his business!" So I sat on his porch and waited for him to come home. I was playin' one of his songs on the guitar when he came up the street. He looked at me. I looked at him. He was pretty friendly. He was a bootlegger. As they said around the neighborhood, "You could always wake up Mr. Pink for a drink!"
>
> Pink had had a stroke a few years before—that's why he didn't play the folk circuit [during the blues resurgence of the mid-'60s], otherwise he would have been a sensation. He was an okay guitar player, but he was really an entertainer who worked traveling medicine shows as far back as 1912. But, by the time I met him, he didn't play much anymore, and his timing was off. He was pretty skinny, so I bought him some groceries and had his phone put back on.

British music fans adored these veteran blues musicians not only for their raw, unvarnished sound but for their hard-knocks life stories, which often elevated them to legendary status in the minds of young, passionate Brits. John Mayall (whose band the Bluesbreakers featured a parade of young guitar virtuosos, including Eric Clapton, Peter Green, and Mick Taylor) took up the mantle for J. B. Lenoir, writing and singing "I'm Gonna Fight for You J. B.," which helped gain a greater recognition and appreciation for the Mississippi-born bluesman after he died in a car crash in April 1967. Cream's thunderous rendition of "I'm So Glad" helped earn Skip James over $10,000 in royalties and paid for the obscure Mississippi singer and guitarist's tombstone following his death in October 1969. But beyond the novelty and bewilderment of adulation from a small cult of English blues fanatics, Pink Anderson and Floyd Council reaped little if any benefit from their association with Pink Floyd, as Roy Book Binder recalls:

> Eventually, we got Pink some gigs in upstate New York, and he was on—like a firecracker! He didn't skip a beat. He was funny and great. There were write-ups in the paper, and he was surprised that people knew who he was. He certainly didn't know who Pink Floyd was! His son went after them for some money, but they never played any of his music. Maybe they could've done one of his songs and tossed him a couple of grand...
>
> Then I heard he died and I didn't believe it. So I went down there and contacted the welfare department, and they showed me where he was buried. I had a tombstone put down on his unmarked grave that said "Pink Anderson—Recording Artist," with a guitar etched into it. Whenever I can, I stop by and clean it off with a little moonshine.

The blues would become the sanctioned soundtrack of London's burgeoning Mod scene, with groups like the Yardbirds covering Howlin' Wolf's "Smokestack Lightnin'" and backing harmonica legend Sonny Boy Williamson on his 1963–1964 British tour. In the summer of 1964, the Animals would top the charts on both sides of the Atlantic as their impish singer, Eric Burdon, bellowed Lead Belly's tale of "sin and misery," "House of the Rising Sun." That November, the Rolling Stones released a smoldering cover of Willie Dixon's "Little Red Rooster," featuring a slinky slide guitar riff played by Brian Jones. Although the song shot to No. 1 on the British charts, a month later it was banned across America, according to Stones bassist Bill Wyman because of its lascivious lyrics.

Everyone from the Kinks and the Who (who covered Sonny Boy Williamson's "Eyesight to the Blind" on their 1969 opus *Tommy*) to the Small Faces and the

Pretty Things played turbo-charged blues and R&B covers in their early live sets. But for a young Syd Barrett and David Gilmour, there was no British band closer to the source than the Rolling Stones.

Syd adored the Stones' original leader, flaxen-haired blues messenger Brian Jones. A brilliant musical innovator, Jones adorned each new Stones album with a surprising sonic palate that included the dulcimer, recorder, saxophone, sitar, Moog, and vibraphone. A decadent dandy, Brian boldly mixed exotic togs from Morocco and India with women's clothes and lizard-skin boots to create a bold and singular fashion style. But his outrageous wardrobe was matched only by his voracious appetite for smoking hash, dropping acid, and gobbling Mandrax (a powerful barbiturate better known as Quaaludes in the states). Beyond Barrett and T. Rex's Marc Bolan, Brian's spirit and style also inspired Jimi Hendrix, who he would introduce to the world at the guitarist's outrageous debut at the Monterey Pop Festival in June 1967.

"The British blues boom injected blues with a shot in the arm which helped propel the music into the future for another thirty years," Violent Femmes bassist Brian Ritchie stresses. "The Pretty Things, Rolling Stones, and Them were all great blues bands by any measure. It was a lazy assumption to say they played a watered-down version of the blues. That claim became a mantra for some people. But how can you blame twenty-year-old enthusiasts for playing the music they loved?"

"It was a strange cultural thing," Pete Brown ruminates. "The blues allowed you to do your own thing with it. But the secondhand British version was still a warm, swinging, and somewhat spontaneous music that was played with love and respect for its black predecessors."

Not everyone was quite so enamored of the Brits' secondhand blues. Led Zeppelin's bassist and multi-instrumentalist John Paul Jones, a dedicated jazz snob, considered the Yardbirds (which featured Jones' soon-to-be bandmate, Jimmy Page) and the Stones a bunch of "blues twits [playing] white R&B, which nobody was into at all. As a musical scene, they just didn't rate. When you'd hear them play 'Little Red Rooster,' you'd go, 'Oh please don't,'" Jones cringed.

Linda Lawrence Leitch (wife of the psychedelic bard Donovan, and former girlfriend of Brian Jones) couldn't disagree more. "I didn't miss a single gig," she said of the Stones' early days. "I was totally blown away because he [Brian] had . . . this thing on his finger and he kept sliding the guitar. It really touched me. The music went deep inside me," she told journalist Simon Dudfield.

Capable of mimicking a human voice or a horn, the slide freed guitarists from the constraints of the instrument's frets while opening doors to new sonic possibilities. Never content with the status quo, Barrett's innovative impulse (or was it simply stoned forgetfulness?) led him to employ a Zippo lighter in lieu of a bottleneck or metal tube and stretch beyond the grinding Elmore James blues riffs that Brian Jones had recently introduced to a new generation of British musicians and fans.

"Country-blues slide players created a whole new vocabulary for the guitar that went way beyond the notes," multi-instrumentalist and avant-garde composer Elliott Sharp points out. "They were suddenly playing microtones that were a pure expressive vocalization of the guitar."

Born in Chicago, Shel Talmy loved the blues long before he arrived in London in 1962 and produced a string of chart-topping early hits by the Kinks, the Who, and Manfred Mann. "I used to see Sonny Terry and Brownie McGhee at the Ash Grove in LA," he recalls. "They were regulars there, as was Odetta."

"I'm certainly not putting them down," Talmy says of the breed of young Brits obsessed with the blues. "Those bands played pretty well. But do I think that any of them played as well as Robert Johnson or Howlin' Wolf? Probably not!" he chuckles. "If you're talking about great [English] blues players, there were very few . . . maybe none. I honestly think you had to grow up in the American South to really understand what that music was all about."

"The Floyd would not have made a great blues band," Rick Wright admitted years later, in a 2001 interview with film director John Edginton. "Syd was *not* an Eric Clapton."

●

Just months after the Beatles invaded America with their stunning debut on *The Ed Sullivan Show* on February 9, 1964, the Blues and Gospel Caravan (road managed by a young, ambitious Harvard student named Joe Boyd) took England by storm with a series of powerful performances by Muddy Waters, Reverend Gary Davis, and Sister Rosetta Tharpe.

At that time, there were few female role models like Sister Rosetta on either side of the pond. While a fervent servant of the lord, she was clearly under no man's thumb. "Can't no man play like me!" she proudly boasted. In her fur coat, high heels, and platinum curly blonde wig, Tharpe had style to spare as she rocked a white 1961 Gibson Les Paul Custom SG, complete with three pickups and a tremolo bar.

On the other end of the spectrum was Willie Mae "Big Mama" Thornton, who howled Lieber and Stoller's "Hound Dog" back when Elvis Presley was still an unknown pup. Weighing nearly three hundred pounds, with razor scars running down her cheeks, Willie Mae was a gender-bender long before David Bowie fell to Earth. She sported men's clothes, her bold plaid hats and flannel shirts foreshadowing Neil Young and a generation of grunge-rockers. Big Mama not only melted microphones with her powerful voice but played impressive blues harp and drums as well. Her pitiful song "Ball and Chain," later popularized by Janis Joplin, was the antithesis of the cheerful fluff chirped by British female pop stars of the day like Helen Shapiro, Cilla Black, and Petula Clark. Only the Scottish-born Lulu (better known as Marie Lawrie to her mother) hinted at any edge when she suggestively sang, "What can I give you in return?" in her 1967 hit, "To Sir with Love."

These liberated women rocked with unbridled passion and soul, provoking the "dolly birds" in the crowd to ponder their own identity. But the roots of '60s feminism had more in common with the outrageous "flappers" of the Roaring Twenties, who publicly smoked and drank, bobbed their hair, and donned skimpy skirts once they were liberated from constraining corsets by Coco Chanel's radical designs.

With her "skinny legs and all," the androgynous waif Twiggy ("The Face of '66," as the *Daily Express* dubbed her) resembled a flapper herself. She singlehandedly redefined a new standard of British femininity, which now favored youth over the matronly shape of a full-figured woman.

"Dedicated Follower(s) of Fashion" (as regaled in song by the Kinks) began flocking to boutiques along the Kings Road in Chelsea, which had transformed overnight into the hub of hip. Hair flowed freely, falling over eyes and ears and down collars of young blokes and birds alike. A new generation began to blur the borders of sexual identity, donning unisex stripes, paisley and polka dots, turtlenecks and wide belts, and shiny vinyl parkas.

Young women in England (and subsequently America, thanks to JCPenney department stores) donned Mary Quant's scandalously skimpy miniskirt, revealing bold, fleshy contours that had been deemed unimaginable only months before. In the *Sunday Times*, tastemaker Ernestine Carter hailed Quant's revolutionary fashion show at her Knightsbridge Bazaar for "jolting England out of its conventional attitude for clothes." Sleek dresses with peek-a-boo holes designed by Zandra Rhodes offered a provocative gape at the wearer's midriff, back, and shoulders. Appropriating exotic Indian and Moroccan fabrics and patterns, Rhodes designed flowing, floral-print caftans worn by glamourous budding rock stars like Marc Bolan and Queen's Freddie Mercury.

This new psychedelic esthetic mushroomed after vintage clothing collector, artist, and musician Nigel Waymouth, along with his girlfriend Sheila Cohen and their partner John Pearse, opened the doors to Granny Takes a Trip in 1966, at the once undesirable location of 488 Kings Road. New boutiques began to blossom overnight like strange wildflowers with intriguing names: Garbo, Kleptomania, I Was Lord Kitchener's Thing, Take 6. A constant procession of shoppers strolled sidewalks alongside a steady stream of Minis, E-Type Jags, and MGs, along with the occasional Lotus Elan and Rolls-Royce, as red Routemaster double-decker buses trundled along, all watched over by bobbies on horseback.

The soundtrack driving this new cultural renaissance had been brewing over the last few years in the laboratory of England's art schools, where young, malcontent rockers like John Lennon, Keith Richards, Ray Davies, and Syd Barrett sought sanctuary (if only temporarily) from a society into which they'd never fit, but for the grace of their songs. Art school offered an experimental bohemian atmosphere where drinking wine, smoking hash, drawing nudes, and exploring one's sexuality was all in a day's work. But not all the players involved in this fomenting new world were such dedicated nonconformists. Mick Jagger, uncertain of his future as a neophyte blues belter, dutifully attended classes at the London School of Economics, where, four years prior to becoming the manager of Pink Floyd, Peter Jenner lectured in sociology.

Before a steady diet of LSD decimated Syd Barrett, his curious mind thrived with innovative ideas and eclectic styles. Beyond his obsession with painting and the blues, Syd soaked up everything from French existentialism to Beat poetry, the *I Ching*, and Zen philosophy.

"With Syd, the [band's] direction changed," Rick Wright told author Barry Miles. The Pink Floyd Sound, as the group was briefly known, took a more experimental and improvisational approach to creating music. While Barrett was clearly "the face" of Pink Floyd, handling lead guitar and vocals, Roger Waters approached the bass "as a lead instrument," while Wright's keyboards began to take on a more "classical feel."

Syd was "terrific to be around and great to be in a band with," Waters later told Joe Smith. But Roger soon began to detect a few unnerving clues that his friend was "in danger of going over the edge."

"There was no question that Syd had something special, but if Roger Waters hadn't been there, I don't think Syd would have been able to find his way to the stage," Pete Townshend observed. Although the Who's dynamic guitarist appreciated the hazy sonic atmosphere Barrett conjured from his reverberating Telecaster, he found his wraithlike presence disturbing: "If Syd was innovative at anything, it was at getting completely and totally out of it. He was the first person I had seen who was totally 'gone' onstage."

The history of rock 'n' roll is filled with legendary doomed stoner iconoclasts, from Moby Grape's Skip Spence to the Rolling Stones' Brian Jones (whom Townshend eulogized as "a man who died every day"). But, Pete believed, "Syd was only able to get away with it" because most of Pink Floyd's fans were "out of their brains as well." While Townshend ultimately deemed Barrett a "pitiful and tragic" figure, he was terrified of Roger Waters' "fearsome countenance, both on and offstage."

Originally home to early gigs by the Rolling Stones, Yardbirds, and the Who, the Marquee Club became the site for the Spontaneous Underground—the strange Sunday-afternoon happenings curated by New Yorker Steve Stollman, filmmaker and younger brother of Bernard Stollman, the visionary producer behind ESP-Disk, home to free-jazz explorers Sun Ra and Albert Ayler as well as anarchist hippie bands like the Fugs, Pearls Before Swine, and the Holy Modal Rounders.

Stollman arrived in London in '65, sent by Bernard to find new acts for ESP-Disk. Finding the scene too "spread out," Steve decided to start his own, by-invitation-only club, renting the Marquee Club to curate a series of Spontaneous Underground happenings. With little to do on a Sunday afternoon in "sleepy

London town," word spread fast. The *Sunday Times* described Stollman as a "revolutionary party organizer." Printing up mimeographed invitations, he encouraged attendees to arrive in "masque and costume of their choice"—whether "ethnic, space, Edwardian, [or] Victorian." His premiere happening promised appearances by Donovan (who allegedly showed up so stoned he had no recollection of singing cross-legged on the stage with a handful of sitarists). Sadly, the legendary Mississippi jazz/blues pianist Mose Allison didn't make it. Ultimately, the Graham Bond Organisation (whose ranks included Jack Bruce and Ginger Baker) kept the party rolling with a percolating gumbo of jazz, roots, and R&B.

It was Steve who gave Pink Floyd their first gig at the Marquee Club, on January 30, 1966. They jammed a three-hour set. In the provocatively titled article "A Child's Eye View of Madness" from the London weekly *Tit-Bits*, a reporter described the wild scene transpiring at the club: "The capital no longer swings, it's gone berserk! With girls stripped to the waist, [and] a man crawling naked through jelly."

Stollman's raves became increasingly outrageous as they progressed, playing a key role in the transformation of the times, particularly after he began to collaborate with Barry Miles, the proprietor and curator of the Indica Gallery (and later author and historian of Beat and '60s culture). Miles, along with John "Hoppy" Hopkins, the visionary behind London's boldly idealistic but short-lived Free School, and Mike Horovitz, poet and editor of London's Beat literature magazine *New Departures*, had recently ushered legendary poets Allen Ginsberg, Gregory Corso, and Lawrence Ferlinghetti across the pond to read at the Royal Albert Hall for the *Poetry Olympics* on June 11, 1965. The famous Beats were joined by likeminded British bards Adrian Mitchell, Alexander Trocchi, Christopher Logue, and Pete Brown. According to Joe Boyd, "The standing-room-only audience recognized themselves [that night] as a counterculture for the first time."

"I've known Barry Miles since he was a kid," Pete Brown recalls. "He was always a very forward-thinking guy. Miles started the Indica Gallery, which was supported by Paul McCartney. The Fluxus group showed their art at the gallery, and John met Yoko there [in November 1966]. I had been making a living from poetry readings at the time, but I wasn't having a very good year in 1964. So,

Miles called me to help him build the place. I was sawing bookshelves when I met all of those people."

Following the limited-run, hand-stapled publication of their underground journal *Global Moon Edition Long Hair Times* in April of '66, Hopkins and Miles joined forces that October to publish the premiere issue of England's first alternative paper, the *International Times* (a.k.a. *IT*), roughly the equivalent of New York's *Village Voice* or *East Village Other*.

"Hoppy was a really big jazz fan," Brown recollects. "He was always around, photographing the great jazz people, both British and American. That was his first claim to fame, as a photographer, and then he got political and helped start the *International Times*. The left-wing underground movement basically grew out of the Campaign for Nuclear Disarmament* and an alliance with the American antiwar efforts."

Beyond Beat poetry, Miles turned Paul McCartney on to the revolutionary periodical the *Evergreen Review*, as well as the free jazz of Ornette Coleman, John Coltrane, Albert Ayler, and Sun Ra. McCartney later referred to Miles' cultural mentoring as "a stoned think tank" where he also soaked up the radical sonic concepts of Karlheinz Stockhausen, John Cage, Luciano Berio, Terry Riley, Pierre Henry, and Pierre Schaffer. In return for Miles' crash course in cultural consciousness, Paul gave *IT* an in-depth interview, which helped raise the struggling paper's profile and expand its readership.

Following the successful launch party for *IT* at the Roundhouse with a night of music by Pink Floyd and Soft Machine, Hoppy and the ubiquitous American road manager and record producer Joe Boyd opened the UFO club at the Blarney Club, an Irish pub located in a subterranean ballroom beneath a pair of movie theaters on Tottenham Court Road. Boyd made a handshake deal with Mr. Gannon, owner of the Blarney, to rent the room for £15 (around $40 at the time) every Friday night for their weekly psychedelic revelries.

Pronounced "You-foh," the legendary psychedelic dungeon was named in honor of Boyd's witnessing a flying saucer hovering above the skies of Puerto Rico when he was fifteen. Apparently, Joe was not alone. The strange sighting,

---

* The CND began in London in 1958. Its founding members included Gerald Holtom, who designed the internationally recognized peace symbol.

he recalled, "was observed by thousands and made the front page of the San Juan daily paper."

◑

Opening on December 23, 1966, the UFO featured music by Pink Floyd and the Soft Machine. Taking their name from William S. Burrough's 1961 novel, the four-piece, Canterbury-based band boasted a jazzy improvisational edge with socially conscious lyrics but lacked a front man with the charisma of Syd Barrett.

During its brief run, the UFO also hosted poetry readings and featured regular screenings of experimental art films by Andy Warhol and Kenneth Anger. Other bands who helped foment the legendary club's surrealist atmosphere included Procol Harum, Tomorrow, the Bonzo Dog Doo-Dah Band, and the Boyd-produced groups the Incredible String Band and Fairport Convention, along with self-proclaimed Dadaist Arthur Brown, famous for wearing his clothes inside out and backward and painting his face years before anyone had heard of KISS. Jenny Fabian, author of the 1969 novel *Groupie*, dubbed the UFO London's "womb of make-believe."

"Each night was a complete buzz because we did totally new things, and none of us knew how the others would react to it," Rick Wright said, describing the UFO's experimental atmosphere.

"In three months, the club went from nonexistent to being *the* club which defined which groups were hot," Joe Boyd later wrote. "By spring 1967, Pink Floyd was already on the record charts. For maybe eight to ten months in all there was a real underground scene coming out of the art schools for the most part, with venues that weren't normal venues, an audience that wasn't a normal audience, and light shows which were not a normal part of presenting groups. And it took less than a year for it to become part of the mainstream of the pop music industry," Boyd bragged.

Not surprisingly, others held less fond and vivid memories of those strange, psychedelic nights. According to the Soft Machine's drummer/singer Robert Wyatt, the crowd at the UFO was comprised of "people who didn't know what year it was, let alone what time it was." In his memoir *Rock Odyssey: A Chronicle of the Sixties*, Ian Whitcomb describes the UFO as "grubby." Finding the light shows "tedious," Whitcomb, no fan of Pink Floyd, dismissed *Piper at the Gates of Dawn* as a "novelty" and felt their early singles were "whimsical" at best. Preferring old school R&B, blues, and hit singles by the Rolling Stones and the Kinks (with whom he'd recently toured), Whitcomb disdained the Floyd's "numbers crammed with aimless guitar solos," supported by "organ chords from a submerged cathedral," while their lyrics "slid from Fairyland to outer space and back again with no time for a breather. . . . The only law they broke was an unwritten one: *Please don't bore.*"

Whitcomb was not alone in his assessment of Pink Floyd's debut LP. Pete Townshend, a regular at the UFO raves, deplored *Piper at the Gates of Dawn*, deeming it "fucking awful in comparison to the band's live shows."

On the other hand, DJ John Peel, champion of London's psychedelic underground, considered *Piper* "a revelation," and Peter Jenner, soon to become Pink Floyd's co-manager, defended his band's penchant for challenging their fans' patience and taste, explaining, "You can't walk around the kitchen humming to the Pink Floyd. . . . If you had the sort of sound they're making in the clubs coming over the radio while you're doing the washing up, you'd probably scream."

Meanwhile, Barrett didn't seem to care or even be aware of what all the fuss was about: "It all comes out of our heads and it's not too hard to understand," he said.

Pink Floyd were not alone in challenging the accepted norms of what designated "entertainment." Unable to find a suitable venue for their outrageous stage act, Joe Boyd willingly gave the Crazy World of Arthur Brown a break and booked them at the UFO. The club, Brown told author Richie Unterberger, was "different from your normal pop atmosphere." He found the crowd generally more open to "more poetic" lyrics and music that explored "an inner landscape," through improvisation and employing electronics. Beyond "a light show which changed color with the mood of the music," Brown's Crazy World employed dance, costumes, and his famous fire helmet, and created "real theater."

One of the Crazy World's biggest fans was Pete Townshend, who showed up at the UFO one night clad in a kaftan and offered to chauffeur Arthur around London in his new Lincoln Continental, to discuss the possibility of signing him to the Who's label, Track Records. Townshend, along with the Who's manager, Kit Lambert, would produce Arthur's single "Fire," which rocketed to No. 2 on the charts, followed by his Top 10 album *The Crazy World of Arthur Brown.*

"I found the UFO to be a bit elite," says Pete Brown (no relation to Arthur, he emphasizes, "just good friends").

> It attracted the avant-garde and the underground, who were mostly quite middle-class . . . myself not included. They were mostly quite educated and interested in the bands playing there—Pink Floyd, Tomorrow, and Procol Harum, who were all developing a following. The UFO began attracting a wider audience, but remember it was only once a week. People I was friendly with went there and I liked the atmosphere. I was already reasonably well-known as a so-called "underground" poet, and part of the political feeling of the times, so I was *persona-grata*. I performed there with my jazz band, called Brown's Poetry [featuring an up-and-coming guitarist named John McLaughlin].

Inspired by wild nights at the UFO, Brown wrote the lyrics to Cream's "Dance the Night Away" (from 1967's *Disraeli Gears*), conjuring visions of Sufis twirling wildly, trying to lose themselves in oblivion.

> I like to go and to jump around a bit. But I was having a bad time. My drink may have been spiked with something or maybe it was due to all the excess. Whatever it was, I wasn't sure whether I was alive or dead. So, I stopped taking everything and got sort of straight and was in a very peculiar state. My idea of reality had changed a great deal. [*laughs*] One of the things that kept me anchored was to go to the UFO and dance with the psychedelic women, which I never did before. I'm not a dancer but I'm rhythmic, having played percussion for years. Sex and dancing got me through that time when I was having panic attacks.

"You couldn't really find music much farther outside the mainstream than what the Floyd were up to in the autumn of 1966," Joe Boyd recalled years later. "Revolutions are, almost by definition, factional, but during those two golden years from June '65 to June '67, the working-class anarchists, vaguely aristocratic bohemians, musicians, crusaders, poets, dropouts, and psychotropic adventurers were united in their respect and affection for Hoppy," he wrote in a 2015 elegy for his old friend. "He was the only true leader the [British counterculture] movement ever had."

●

"Was it merely a vast fashion aberration, or were we seeing a brand-new mass art movement like the Pre-Raphaelites or the Aesthetes?" Mick Farren, singer with the Deviants, ruminates in his 2001 memoir, *Give the Anarchist a Cigarette.* "An alternative society was actually coming to pass, but at a frightening and uncontrolled rate, like a virtual culture growing exponentially, [with] each cell dividing and reproducing over and over again."

Some striking and uncanny parallels can be drawn between London's UFO club and Zurich's infamous Cabaret Voltaire. Fifty years after the German poet Hugo Ball persuaded Ephraim Jan, the proprietor of the Holländische Meierei, to allow a group of writers to meet on a once-a-week basis at his club, the Blarney's proprietor, Mr. Gannon, rented out his grubby basement pub to a pair of fledgling counterculture entrepreneurs for their weekly psychedelic soirees on Friday nights. Within a month, both the Cabaret Voltaire and the UFO became home to a thriving new revolutionary scene.

European artists seeking sanctuary from the escalating madness of World War I fled to Switzerland. Zurich soon became a refuge for exiled musicians, artists, writers, and all stripes of dissidents with a flair for absurdity. With the aid of Romanian poet/performance artist Tristan Tzara, who drew up a list of left-wing "Dada presidents"—including artists Max Ernst and Jean Arp, cutting-edge composer Igor Stravinsky, and surrealist poet André Breton—Hugo Ball began to shake up an already shook-up world. The absurdist concept behind Dadaism was "terribly simple," he explained. "In French it means 'hobby horse.' In German it means 'goodbye.' In Romanian it means 'yes, you are right.'"

"Cabaret Voltaire was where they wrote and first read the Dadaist manifesto publicly, in July 1916," neon sculptor and musician Cork Marcheschi notes. "It was where [German collage artist/poet] Kurt Schwitters stood on a tabletop and held up the letter *W* written on a piece of cardboard and recited his 'W Poem,' repeating the letter *W* 250 times. He screamed it ... 'Waaah!' and hollered it . . . 'Whoo!' until he threw it on the ground and proclaimed it the greatest poem ever written!" (Attempting to explain his baffling performance, Schwitters declared, "The basic material of poetry is not the word, but the letter.")

More bizarre events followed when Hugo Ball questioned a small crowd, "How does one achieve eternal bliss? By saying Dada! How does one become famous? By saying Dada. With a noble gesture and delicate propriety. Till one goes crazy. Till one loses consciousness."

Like Ball before him, Hoppy Hopkins created a platform for a flock of social misfits who advocated free speech and free love, along with a ragtag crew of political revolutionaries, recreational druggies, and publishers and purveyors of "obscene" literature (as *IT* was promptly deemed by the Establishment), while providing a home for some of the greatest music to come out of England in the 1960s.

Following a performance of the Spontaneous Underground at the Marquee Club on June 13, 1966, Pink Floyd would meet Peter Jenner, a fan of avant-garde music who had previously recorded the experimental group AMM with expat soprano saxophonist Steve Lacy. But Jenner soon realized there was no profit in producing jazz, so he went looking for an edgy rock band like the Velvet Underground who might break into the mainstream. Jenner had even reached out to John Cale about managing the band before learning that Andy Warhol had already got them signed to Verve Records and was producing their first album.

Mesmerized by the Floyd's burbling, psychedelic cauldron of sound, Jenner and his partner Andrew King (who'd been teaching cybernetics at the time) would form Blackhill Enterprises and offer to manage the band. With little experience but a bundle of family money to play with (which they quickly spent on new equipment for the band), they formed a six-way equal partnership, split between themselves and the four members of Pink Floyd. Their secretary, June Child, would later go on to manage and marry Marc Bolan.

While Pink Floyd's budding popularity helped Jenner and King find higher-profile bookings, the band bemoaned having to whittle down their expansive jams to under three-minutes to fit the demands of the pop singles market. Despite their paisley and satin togs and the mesmerizing light shows that swirled around them as they played, Pink Floyd disavowed the trendy "psychedelic" moniker, if for no other reason than trying to keep the bobbies at bay after John Lennon and Yoko Ono, Keith Richards, and Donovan were all busted by Sgt. Norman Pilcher's celebrity-seeking drug squad.

Syd was the only member of the band who truly lived the life (albeit to the point of excess), while the others were self-described "weekend hippies." Clad in Carnaby Street gear, Roger looked about as hip as a TV-show detective. It's interesting to note that, with Barrett's departure, so went the band's brief dalliance with fashion. Waters, Wright, and Mason soon dropped all vestiges of psychedelia, replacing their bright silk kerchiefs and satin shirts with a more "laid-back West Coast look" comprised of T-shirts, jeans, and the occasional buckskin fringed jacket. Besides, Barrett, who continually challenged the status quo was all but done with the trend by the time he confessed to looking like "a jerk" all done up in paisley and velvet in his free-associative lyrics to "Vegetable Man."

With the hazy dawn of 1967, Pink Floyd signed to EMI for a £5,000 advance. Joe Boyd, who produced the new wave of British folk-rock albums by the Incredible String Band, Fairport Convention, and Nick Drake, was chosen to shepherd the band's debut single. "My philosophy as a producer is to set as good an atmosphere as possible for the artists to play their best and put them in front of a microphone and record them as faithfully as I can," he told the UK pop and rock monthly *Beat Instrumental* in December 1968. "I don't want to impose my personality on the record, and I don't like using electronic trickery."

Beyond Rick Wright's exotic "Turkish delight" Farfisa organ riffs and a schmear of reverb on Syd Barrett's voice, Boyd managed to stand clear of all surplus effects and let the song stand on its own two wobbly feet. At the same time, Boyd also produced "Granny Takes a Trip," a turbo-charged jug-band number by the Purple Gang that was immediately banned by the BBC for its alleged LSD reference, despite it also being the name of the popular boutique on the Kings Road. With its kazoo, tack piano, and harmonica, the tune evoked the nostalgic ragtime of Boyd's old Cambridge (Massachusetts) pals the Jim Kweskin Jug Band, as well as a few of the old-timey moments heard on the Rolling Stones' recent *Between the Buttons*, like "Cool, Calm, and Collected" and "Something Happened to Me Yesterday," which feature buzzing kazoos and an oompahing tuba from the ever-versatile Brian Jones.

In their earliest incarnation in 1964, the Grateful Dead—featuring Jerry Garcia, Ron "Pigpen" McKernan, and Bob Weir, and originally known as Mother McCree's Uptown Jug Champions—shared a passion for the obscure music of 1920s and '30s, played many of the same instruments, and covered a similar repertoire to the Purple Gang. One must wonder if Syd Barrett had been inspired by the sound of this Stockport-based group when he wrote his brilliantly demented "Jugband Blues."

Meanwhile, having graduated college in 1966, Ivan Pawle (who played bass and keyboards with the Irish psychedelic folk-rock band Dr. Strangely Strange) fled Dublin and headed for London, seeking employment as a teacher. But he soon realized he lacked the temperament necessary for the calling. At the time, London was in the thick of a cultural renaissance, and Ivan joyfully devoured it all. Finding a flat off the Portobello Road, he recalls passing "All Saints Hall, where Pink Floyd rehearsed with their light show. They sounded good! The *International Times* was also starting up, and there were regular Sunday night benefit gigs, featuring the current crop of bands at the Roundhouse, which became London's center for the Summer of Love."

Ian Whitcomb described the Roundhouse in Chalk Farm, formerly used by British Airways as "a storage shed," as a "ramshackle" version of Bill Graham's Fillmore West auditorium, where counterculture happenings were staged by the local underground.

"The Roundhouse was an icy cold cavernous venue," recalls Marijke Koger-Dunham. "Wrought-iron arches supporting the domed roof, the sound system blasting with mind-blowing performances by the Soft Machine and Pink Floyd, enhanced by colorful hallucinatory projections of oil and water slides," all helped to create its "groovy psychedelic ambiance."

"It was a small but potent scene," Pawle continues. "I saw John Lennon and met Yoko Ono briefly, at the opening of a macrobiotic restaurant at the Buddhist Society on Church Street in Kensington. I passed Paul McCartney on the stairs in Southampton Row and attended such events as the 14-Hour Technicolor Dream at Alexandra Palace."

Organized by Hoppy and dubbed "A Night Out of Time" by the *International Times*, the 14-Hour Technicolor Dream began on the evening of April 29, 1967. Upon entry, members of the crowd of between five and eight thousand "tripsters" were told to randomly reset their watches, to create a new alternative dimension where time was irrelevant. The musical marathon kicked off with a set by the Crazy World of Arthur Brown, followed by the Soft Machine, the Pretty Things, Pete Townshend, and Yoko Ono. Pink Floyd, who topped the bill, began their set at sunrise, having just returned from Amsterdam.

Peter Whitehead (best known at the time for his cinema-verité documentary of the Rolling Stones' 1965 tour, *Charlie Is My Darling*), documented the events in his 1967 film *Tonight Let's All Make Love in London*. One scene portrays a stoned John Lennon, mustachioed and bespeckled, wandering among a crowd of writhing dancers while Yoko Ono directs a "happening," handing out scissors to puzzled audience members who snipped away at a paper dress worn by a nervous, lithe model.

Charming and odd as it all now seems, it didn't take long for the hippie honeymoon to spiral out of control. Ivan Pawle laments:

> Some of my colleagues quickly graduated from smoking dope and dropping acid to doing heroin and methedrine. I wound up moving back to Dublin, to a cooler, less frantic environment, and got involved in musical endeavors, which led to Joe Boyd producing our first [Dr. Strangely Strange] album, *Kip of the Serenes*. We were managing ourselves and did gigs in universities and folk clubs. At the time, Joe was very busy with the Incredible String Band, Fairport Convention, John Martyn, and Nick Drake, not to mention Sandy Denny! In fairness, he gave us a lot more attention than we truly deserved. But it was a privilege to be recorded by Joe Boyd at Sound Techniques Studio with [engineer] John Wood. Joe had an unerring ear for pitch. Our first album was released by Island Records. But Joe was already winding down his time in London, and [he] sent Roger Meyer over to Dublin with [Fairport Convention drummer] Dave Mattacks for two days to complete our second album, *Heavy Petting*.

Back in 1966, the ever-busy Boyd had attempted to land a contract for Pink Floyd with Elektra Records, for whom he had recently recorded the Incredible

String Band, but the label's director, Jac Holzman, passed on the band. A folk and blues producer, Holzman didn't connect with the burgeoning psychedelic scene . . . until he signed the charismatic Arthur Lee, whose band Love had ignited the Sunset Strip with a combination of soul and psychedelia. Holzman, who then signed the Doors, had an uncanny intuition and lived by the maxim, "Never make a record you're not passionate about."

Frustrated, Boyd had left Elektra by the end of 1966. He recorded Pink Floyd independently, having previously "learned the studio" from Paul Rothchild—best known for producing the Doors, Paul Butterfield, and Tim Buckley—who helped bolster his confidence and "demystified the process" of making records.

Recorded in February and released on March 10, 1967, Pink Floyd's first single was "Arnold Layne," who according to the band was "a nasty sort of person" with "a strange hobby." No one expected an ode to a creepy neighbor with a panty fetish to soar to No. 20 on the UK charts, but that's exactly what happened.

"'Arnold Layne' was very big for me. I absolutely adored that song," says Pete Brown. "It was very innovative in that it had this completely British subject about British perversions. Not everyone understood it, but eventually they came around. It was a great song, although the band didn't play it live very well, apart from Syd. They'd mostly been in blues bands when they suddenly transformed into doing this new psychedelic thing."

Common in the British theater since the days of Shakespeare, cross-dressing eventually became a short-lived trend when glam rock went mainstream in the UK (and to a lesser extent in America) in the early '70s. Just a few years earlier, the Rolling Stones could be seen done up in drag on the outrageous cover to their 1966 single "Have You Seen Your Mother, Baby, Standing in the Shadows," while Van Morrison sang a heart-wrenching ode to the high-heeled transvestite "Madame George" on his 1968 masterpiece *Astral Weeks*. While Syd Barrett and Marc Bolan fearlessly donned frilly lace cuffs and gobs of black eyeliner, David Bowie not only looked fabulous in a floral dress designed by Michael Fish but also shocked the world when he boldly announced he was gay in a January 1972 interview with *Melody Maker*.

Essential, too, to the surreal hilarity of *Monty Python's Flying Circus* (first aired in October 1968), cross-dressing would also inspire the Kinks' 1970 chart-topping ode to the sexually ambiguous "Lola." And, having gone solo following the demise of the Velvet Underground, Lou Reed released *Transformer* in 1972, with "Walk on the Wild Side," which recounted the odyssey of "Holly" (Woodlawn, the Puerto Rican actress and star of Andy Warhol's film *Trash*), who shaved his legs and plucked his eyebrows while hitchhiking en route to New York from Miami, thereby becoming a she. The gender-bending fad embraced by Mott the Hoople, Slade, Roxy Music, and the New York Dolls would peak in 1975 as fans of *The Rocky Horror Picture Show* filled movie theaters from coast to coast, sporting lipstick, girdles, garters, stockings, and heels, to act out the film's scenes in real time.

◐

With Blackhill Enterprises now in charge of Pink Floyd's affairs, Jenner and King quickly ousted Joe Boyd as the band's producer and appointed the Beatles' former engineer Norman Smith (or "Normal," as John Lennon called him) to the task of overseeing the band's next single.

From the start, Pink Floyd's fans seemed to resent the band's increasing success, believing they should remain a cherished secret of the London underground. After the band signed their first record deal and moved on to larger venues, one angry fan scrawled "Pink Finks!" on the UFO's bathroom walls. As Roger Waters told Connor McKnight of *ZigZag* magazine in 1973, "Freaks [were] standing by the side of the stage screaming that we'd sold out." Nick Mason recalled the abuse being hurled by the other band sharing the bill that night, the Brothers Grimm, along with "their lady friends. I remember that well because it hit hard."

With the band branded "sellouts" for signing a record contract, David Gilmour pondered the predicament of being hip versus having a hit. "It seems if you have a record in the charts, you are rejected by the underground movements. Hit parades do spell death for our sort of group. Myself," he added ironically, "I don't think we'll ever get through to the masses."

While the members of Pink Floyd considered themselves to be UFO's house band, according to Nick they were "known to live in a world of their own."

They were not "into the lifestyle" and were not part of the larger, burgeoning underground community that Hoppy, Boyd, Barry Miles, and Bob Fraser helped to organize.

Whereas San Francisco bands like the Jefferson Airplane and Grateful Dead contributed to the neighborhood and culture of Haight-Ashbury, "The Floyd were neither psychedelic or underground," Barry Miles later wrote. "The underground was [just] a convenient stepping stone, to be used and discarded."

Awash in a sea of reverb and whimsy, Pink Floyd's second single, "See Emily Play," was released on June 16, 1967, and was said to be inspired by "the psychedelic schoolgirl" Emily Young, a habitué of the UFO. Producer Norman Smith later claimed "Emily" was his favorite Pink Floyd track, as he was able to make "some alterations and dress that up in a more commercial way than they had in mind. And it turned out to be a big hit."

It was, Pete Brown enthuses, "such a beautiful, lyrical song":

> It really revolutionized a lot of stuff, along with [the Beatles'] "Eleanor Rigby." Everyone had been into this soul thing at the time, which was very good at first, but it wasn't very original. They were just copying Americans. Then suddenly there were bands popping up like Tomorrow, Pink Floyd, and a few others who were doing very British material, driven in part by "Strawberry Fields Forever" and "Penny Lane," which opened up a whole new spectrum of what was possible musically and lyrically, because it was closer to home, it was kind of easier than trying to sing like Wilson Pickett, which we all wanted to do, whether we were capable to, or not. [*laughs*]

Deeply cynical of show business, Roger Waters would complain that there was "more to playing rock 'n' roll than 'Johnny B. Goode.'" Following the band's initial string of singles, he announced that they had no further intention of recording and releasing three-minute pop confections designed for the hit parade. In addition, they refused to play "Emily" live. "Not out of spite," Rick Wright politely explained to documentary director John Edginton. "[But] that of course caused huge problems," he added—not just with EMI, their record company, but with frustrated fans who expected to hear familiar songs at their shows. "There were a few beer glasses flying around," he chuckled.

In an interview with *ZigZag* magazine, Roger Waters recalled a group of rowdies at the California Ballroom in Dunstable, "pouring pints of beer onto us from the balcony," along with "broken beer mugs smashing into the drum kit. . . . That was most unpleasant and very, very dangerous too."

Hardly calm, Syd Barrett stood at the center of this swirling cultural hurricane, taking it all in with his sparkling eyes wide open. Between the sudden onslaught of rock stardom and the smorgasbord of drugs he voraciously consumed, Syd's nervous system began to tilt as he teetered on the tightrope of sanity. Initially, no one seemed too concerned about the strength and purity of the LSD passed around London's underground scene. But by the summer of 1967, Joe Boyd pointed out, "It was often heavily adulterated, with amphetamines and other substances cranking up the rate of 'bad trips.' There may have been more to it than that, but I am not the one to suggest another source of Syd's collapse."

As Roger Waters summed it up to Connor McKnight, "There was so much dope and acid around in those days that I don't think anyone can remember anything about anything."

Whether Dadaists gathering at the Zurich's Cabaret Voltaire or the psychedelic explorers who comprised the original underground at the UFO, such scenes are never built to last. In Hoppy Hopkins' case, retribution came swift and hard for challenging societal norms. Topping the list of persecuted counterculture celebrities, Sgt. Norman Pilcher's Narco squad's next target was the cacophonous "hippie vice den," as the UFO was branded by the London press.

"Hoppy was potentially a very, very good leader," Pete Brown stresses. "But I think his power was ultimately reduced by acid. He took quite a lot, and it didn't do him any favors. That was my impression, anyway. . . . And then, of course, there was the bust."

Arrested after a small chunk of hashish was discovered in his flat, Hoppy was unceremoniously hauled before a judge and handed a nine-month jail sentence. *Free Hoppy* graffiti appeared on city walls overnight, and Paul McCartney bought a full-page ad in the *Times*, supported by a host of London luminaries, demanding fair treatment for Hopkins.

The so-called "Summer of Love" began with Hoppy behind bars in the notorious Wormwood Scrubs prison, where Keith Richards and Mick Jagger wrote the sardonic "We Love You" after famously spending a night in jail following their celebrated bust at Richards' Redlands home on February 12, 1967.

According to Peter Jenner, Hoppy's bust was "a tragedy for the hip community . . . I don't think it ever recovered. . . . His energy which fired so many schemes . . . held everything together and helped to maintain a unity." Due to "internal bickering, police harassment and better-funded competition," the UFO soon "lost its way," Joe Boyd lamented, and was closed by October.

◐

Meanwhile, the psychedelic scene in California had exploded with a new breed of groups with long, strange names like the Grateful Dead, Jefferson Airplane, Quicksilver Messenger Service, Country Joe and the Fish, and Big Brother and the Holding Company, who, true to their egalitarian spirit, played free concerts in local parks. Inspired by the modal improvisations of John Coltrane and fueled by copious amounts of pot, LSD, booze, and various pharmaceuticals, they stretched the parameters of popular music, along with their minds and various societal taboos. Like Pink Floyd at the UFO, the Dead became the house band for the celebrated author Ken Kesey's "Acid Tests," where they routinely extended their songs to seven, ten, or fifteen minutes, as their mesmerized crowd swayed and swirled themselves to the threshold of oblivion.

But not everyone was gleefully "floating around on the belladonna clouds" of peace, love, and dope. Peter Stampfel of the anarchist string band the Holy Modal Rounders (best known for their off-kilter waltz, "Bird Song," from *Easy Rider*) claims, "The Summer of Love was stupid! I called it the 'Somber Blub Blub.' It annoyed the hell out of all of us. Sam Shepard"—the Rounders' drummer, before finding fame as a distinguished playwright and actor—"got a crew cut in protest at all the shenanigans."

Looking like he was about to be shipped off to Vietnam, Shepard suddenly no longer conformed to the hippie ideal of cool. In response, ESP-Disk's Bernard Stollman, the arbiter of the avant-garde, refused to allow his image to appear on the new Holy Modal Rounders album cover. After all, until Charlie Manson came along, hair length was a handy yardstick by which many (no matter how misguidedly) measured the depth of their peers' character.

Within a year, the Summer of Love had withered on the vine as the riots raged at the Democratic Convention in Chicago, and the Rounders would drive to San Francisco to open for Pink Floyd at the Avalon Ballroom. Stampfel recalls:

> We picked up a couple of thirteen-year-old hitchhikers on the way. They were complaining about the price of weed! I thought this drug business was getting out of hand. I didn't think kids should be smoking pot. So, we decided to make some sort of gesture. Rather than smoke weed, we got some booze—bought a few hip pocket bottles of Jack Daniels. In turn, this outraged the San Francisco hippies because we were using "a bad drug"! I guess someone, somewhere had decided there were "good drugs" and "bad drugs." That little escapade inspired our song "Bad Karma," which was a fuck-you to the hippies. But worst of all, the only San Francisco–style poster to ever feature our name on it was black-and-white, which was weird. But that was the luck of the Rounders.

Despite whatever drink or drug musicians chose to enhance their reality, the blues always remained a key component of the music. Even when augmented with a new palate of electronic sounds, the blues' simple, infallible structure provided a sturdy foundation on which to build endless psychedelic jams for groups as diverse as the Grateful Dead, the Pretty Things, and the Mike Bloomfield–era Paul Butterfield Blues Band. You could hear the blues burbling just below the shimmering surface of new "space rock" tunes like Pink Floyd's "Interstellar Overdrive," or the soul-freezing isolation of the Rolling Stones' "2000 Light Years from Home."

The Byrds were actually the first band to scrape the stratosphere, with their John Coltrane–influenced "Eight Miles High," released in March 1966, followed by the country-rock prototype "Mr. Spaceman."

In the spirit of polar explorer Richard Byrd, for whom the Byrds were named, Roger McGuinn, in the fall of 1967, invited Paul Beaver of the famed electronic duo Beaver and Krause to play Moog synthesizer on their most innovative album, *The Notorious Byrd Brothers*. After learning the intricacies of the Moog from Beaver, McGuinn added swooshing atmospherics to a droning Irish folk melody to create the mesmerizing "Space Odyssey." Freely jumping continents, McGuinn then dialed up India on the innovative "Moog Raga."

Following the Byrds' Gram Parsons–led expedition into the new and as-yet-unnamed genre of Americana with *Sweetheart of the Rodeo*, McGuinn returned to experimenting with his beloved synthesizer. Combining a clawhammer-style banjo and Terry Riley–style bubbling keyboards, Roger reinvented the traditional Appalachian tune "Give the Fiddler a Dram." While Gid Tanner and His Skillet-Lickers, who first recorded the song in 1926, would never have recognized it, Roger's mischievous mashup sadly remained unreleased due to the objections of his bandmates. Although it was never finished, the track was stronger than much of what appeared on the Byrds' 1969 album *The Ballad of Easy Rider*.

O

"For the previous decade or more, modern composers had been seeking 'new sounds,' which was a simple request but hard to reach given the limited technologies of the '50s and '60s," Brian Kehew explains. "Pushing the boundaries of standard instruments, effects, and studio options became a mindset. The early Pink Floyd was born of the psychedelic age, basically an audio movement that set out to simulate/create the sounds of a drug trip using sonics."

Synthesizers aside, Roger Waters wanted nothing to do with "space rock," a genre his band helped to define. "Syd had one song that had anything to do with space," he groused. "'Astronomy Domine' [was] the sum total of all Syd's writing about space, and yet there's this whole fucking mystique about how he was the father of it all."

Yet Waters' attempt at distancing himself from the space-rock handle seems hypocritical, as Pink Floyd's music constantly evoked both the sound and imagery of the starry dynamo with the band's love of the latest electronica and song titles like "Interstellar Overdrive," and his own "Set the Controls for the Heart of the Sun" and "Cirrus Minor."

Just two days after Pink Floyd headlined the legendary Games for May concert at Queen Elizabeth Hall on May 12, 1967, the group appeared on BBC's Sunday night show *The Look of the Week*. The program began with Syd standing at the mic, bathed alternately in bright light and dark shadows, mouthing a drumbeat, "beatboxing" decades before anyone had a term for it. Suddenly,

Roger let out a banshee howl (exemplifying the wild false-face, masked spirit that Pete Townshend previously found so fearsome) as icy strobes flashed and large abstract florescent amoebas slithered up and down the wall behind them. (For the full effect, listen to Waters' blood-curdling scream on "Careful with That Axe, Eugene," from their 1969 double album *Ummagumma*.) Even Nick Mason, Waters' closest friend among the band members, had to admit he occasionally found Roger "frightening."

The fun was suddenly cauterized the moment the camera cut to the smug, cigarette-clutching Austrian musician and critic Hans Keller, who claimed he had no intention of prejudicing the viewer's opinion. But, a moment later, he bitterly complained of the band's volume and repetitive music. Waters and Barrett politely endured the haranguing interview as their condescending host likened their art to no more than a display of childhood regression.

Syd didn't seem particularly more stoned, incoherent, or aloof than any other rock star of the day. In fact, he appeared rather charming and considerate toward Keller, who was obviously unnerved by the sonic onslaught of Pink Floyd's "Astronomy Domine."

☾

That May, David Gilmour dropped by Abbey Road while Pink Floyd were in the thick of recording "See Emily Play." He had not seen his old friend in quite a while, and it was clear that Syd had experienced a profound change. Joe Boyd concurred, claiming to have watched, crestfallen, one night as a burned-out Barrett was led through the crowd outside the UFO by his girlfriend, Lynsey Korner (whom Syd eulogized in "Apples and Oranges"). Onstage, the doomed dandy stood motionless before the microphone, his "arms by his sides, staring into space," as Boyd described it. The light that once beamed so brightly from his eyes had inexplicably been extinguished. "Something had happened," Rick Wright explained. "[There was] a total difference. He was still looking the same, but he was somewhere else."

Aubrey Powell, who shared a flat with Syd in South Kensington in London, recalled Barrett's ever-shifting moods from "extremely aggressive and then passive with completely a dead look in his eye the next. It was frightening and I watched this person just sort of slip away into somebody who could no longer play the guitar. . . . He would sit there with a guitar in front of him, try to strum it, but his fingers wouldn't touch the strings. It was tragedy beyond, and then he left London and went back to live with his mother in Cambridge."

Despite Syd's darker moments, Powell remembered his deeply troubled friend with "great affection." After all, it was Barrett who gave Hipgnosis its clever name, carving the strange word into their office door with a ball point pen. Powell explained how Syd's brilliant mashup came about: "Hip meaning cool, groovy, and gnostic meaning wise. . . . We thought that's a very great name for a company. What a great title. . . . He was a wordsmith. He loved to tear up newspapers and tear up the words and throw them up in the air and wherever they land he'd create songs out of them. All those wonderful sort of little ballads that he made up, that were very much kind of fairy tale songs, were often formed from things that he found."

Since their early days at the UFO, Pink Floyd's visual esthetic had always played a key role in the band's appeal. Vic Singh's photograph that graced the cover of *Piper at the Gates of Dawn* portrayed the band as a pack of sinister dandies, clad in satin shirts and silk scarves. His kaleidoscopic lens perfectly mirrored the music's otherworldly sound.

Everything about *Piper at the Gates of Dawn* made one stop momentarily to wonder about the sugar cube they just dropped in your teacup. Inspired by Kenneth Grahame's *The Wind in the Willows*, *Piper* (whose original title had been *Projection*) was recorded at the same time and in the same studios as *Sgt. Pepper*. A concept album in theory, *Pepper* took a nostalgic glimpse back at life (both real and imagined) in the Fabs' hometown of Liverpool, while Barrett's lyrics stretched the parameters of pop music with a smattering of fantastic visions inspired by C. S. Lewis and J. R. R. Tolkien. Gnomes and unicorns frolicked throughout, along with visions of unexplored galaxies and fragmented memories of his Cambridge childhood.

Like John Lennon, Barrett greatly admired Lewis Carroll, author of *Alice in Wonderland* and *Through the Looking-Glass*. Lennon's nonsensical "I Am the Walrus" obviously owed its inspiration to Carroll's poem "The Walrus and the Carpenter," and the Beatles included his image among the curious crew that comprised the cover of *Sgt. Pepper*, despite mounting accusations that the beloved author was a pedophile.

While whimsy and mythology were de rigueur in rock lyrics by 1967, in Barrett's case his songs often sprang directly from personal experience. According to Andrew King, Grantchester Meadows served as a muse for both Roger Waters' lilting pastoral ballad by the same name and Gilmour's "Fat Old Sun," from *Atom Heart Mother*. For Waters, the mythical meadow was where he spent "many happy hours" riding his bike and fishing in the River Cam. It was also on that same swatch of fertile earth that Syd allegedly encountered the cloven-hooved/goat-horned/pipe-blowing god among its golden weeds and bare trees. Barrett believed this extraordinary meeting with Pan gave him "insight and understanding into the way nature works."

As Gilmour later told broadcaster Sue Lawley when appearing on BBC Radio 4's *Desert Island Discs* on April 6, 2003, "Syd had a wonderful way with words and could write words so easily that always had such a poetic sort of edge to them. He was a lovely guy."

Barrett's ethereal tunes, as Joe Boyd once said of the Incredible String Band, were built on "wonderful and enchanting melodies, capable of transporting you into a kaleidoscopic parallel world cleansed of the ugliness of everyday life, of violence: each note of them is an invitation to enjoy life ... to love and dance."

"Wonderful and enchanting" or not, Norman Smith, a former struggling jazz trumpeter turned engineer, had a hard time relating to Pink Floyd. "There was nothing in their music that appealed to me that much," he grumbled. But from a business perspective, Smith believed Pink Floyd might sell some records after seeing the crowd's overwhelming response to the band's performance at the UFO, enhanced by their dazzling light show. Smith eventually convinced EMI to put up the money to record *Piper at the Gates of Dawn*.

"Some of it was particularly difficult. Particularly with a gentleman called Syd Barrett!" said Smith, who later described Barrett as "extremely difficult to get through to with any suggestions I might make."

○

While hardly a virtuoso, Syd's inventiveness on the guitar remains undeniable on numbers like "Interstellar Overdrive" and "Astronomy Domine," which begins with Pink Floyd's manager, Peter Jenner, calling out a list of the planets through a bullhorn.

"I found Syd's approach to guitar revolutionary," says Gary Lucas, songwriter and guitarist of Captain Beefheart and Jeff Buckley fame. "His angular, slashing, rave-up style of guitar playing, coupled with judicious use of effects (primarily Echoplex with slide, plus lots of studio/time manipulations courtesy of Beatles engineer turned producer Norman Smith) just sent me. I'd put him up there with Lou Reed and Jimi Hendrix. While Jimi was truly also a technical virtuoso, Syd and Lou were not. But in terms for going for the Godhead, Syd was the one for me!"

Decades later, Gary remains awed by the whimsical "See Emily Play": "Those opening splashes of guitar color, splattering notes with his slide and echoplex like a sonic action painting and then soaring into the blue empyrean on the guitar solo with grinding fuzz guitar underneath, still instills a sense of wonder. He has the purest feeling. And there is an unfailing sense of the placement of his guitars in the overall sonic canvas!"

Elliott Sharp credits the innovative Sun Records session guitarist Pat "Auburn" Hare, who played on early records by Howlin' Wolf, for being one of the first to stretch the boundaries of the electric guitar:

> He was a brilliant, weird, noisy guitar player, whose use of tremolo was onomatopoeic, a forerunner to the way psychedelic bands would use feedback. Hare and Link Wray both influenced Syd, and lots of other British guitarists of the day. Then, of course, there was Jimi Hendrix, who was playing with Curtis Knight when he was first discovered by Les Paul and his son, Les Jr. They were driving into the city when they stopped to hear them at the Club 20 in Hackensack [New Jersey]. But when they went back to see him again, he was gone. There was a whole slew of noise guitarists, doing what was inevitable. Like Roy Buchannan, who stuck a knife into a speaker cone to create fuzz tone and played purely onomatopoeic noise.

Elliott emphasizes the influence of Stockhausen, Cage, and Henry Powell, as well as the improvisational group AMM, on groups like Pink Floyd and Soft Machine. "Keith Rowe was actually a really good guitarist," he stresses.

Rowe, who began his career as a jazz guitarist in the mold of Wes Montgomery and Jim Hall, soon grew bored with using melodic song forms as a vehicle for improvisation. No stranger to the avant-garde, he had already explored the world of musique concrète, employing radios and saws in his sound. Much to the chagrin of his bandleader, pianist Mike Westbrook, Keith made a radical New Year's resolution: to stop tuning his guitar and to play it lying flat on his lap, using every fret of the instrument to discover new sounds beyond the predictable music he'd now turned his back on. Rowe recalled how he would "cut out images from magazines and fruit pie packets and glue those onto [music] scores." He claimed to find more inspiration for his unorthodox guitar solos "from the fruit pie covers" than from standard notation.

"Barrett and the whole London scene interfaced with the Fluxus scene, which included composer Anna Lockwood and Harvey Matusow, who had been Roy Cohn's right-hand man," Elliott continues. "After going to jail for perjury, Matusow went to England [and] became an expat and an avant-garde prankster who was involved with piano burnings and various happenings with *Oz.*"

While Barrett's innovative guitar work was crucial to defining the early Pink Floyd Sound, "none of this would have amounted to a hill of beans without Syd's ingenious and fiendishly brilliant songwriting, which still stands tall in the canon of art-rock achievements," Gary Lucas emphasizes.

No one might have imagined the enormous influence that pop songster Burt Bacharach had on the space rock opus "Interstellar Overdrive," but Barrett allegedly composed the instrumental after struggling with the riff to "My Little Red Book," a song written by the same gent responsible for such enduring pop confections as "Raindrops Keep Falling on My Head," and "Do You Know the Way to San Jose?"*

O

Just months after *Pepper* and *Piper* were recorded, the Pretty Things took over Abbey Road's Studio 3, with Norman Smith, to create rock's first opera, *S.F.*

---

* Syd's inspiration for "Interstellar Overdrive" is most often said to be Arthur Lee's rendition of "My Little Red Book" on Love's March 1966 self-titled debut, yet Manfred Mann had previously cut the song a year earlier for the soundtrack to *What's New Pussycat?*

LUNACY

Sorrow, fourteen months before the Who's groundbreaking *Tommy.* With its release subsequently delayed by the band's American label, Tamla/Motown, the Pretty Things were accused of "jumping on the *Tommy* bandwagon," Pretty Things front man Phil May later recalled.

While the Pretty Things found Smith easy to work with, Pink Floyd's experience was a different story. "It was hard [working with them]," May told journalist Richie Unterberger. "Roger [Waters] was such an egoist. I mean, the minute he could get rid of anybody who was doing anything in the Floyd, he would." May believed "Roger wanted the Floyd for himself. And he was a very powerful bloke. I've got a lot of respect for Roger. He did some great things. But it was [all about his need for] control."

Such criticism was lost on Waters, who, in his own defense, said, "You've got to be competitive, aggressive, and egocentric—all the things that go to make a real star."

Alan Parsons, Pink Floyd's future engineer (and de-facto producer), claimed he "wasn't terribly impressed" upon first hearing *Piper at the Gates of Dawn.* "If this was to be the music of the future, I wasn't looking forward to it," he grumbled.

Like everything else in the '60s, musical trends changed fast—from trad. jazz to blues and soul to the mushrooming psychedelic scene. As Pete Brown recalls, "There was a soul band known as the In-Crowd who'd been doing well on the circuit and, almost overnight, they became quite successful as Tomorrow. Suddenly their Mod haircuts were gone, and they stopped singing 'In the Midnight Hour.' They started wearing white suits and were singing 'My White Bicycle'—which was a good song, don't get me wrong. They were good musicians and sang well, but it was weird …"

Speaking of "weird," Andrew King found Syd's unique approach to mixing *Piper* quite unusual. "He would throw the levers on the board up and down apparently at random, making pretty patterns with his hands. He wouldn't do anything unless he thought he was doing it in an artistic way."

○

Peter Jenner found the lyrics to Syd's loopy new tune, "Jugband Blues," disturbing. Whimsical as it seemed, Barrett's disjointed ditty contained a casual confession of his encroaching schizophrenia when he sang, "I'm most obliged to you for making it clear, I'm not here." While actors, painters, writers, musicians, and dancers regularly refer to themselves as "empty vessels," intent on staying out of their muse's way, so their expression remains direct and pure, Syd's strange plea for help alarmed his manager when he sang, "I'm wondering who could be writing this song."

Originally intended as the single from Pink Floyd's second album, *A Saucerful of Secrets*, "Jugband Blues" begins with Barrett strumming an off-kilter waltz on an acoustic guitar as Rick Wright embellishes his surreal verse with a plaintive (and slightly out of tune) recorder. The tempo suddenly stumbles into a drunken marching 2/4 rhythm as Nick Mason buzzes a kazoo, while members of the North London Salvation Army Band (whom Barrett had invited to the studio) blow disjointed shards of free jazz, much to Norman Smith's chagrin.

The video made for the song perfectly reflected Syd's state of mind. With his dark eyes vacant, Barrett sings and strums his guitar, while Waters' fingers barely move as he mimes playing the tuba. It's no surprise the promotional clip disappeared for thirty years, before inexplicably turning up in 1999.

Barrett's peculiar behavior attained a new level, stretching beyond such quaint labels as "eccentric" and "odd." His bandmates finally came to realize that Syd's antics were no longer simply contrarian or self-sabotaging but downright deranged. "There was something seriously amiss," Roger Waters confessed, in a candid interview with documentary director John Edington. "It was quite clear [Syd] was no longer with us in any real sense."

Aubrey Powell believed Barrett was "not cut out for the music business. Apart from all these stories about overdoses of LSD and stuff like that, which are probably true—he took quite a lot of LSD—I think that he really did not like the music business, in the sense that he felt he was having to pander to it.... He was under immense pressure to keep coming up with the goods."

At the time, personnel changes in pop bands were second only to death for devout music fans. But Syd Barrett could no longer handle the constant grind of the pop star "machine" that Roger Waters would later brilliantly lampoon in "Have a Cigar."

Publicist Derek Taylor might have been describing Syd Barrett's predicament when he announced that singer/songwriter Gene Clark had abruptly quit the

Byrds on March 1, 1966: "He left because he was tired of the multitude of obligations facing successful rock 'n' roll bands ... tired of the travel, the hotels, and the food ... bothered by the photographs and interviews, and exhausted by the whole punishing scene."

Clark's standing within the Byrds had been shaky from the start due to Roger McGuinn and David Crosby's mounting jealousy over the money and attention lavished on Clark as the band's most prolific songwriter. Gene's intense fear of flying, fueled by a steady diet of dope and booze, didn't help matters. Halfway through recording their third album, *Fifth Dimension* (1966), "Prince Valiant," as bassist Chris Hillman dubbed him, quit "The American Beatles" and headed back to his hometown of Kansas City, where he began writing new songs for his first solo album, oddly enough titled *Echoes*.

○

Whether due to their management's incompetence or uptight authorities at the Department of Immigration, Pink Floyd's visas for their first American tour had been delayed, forcing them to cancel two shows at the Whisky a Go-Go on Sunset Strip. They also faced problems at Bill Graham's Fillmore West and were forced to bow out of a headlining set at radio station KPFA's Benefit Halloween Ball with Sopwith Camel (who apparently shared Pink Floyd's lunar obsession, as they titled their 1973 comeback album *The Miraculous Hump Returns from the Moon*).

The Floyd had been scheduled to appear at Winterland Ballroom on November 2 and 3, with Big Brother and the Holding Company and the soulful folksinger Richie Havens, who did his best to fill in for the missing Brits.

Years later, in June 2009, Havens recalled the scenario to me:

> After my set at the Berkeley Folk Festival, they asked me to be on this panel about show biz in this big auditorium. So, I'm sitting there, listening to all these guys—promoters and lawyers—and there's me, the artist. I'd never done one of these panel things before. I guess I was supposed to say something, so I finally said, "If you take away the artists, there wouldn't be a music business."
>
> Afterward, this guy comes up to me, and said, "Y'know, Richie,

you were really right. I hope to work with you sometime." It was Bill Graham. Two hours later, I'm back at the hotel when I get a phone call. It's Bill, and he says, "Richie, I need to ask you a favor. Pink Floyd is supposed to be here to play, but they're stuck at the airport with all this equipment that I told those assholes to leave at home … I'm gonna kill them when they get here, but could you sit in until they arrive?" So that was a good break. It was really a magic time.

Pink Floyd finally made their American debut at Winterland on November 4, opening for Big Brother, before heading to LA for a disastrous live taping of *The Pat Boone Show* the following afternoon, when Syd answered the "Safe as Milk" host with nothing but blank stares.

The band played two shows later that night at the Cheetah Club in Venice Beach. According to the *LA Free Press*, the first set went swimmingly: "Even the seaweed was swinging," the critic cheered. With the second set came one of the more "mind bending" (*LA Free Press* again) stories in the annals of rock mythology. Not surprisingly, accounts vary wildly, and there are no blurry home movies posted on YouTube to help us decipher the details of this "Grassy Knoll moment" in which Syd seems to have played both Lee Harvey Oswald and JFK.

Before a small crowd comprised of approximately fifty fans, Barrett is said to have appeared with his head glistening with gobs of hair gel. Having allegedly gobbled a handful of barbiturates (or was it acid?) before taking the stage, he apparently stood completely still, frozen like a deer in headlights, staring into the void, his arms dangling limp by his sides unable and uninterested in playing his guitar. Others claim he'd hypnotized himself, putting himself in a trance with a series of long droning tones from his guitar. Either way, the rest of the band soldiered on through the set without him.

Eyewitnesses claim Barrett was inert, either shocked by his equipment during the set or simply in a state of shock that night. Whatever the circumstances, Pink Floyd could no longer rely on their fractured front man.

Following Pink Floyd's appearance on *American Bandstand* on November 6, 1967, Waters refused to make any further appearances on commercial television. He found the experience insufferable, and he could no longer bear the thought of white-bread TV hosts like Dick Clark asking daft questions about cheeseburgers and sightseeing destinations. It was no surprise that the group were not invited back after a hollow-eyed Barrett barely lip-synched the words to their latest single, "Apples and Oranges." While commonly dismissed as a knockoff written under industry pressure to produce another hit, Syd's lilting, sparkling song (which remained unreleased in America) was far from anything one might consider "commercial."

Frustrated and unnerved by Barrett's increasingly strange antics, the band canceled the remainder of their American tour dates and beat their retreat to London. But it was just a matter of days before Pink Floyd again found themselves on the road, this time third on a bill of seven bands, supporting the Jimi Hendrix Experience and the Move on an old-school "package" tour for which their allotted time was a brief twenty minutes.

Barrett, to everyone's surprise, managed to rise to the occasion for "The Alchemical Wedding," as the first night of the tour, November 14 at the Royal Albert Hall, was billed. But the tour soon took a serious toll on "Smiling Syd," as Jimi Hendrix dubbed the Floyd's strangely aloof front man. When Barrett became incapable of functioning, he was replaced by guitarist Dave O'List (of the Nice), whose identity was well concealed as he stood onstage, a darkened silhouette in the glow of Peter Wynne-Willson's mesmerizing lightshow.

As Syd's increasing chaos became a liability to the band's future, his old friend from Cambridge, David Gilmour, was quietly ushered in as the "Fifth Floyd" to cover when Barrett, in the throes of a psychotic stupor, might unpredictably bash the strings of his guitar in an ear-splitting cacophony or simply refuse to play at all. Barrett, in the understated words of Nick Mason, had become "a loose and hallucinating cannon."

On December 20, Pink Floyd played live at the BBC Maida Vale Studios. The tapes, broadcast on *Top Gear* on New Year's Eve, reveal some lovely if murky renditions of Syd's latest strange gems: "Jugband Blues," and "Vegetable Man," whose lyrics Peter Jenner likened to "words from a psychiatrist's chair." Barrett's harrowing sense of alienation had become apparent for all when he sighed, "I've been looking all over the place, for a place for me / But it ain't anywhere."

Billed as "Christmas on Earth Continued—An All-Night Christmas Dream

Party," the concert began at 8 p.m. on December 22 and featured a cornucopia of cool, with the Jimi Hendrix Experience, the Who, Eric Burdon's New Animals, Soft Machine, and, of course, Pink Floyd, in the last throes of their Syd Barrett incarnation, teetering on their wobbly legs before the Olympia crowd of fifteen thousand ripped revelers.

The turning point finally came, following a short holiday break, at a gig at Southampton University on January 26, for which the Floyd shared the bill with the Incredible String Band and Tyrannosaurus Rex. Filled with trepidation at the thought of what another performance with Syd might bring, Roger Waters took a quick vote. Finding no protests among his bandmates, he remarked, "Let's not bother [to pick up Syd]." While they considered Barrett their friend "most of the time," Waters admitted there were more than a few occasions when they all "wanted to strangle him."

One might easily imagine Syd sitting alone at home, waiting for the van to come, lost in reverie, gently strumming the chords to a new song with the evocative title of "Dark Globe," lonely and confused, as he sang, "Won't you miss me, wouldn't you miss me at all?"

According to David Gilmour, there came a point when nobody was willing to risk booking Pink Floyd if Syd Barrett remained in their ranks. "It had become a totally impossible situation," he explained. "After the success of the summer of '67, the band sank like a stone. The only way out was to get rid of Syd."

While the disappointing response to "Apples and Oranges" signaled the end of Pink Floyd's viability as a singles band, the accompanying video, shot along with six others over the course of February 18 and 19, 1968, for Belgian TV, is perhaps a more telling (and somewhat creepy) document than anyone realized at the time. Syd is nowhere to be seen; a bemused David Gilmour strums his guitar, surrounded by crates of fruit, as Roger Waters lip-synchs the vocals, seemingly gleeful at being the center of attention. The other songs filmed in Brussels' Parc de Laeken that chilly February included Rick Wright's moody "Paint Box," along with three additional Barrett numbers: "The Scarecrow," "See Emily Play," and "Bike."

Back home in Cambridge, the band's isolated visionary was no longer needed, the groundwork for the new Pink Floyd having been laid with an awkward appearance on *Tienerklanken* (a.k.a. *Teen Sounds*), broadcast on Belgian TV on

March 31, 1968. A week later, on April 6, the news broke: Syd Barrett was out. Yet he would remain as integral to Pink Floyd's mythology as their flying pig, "Algie," which also broke loose from its moorings and drifted off, beyond anyone's reach.

○

Barrett's storied madness would continue to inspire great songs and albums from the Floyd as well as his own first solo flight, *The Madcap Laughs*. Chock full of whimsical imagery and baffling perspectives, the *Madcap* sessions were produced to the best of Dave Gilmour's ability, despite Syd's increasingly erratic behavior. The record took a year to finish and was finally released in January 1970. Just twenty-two, Barrett had sadly fallen victim of his own debauchery.

Hoping to downplay Syd's sorry condition to the *NME*'s Nick Kent, Gilmour implied that his old friend "functions on a totally different plane . . . a higher consciousness," while Waters continued to stoke the "genius" myth.

Despite the support of engineer John Leckie and EMI—who provided studio time at Abbey Road, along with a batch of new guitars—Syd remained fractured, unfocused, and unpredictably brilliant. The various bits and pieces that Gilmour and Rick Wright managed to cull from the sessions (which ran a bit more efficiently than on their first outing) would comprise his second offering, *Barrett*, released in November 1970.

Syd's story was hardly shocking to anyone in the entertainment world. Since the advent of Hollywood scandal sheets, the troubled lives of movie stars grappling with addiction, divorce, bankruptcy, and madness in the wake of sudden fame made great front-page fodder for newspapers and magazines long before rock 'n' rollers came along. Living vicariously through their doomed hero's triumphs, losses, and emotional messes, the public often forgets or ignores the vulnerable person who dwells beneath the shiny armor of fame, let alone the heartbreak and abuse their loved ones are forced to endure.

The list of fallen young heroes from the '60s is staggering—from Brian Jones to Jimi Hendrix, Janis Joplin, Al Wilson, Jim Morrison, Gram Parsons, and Keith Moon, to name just a few. Syd Barrett managed to live to the ripe old age of sixty, although he was lost in *The Twilight Zone* for most of it. Yet, to this day, he remains a fascinating enigma, particularly for the new generations who continue to discover him. His songs still reverberate like cryptic texts from a lost era, while tales of his brief, exuberant burst of creativity and imagination, followed by his tragic, rapid decline, read like a gloomy, moralistic fairy tale from the sixties.

Anthony Stern recalled Syd as "a very thoughtful man . . . until he spiraled [out of control]. I've spent my entire life avoiding being famous because I saw how bad it was for Syd Barrett," he explained. "I saw him go into decline. He wanted to do the music. He didn't want to do *Top of the Pops*."

"The legend, the martyr, the painter, the piper, the seer of visions," Derek See of the Rain Parade says reverently.

> We'll never know exactly what happened to this absolute genius, but he truly epitomized an earthbound shooting star. His brilliance shone so brightly, so briefly, and in so many ways he influenced practically everything cool that followed in his trail, either directly or indirectly. His lyrics and otherworldly guitar playing give us a free ride to the cosmos, and his painting was just as brilliant (the only material possession I dream of owning at this point in my life is one of his paintings). I've been hypnotized and influenced by his music since I was a little kid, thanks to my uncle's record collection, and his work somehow seems to get better and better over time.

"Syd's story is a sad story romanticized by people who don't know anything about it," David Gilmour imparted solemnly. "They've made it fashionable, but it's just not that way."

"People just didn't know what the limits were," Pete Brown exclaims.

> They didn't know when to stop, and in the end, it stopped them! I was always suspicious of Timothy Leary and wondered if he worked for the CIA as LSD had been developed as a weapon of war. Acid was very damaging and dangerous. Not that I'm a rabid conspiracy theorist but there seems to be enough evidence to prove that the British underground was very undermined by LSD

in particular. It was made to look very desirable, but it caused a hell of a lot of trouble. It killed a lot of brains that could have been very useful in really changing society.

An entire generation's drive to create a new world of possibility had initially been sparked by the space race and reinforced by momentous events like the moon landing and the surprise party of Woodstock. But soon, such optimistic aspirations were derailed by the escalating war in Vietnam and the proliferation of hard drugs. Short-lived and naïve as it might appear, there was a shared notion of a new alternative lifestyle that could evolve from a wardriven, consumer society to an ideal civilization whose currency was based on peace, love, and cooperation. The psychedelic experiment had flung wide the doors of perception, but the hallucinations it revealed were not always of the mystical, enlightening variety.

At the first handful of gigs he played with Pink Floyd, Gilmour, "the new guy," performed with his back to the audience, and he later confessed to having been "nervous" and "very embarrassed." While having "consciously learned" his old friend's riffs and style, he hadn't done much psychedelic jamming with his former band, Joker's Wild. Initially, he found the entire experience frustrating. For the first six months, he claimed to have only "played rhythm to help it all along." He admitted to feeling "pretty paranoid . . . I don't think the band had fixed ideas of what I should do or how I should do it . . . they never ever said, 'Play like Syd Barrett.' That was the last thing they wanted."

Most people didn't know that David Gilmour had originally taught Syd how to play Rolling Stones riffs back in their early days, or that he'd used guitar echo effects before Barrett became famous for conjuring a wild new frontier of space sounds.

Not surprisingly, Syd's dismissal triggered a bitter backlash from friends and fans who were outraged by the absurd notion of Pink Floyd continuing without him. As their original manager, Peter Jenner, observed, "One thing I've always taken into consideration, and which sums up, for me anyway, the fundamental personality crisis inherent in the old Floyd, is that Syd was an artist and the other three were all student architects. I think that says an awful lot, particularly when you study the kind of music the Floyd have gone on to play since that time."

No one personified the disappointment of Barrett's vanishing act more than Peter Stampfel, who shared a bill with the "new" version of Pink Floyd with his band, the Holy Modal Rounders, and Seattle-based prog-rock pioneers Crome Syrcus, at the Avalon Ballroom on August 2, 1968:

> In early 1967, Pete Frame* sent me this great reel-to-reel mix tape with a whole lotta stuff I'd never heard before, like "Arnold Layne," "Granny Takes a Trip" by the Purple Gang, and the Pretty Things. The Incredible String Band were also on it, along with Denny Laine's "Say You Don't Mind," and it was the first time I heard [the Kinks'] "Waterloo Sunset." I was really impressed with "Arnold Layne" and "See Emily Play." But then I heard that the guy responsible for those songs had left the group. I didn't know the details, but I was totally pissed-off about it. I was like, *Fuck Pink Floyd without Syd Barrett!* So, I didn't listen to them when we played at the Avalon Ballroom. In retrospect I wish I had. I never even heard *Dark Side of the Moon* when it came out, but I was aware of the huge kerfuffle it made.

"Syd sightings," whether imagined or real, immediately quickly became part of rock 'n' roll's mythology. The most notorious incident occurred on June 5, 1975, when Barrett, in a near-catatonic state, unexpectedly appeared at Abbey Road Studios one night, bald and plump as an eggplant. Shocked upon recognizing him, his former bandmates were aghast at how quickly Syd had degenerated in such a short time.

While chiding himself over his lack of compassion for Syd, Roger Waters made it clear he did *not* write "Shine On You Crazy Diamond" for his fallen friend. The song, Waters stressed, "is not really about Syd. He's just a symbol for the extremes of absence some people have to indulge in because it's the only way they can cope [with the sadness of modern life]."

Less dramatic, but just as telling, is Pete Brown's memory of a mysterious

---

* The British music journalist and historian known for creating the rock family trees which traced the lineage of '60s pop bands.

guitarist and voice in the crowd at a poetry reading he gave in Cambridge in October 1974, which helps put Barrett's post-Floyd years in perspective:

> Jack [Bruce] arrived to collect me after the reading and take me to his place to write, not so far away. I got there a bit late, and Jack was early. Someone had recognized him and handed him a standup bass, and he was jamming with the house band when I got there, alongside a very interesting guitarist. They were sort of playing jazz. Later, when I did my poetry set, I dedicated it to Syd, calling him something like "your [Cambridge's] great local poet." The guitarist, who was in the audience, stood up and said, "Oh, no I'm not." It was indeed Syd!

THE PLASTIC PAISLEY
PIPER INTERLUDE

Inspired by early Pink Floyd, the Milwaukee-based neo-psychedelic band Plasticland didn't play songs, per se, as much as "long pieces, improvisations, and unbridled wildness," as their bassist and songwriter John Frankovic explains.

> *Piper at the Gates of Dawn* was a big influence on most of the musicians I knew at the time. Syd was one of the greatest lyricists ever. I also thought *Ummagumma* was an excellent album, and we covered "Careful with that Axe, Eugene." But I was more into German avant-garde and space-rock bands like Amon Düül and Ash Ra Tempel and grew less interested in Pink Floyd as they became hugely successful. They didn't really need my attention once they got their due. But always I liked that *Dark Side* was about Syd.
>
> When Plasticland formed in 1980, it was outrageous, because punk was happening, and we had really long hair and dressed in flamboyant clothes and colors—not in black jeans and leather, like everyone else. You'd never have known we came from Milwaukee! We were the only ones dressing like that at the time. Then, in LA, the Paisley Underground started to happen.

"The new frontier of psychedelia only lasted a couple of years," Plasticland vocalist and guitarist Glenn Rehse adds.

The roots of a new psychedelic culture began to sprout its strange colorful tentacles once again in California, this time in Los Angeles in 1982. As the Dream Syndicate's Steve Wynn recalls:

Psychedelia could mean anything, from fashion or production techniques or art and design. It could exist in bubble gum, Top 40 radio, album-side-long tracks of indulgence, in free jazz, onstage, or in the audience, in sound or their response to sound.

Our Paisley Underground scene was united by and branded by a very broad-brush stroke of psychedelia. It really is a very broad stroke. The term could include everything from tie-dyed T-shirts and go-go dancers in Day-Glo miniskirts to fuzz pedals and backwards guitars, from the brain and psyche damaging bad acid trips of Brian Wilson and Syd Barrett to the enlightened mumbo jumbo of Timothy Leary, from Bubble Puppy to John Coltrane's deepest *Sun Ship* explorations into space.

For me, psychedelia simply meant being transported. It meant being taken from one state of being to another. It was about the trip along the way, the new places and state of mind at the end of the destination. You trip out in any way you wanna trip out. . . . I often wondered how many of my paisley compatriots had actually done acid. That's not to say they hadn't. Maybe all of them dropped every day. And it's not to say that I was well versed in the lysergic arts, having only taken acid a handful of times, although one of those times mostly consisted of listening to [the extended electric raga] "East-West" by the Butterfield Blues Band on repeat and thus figuring out much of what I wanted to do on stage and in studios for the next forty years.

"I'm not the 'mono version that was only released in Belgium' kind of guy," says Rain Parade's Matt Piucci, summing up the record nerd/snob syndrome.

I was raised on records my brother had, compilations and double albums like the Rolling Stones' *Hot Rocks*, Bob Dylan's *Greatest Hits Vol II*, the Doors' *Absolutely Live*. I don't know why my strict parents allowed my older brothers to take me into Chicago to see concerts, but they did. I was fourteen when I saw my first show—Alice Cooper and Wishbone Ash. It was fucking amazing!

Later that year, he took me to see the Byrds and Commander Cody at the Aragon Ballroom. We had great seats. Somebody handed us some acid, and I was never the same after I saw Roger McGuinn's head floating above the stage during a twenty-minute version of "Eight Miles High." They were improvising. It was jazz-influenced but full of otherworldly sounds. Psychedelic music takes on many forms, like Ornette Coleman's album *Skies Over America.*

So, that was it! I started to learn how to play guitar. I was in high school, and *Dark Side of the Moon* was everywhere. How could you miss it? I wasn't stupid into it. I thought it was cool but then punk hit. I went straight from hippie to punk. Skipped disco... I went to see Talking Heads and cut my hair the next day! But punk was a misnomer. The New York bands weren't *really* that punk—Blondie, Talking Heads—and Patti Smith wasn't really punk: she was into older stuff like [French symbolist poets] Charles Baudelaire [and Arthur] Rimbaud, and the Doors. And the Ramones, as Johnny said, were "just twisted bubble gum music." Once it hit England and got politicized—the Clash, the Damned, Sex Pistols... *that* was punk!

So, I started writing my own stuff [while in college in Minnesota] and formed Rain Parade with David Roback, who later went on to form Mazzy Starr. Both Dave and I loved surrealistic art. We loved the Beatles, the Byrds, and Pink Floyd. We played early '60s surfy stuff. Listened to Love and some real obscure psychedelia, and I went back and listened to *Piper* and was seriously influenced by their tempo changes and weird chords.

Piucci was fascinated by Pink Floyd's unique approach to creating sound.

They played by different rules or by none at all. They used whole tone scales! Their songs would go up chromatically or slide down a half-step. The tempo would slow down, or they'd throw in stops for no apparent reason. Rain Parade learned to play "Lucifer Sam,"

"Interstellar Overdrive," and "Astronomy Domine." For me, it was all about *Piper* . . . and Syd Barrett's solo albums, which were a totally different thing, totally weird, heady music. We were just journeymen in the landscape that Pink Floyd laid down. I'm an ant, they were giants.

2

LET THERE BE
MORE LIGHT

With their flamboyant front man "long gone," the remaining members of Pink Floyd appeared anonymous onstage, blurry figures moving slowly, as if operating machinery or lifting heavy equipment, as their mesmeric light show swirled behind them.

The practice of projecting and reflecting light to enhance the atmosphere of religious rituals can be traced all the way back to ancient Egypt and Greece, while magic-lantern theater techniques are said to have originated sometime in the mid-1600s. Three hundred years later, by the mid-1960s, liquid light shows had become integral to the psychedelic music experience. Elias Romero, an art student from LA, is credited with creating the earliest prototypes in the late '50s when he projected images to live jazz at parties, galleries, and coffeehouses around San Francisco.

"While Tony Martin is probably best-known for his light shows in California, he was inspired by Elias Romero, who used a variety oils and liquids to create the effect," Cork Marcheschi points out. "Tony had a regular Sunday-night gig with the San Francisco Mime Troupe at an old church in the Mission and also created light shows for Berkeley's Open Theater, projecting shapes and colors onto nude dancers."

With a dazzling palate of pigments and oils, Martin conceived of the light show as "painting in time." Bill Graham soon hired him to transform the Fillmore West stage into a swirling, luminescent canvas for performances by the Grateful Dead and Jefferson Airplane. But Martin's stint in the rock world was short-lived: he believed his innovations better suited the sonic innovations of avant-garde composers like John Cage and Toshi Ichiyanagi (Yoko Ono's first husband).

Cork continues:

> Ramon Sender was a writer and electronic musician who cofounded the Mills College Tape Music Center with Morton Subotnick in 1962. Ramon brought Tony in to create visual images to go with their music, along with experimental composers like Pauline Oliveros and Terry Riley. His real-time painting would inspire Abstract Illusionist artists [like James Havard and Jack Reilly] who later became popular in the 1970s. When Tony connected with Bill Graham and did light shows at the Fillmore West, he used ten projectors at a time on the same screen. The colors were made from marking pen ink, which was so rich and transparent. They would drop the ink into oil or shoot it out of ketchup and mustard squeezers and swirl it around. I think those people's hands were stained forever. It's like they got tattoos without needles. But honestly, I was never that interested in the light shows. They projected them all over us when we played, and people couldn't see what we were doing. Besides, lots of people were doing them. It was like you couldn't do it wrong! You had a band playing with a bunch of stoned people dancing. You could've melted a Hershey bar up there and people would've gone, "Whoa!"

The problem with liquid light shows, Anthony Stern concurred, is their inability to "hold your attention … they're not conventionally structured, they just happen. And if you're stoned or dancing … it doesn't matter at all, you just enjoy the imagery."

Perhaps critic Roy Shipston had a point when he groused, in the November '69 issue of *Disc and Music Echo*, he "was convinced that the beautifully coloured bacteria shapes on the backcloth were only to draw attention from the row [Pink Floyd] was making."

Christoph Grunenberg, an art historian and director of the Kunsthalle in

Bremen, Germany, considered the Joshua Light Show "the most complex and sophisticated" of all the '60s liquid light shows. From March 8, 1968, until its closing on June 27, 1971, Joshua White and his crew transformed New York's Fillmore East into a bubbling cauldron of wonderous visions with their "stoned-age technology." To achieve this mesmeric effect, White combined three film projectors, two banks of four-carousel slide projectors with three overhead projectors, hundreds of color wheels, motorized reflectors crafted from aluminum foil, sheets of Mylar, and broken mirrors, along with two hair dryers, watercolors, colored oil, alcohol, glycerin, two crystal ashtrays, and dozens of clear glass clock crystals. White and his crew of between six and eight assembled several tons of equipment on two elevated platforms, approximately twenty feet behind the Fillmore stage.

Initially interested in theater lighting, White had an epiphany at age fifteen after going to New York's Museum of Modern Art, he recalls, "to see all these great works [including Picasso's] *Guernica*, Jackson Pollock, and Monet's *Water Lilies*. But down in the basement, in a dark corner, was a weird piece about the size of a small TV set. It was a beautiful abstraction by Thomas Wilfred," whose unique visual explorations date back to the 1920s. "You couldn't see how he did it, but it was hypnotic. I loved to sit in that room and just stare at it. I never knew how it was done, but when you looked into it, it went on forever. Everything I did afterwards was informed by Thomas Wilfred."

White's assortment of colored lights was rear-projected onto a twenty-by-thirty-foot vinyl screen, by a twelve-hundred-watt airplane landing-strip light, through various handmade and modified devices. Employing slides of paintings one might see in an art-history class—Goya and Manet—he also projected famous quotes from Marshall McLuhan and Andy Warhol on the screen. Hand-painted slides, slides of geometric patterns, film clips, hand-etched film loops, and segments from commercial cinema were also employed. White eventually used closed-circuit video to project enlarged images of the musicians performing onstage in real time.

Anthony Stern, who worked alongside Peter Wynne-Willson at the UFO light shows, described the experience as "a very inky business. But the results were wonderful, [creating] crashing galaxies [and] microscopic universes. . . . The experiments at the UFO performed by Pink Floyd and Peter Wynne-Willson were the first fusion of music and image where ultimately neither was complete without the other," Stern told *LUX* magazine in 2014.

The resourceful and inventive Wynne-Willson began creating light shows when he stretched a condom across a wire frame and then dripped oil paint over the transparent latex while illuminating it from behind. He also fashioned a unique pair of spectacles from welding goggles after replacing the lenses with prisms, which literally provided the wearer with the "kaleidoscope eyes" that John Lennon describes in "Lucy in the Sky with Diamonds."

The psychedelic experience begins when "you open the portals of the eyes and the portals of the ears, and something happens inside where they came together," Stern theorized. "It is a kind of explosion that takes you outside your head and a third art form happens."

But in the case of Syd Barrett, the constant onslaught of sensory "explosions," amplified by his steady diet of pot and acid, only exacerbated his already fragile psychological state and helped to throw him over the hedge into a suburban no-man's land.

Curiously, little has been said whether Syd might have suffered from what is called the Bucha effect—an extreme state of disorientation induced by exposure to flickering or flashing bright lights. In the 1950s, Dr. Bucha experienced a profound moment as he gazed through his car window at sunlight flashing between a row of trees. Through a series of experiments, he discovered that light strobing between 1 and 20 Hz (approximately the same frequency of human brainwaves) could induce vertigo, epileptic seizures, temporary amnesia, and, at the very least, nausea. Occasionally, helicopter pilots have become hypnotized by the light flickering through the spinning blades above them, causing them to crash their aircrafts.

○

Having become "crazier and crazier," Syd eventually returned to Cambridge, where he led a quiet, isolated life with his mother, Winifred. In the wake of his breakdown, Pink Floyd became something of a rudderless ship adrift in the perilous waters of the music business, offering a series of patchy experimental albums until Roger Waters began commandeering the band.

"From *Meddle* on, I made all the decisions," the bassist asserted. Then-manager Peter Jenner concurred: "Roger was the organization . . . the one you went to for sorting out practical issues." And although David Gilmour often felt Waters' personality and ambition was overbearing, he later conceded that "Roger was the ideas man and the motivator and helped to push things forward."

With Gilmour bolstering the erratic Barrett at live performances, Pink Floyd had no choice but to move on, recording *A Saucerful of Secrets* over the course of the next year (May 1967 through May '68) at Abbey Road Studios. In the meantime, their once-charismatic leader, Syd, had abruptly fallen to the rank of stoned mascot within the band, offering a minimum of input.

Along with the trend of ingesting mind-expanding drugs, it seemed like insanity had become a common theme of many mid-to-late-sixties songs, led by the lunatic march of "They're Coming to Take Me Away Ha-Haaa!," a disturbing novelty number by Napoleon XIV (a.k.a. recording engineer Jerry Samuels). The song, which was more like a maniacal monologue (backed with "!aaaH-aH ,yawA eM ekaT oT gnimoC er'yehT"—yes . . . the same tune, only backward), instantly shot to No. 3 on the *Billboard* charts on August 13, 1966, but it was immediately dropped from Top 40 New York playlists by WMCA and WABC, as well as by the BBC, following a flurry of complaints from mental-health organizations. Ironically, the song's final verse reveals that the potty protagonist has been driven to the brink of madness not by his sweetheart's betrayal but due to the misbehavior of a "mangy mutt," which the singer threatens will spend its final days locked away in a cage at the local the ASPCA.

On a more serious note, Leonard Cohen's hypnotic, finger-picked ballad enchanted listeners with tale of the "half-crazy" "Suzanne," who "takes you down to the river," to discover vestiges of truth and beauty "among the garbage and the flowers." According to Joni Mitchell, Cohen's soft-spoken "Suzanne" was "one of the greatest songs I ever heard. . . . All my songs seem so naive by comparison. It raised the standard of what I wanted to write," the Canadian chanteuse told Malka Maron in her book *Joni Mitchell: In Her Own Words*.

Meanwhile, the Rolling Stones' "19th Nervous Breakdown" slammed a ditsy dolly bird on the edge of collapse, and Dylan's bewildered watchman in "Visions of Johanna" wondered whether it was himself or them that "is insane."

In February 1967, John Lennon coaxed an entire generation disillusioned with war and the evils of society down to the eternal meadows where his childhood imagination had blossomed in the ethereal "Strawberry Fields Forever," where "nothing is real."

One glance at Joel Brodsky's eerie photo of the Doors on the iconic cover of their 1967 debut album revealed that all was not peace and love in California. The message was loud and clear as Jim Morrison bellowed "All the children are insane!" in his Oedipal opus, "The End."

Jefferson Airplane's "Lather"—written by Grace Slick and allegedly inspired by her boyfriend at the time, the band's drummer, Spencer Dryden—portrays an aging child who, despite having reached his thirtieth birthday, was incapable of coping with the changes of our mechanized/materialistic society.

"Be kind to a child in a fantasy wild / It's the best thing you can do," Richie Havens advises in his somber, minor-keyed ballad "From a Prison," pegging the escapist attitudes of his generation in just a few words.

The baby boomers whom Welsh poet Dylan Thomas had warned "do not go gentle into that good night" clearly wanted no part of the "Comfortably Numb" world their parents had carefully constructed for them. Yet, the prospect of insanity has always lingered in the shadowy fringes of American consciousness, whether due to copious drug consumption or simply as a tool to avoid the draft.

At the time, the future of an entire generation of young men was being systematically derailed by America's escalating involvement in Vietnam. Too young to drink or vote, most of the boys required to serve their country faced the prospect of either being drafted or seeking sanctuary in Canada or Sweden if they objected to partaking in what they deemed an amoral and unjust war. But dodging the Selective Service took great cunning and courage, and it carried consequences of stiff fines and prison sentences, along with the stigma of being branded a coward.

For a brief time, college students were permitted an exemption. But if their grades were below average, or their parents weren't wealthy or influential enough to wangle a medical deferment, their fate was all but sealed. In a last-ditch effort, you could always show up out of your head at the local draft board, in hopes of being classified 4-F (unfit for service). Feigning insanity was best accomplished after binging on high doses of LSD and speed for a few days. Another surefire way of exemption was by claiming to be gay. Arlo Guthrie's hilarious rambling eighteen-minute talking blues, "Alice's Restaurant," was nearly a user's manual on dodging the draft.

Labelled "freaks" by the Establishment, a generation of long-haired baby boomers had plenty of reasons to fear the future. "Paranoia" had quickly usurped "peace" and "love" as the buzzword of the day. "Into your life it will creep," Stephen Stills warns in Buffalo Springfield's ominous 1967 hit single, "For What It's Worth," while King Crimson's lyricist Peter Sinfield found himself at "paranoia's poison door" in "21st Century Schizoid Man," which kicked off their stunning 1969 debut album, *In the Court of the Crimson King*.

A year later, in 1970, Black Sabbath's "Paranoid" teemed with fear and loathing, while the Kinks' Ray Davies bemoaned suffering from "Acute Schizophrenia Paranoia Blues" over an old-timey wailing Salvation Army band on his band's 1971 foray into Americana, *Muswell Hillbillies*.

While some wrote and sang odes to insanity, others simply lived it. Larry "Wild Man" Fischer grew up in LA, dogged by severe mood swings. Diagnosed as schizophrenic, he spent most of his life ping-ponging between institutions and living on the street. Heavily medicated and occasionally under control, the Wild Man performed his uniquely twisted, self-penned tunes for spare change on Hollywood sidewalks. He soon found himself in demand as a novelty act, opening shows on the Sunset Strip for the Byrds and Iron Butterfly.

Having launched the appropriately named Bizarre Records label in 1967, Frank Zappa released new albums by his own band, the Mothers of Invention, while producing a slew of left-field artists including Alice Cooper, Captain Beefheart, the GTO's (Girls Together Outrageously), and Fischer, whose 1968 double album *An Evening With . . .* pioneered a new genre of "outsider" music, opening the back door for musical misfits including the Shaggs and Daniel Johnston.

Zappa once described his music as "specialized entertainment for people who are tired of other types of entertainment." But one must wonder where the line between "specialized entertainment," exploitation, and morbid fascination (certainly the case with Syd Barrett's post–Pink Floyd career) is drawn. While Zappa helped shepherd Wild Man Fischer into the public's consciousness by producing Larry's "Merry Go Round," he immediately cut him off after Larry, in a moment of psychosis, threw a bottle at Zappa's daughter, Moon Unit. (It smashed just inches above her head.) The following year, a pack of oddballs dubbed the Crazy People kicked off their *Bedlam* LP with the loopy number "Parade at the Funny Farm," featuring a guest vocal by Fischer, who loaned a genuine credibility to their brand of crazy.

O

Not all lunatics can be found "raving and drooling" on street corners. Appearances are often deceiving, particularly in the case of Porter Wagoner. The great country star seemed to have it all: gussied up in his Nudie suit, with a gleaming blond coif, he topped the country charts while hosting his own TV show. But inside he was a wreck of a man, tortured by the beauty of a woman he loved but could never completely possess—that curvaceous country siren, Dolly Parton. His love and obsession for Dolly would eventually lead him down the white sanitized corridors to his own private cell at the local mental hospital. That blinding smile was transformed into a feral jigsaw of gnashing teeth.

While most folks wouldn't consider Porter's 1972 LP *What Ain't to Be, Just Might Happen* to be a concept album, it contains a couple a number of songs that were concept albums unto themselves, including "Waldo the Weirdo," in which Wagoner solemnly preaches the moralistic tale of an outsider who lives alone in a shack on the edge of town; along with his reverb-drenched classic, "The Rubber Room."

"I had heard some songs that were scary but entertaining," Brian Ritchie explains. "Syd Barrett comes to mind. He sounded unhinged and, in that case, we know how the story ends. But still, there was lightness and some fun involved, so I consider Barrett to be easy listening. It wasn't until I heard Porter Wagoner's 'Rubber Room' that I was actually scared by a song. The lyric was so matter of fact and unadorned, an artless description of madness that one can't conclude it's a literary work. It's simply a raw and rotting slab of autobiographical writing. One that makes you think, please don't let this ever happen to me."

"No one tells a story like Porter Wagoner," Johnny Cash boasted. Lust, madness, and murder were the man's modus operandi, and "The Rubber Room" was about as dark and riveting as country music has ever gotten.

Virtuoso guitarist and producer Chet Atkins, the creative engine behind RCA's Nashville division, greatly appreciated Wagoner's unflinching stance and encouraged him to mine his dark side for inspiration. Wagoner never tried to dodge disappointment or sugarcoat misery but confronted heartache and tragedy head on at 90 mph in songs like "Sorrow on the Rocks" and "The Cold Hard Facts of Life."

"When I wrote 'The Rubber Room,' [Chet] just flipped out," Wagoner recalled. While Atkins believed "country people won't like it," he predicted, "There'll be a rock group [doing something like] that one day, and it'll be a giant song." A year later, Pink Floyd made Atkins' prediction a reality with "Brain Damage."

With "Time," Roger Waters punched a hole in the pervading silence and denial that has gagged British society for centuries with his classic observation, "Hanging on in quiet desperation is the English way." But his sardonic societal commentary was hardly the first in English pop music. Following a string of early proto-punk rockers like "All Day and All of the Night" and "You Really Got Me," the Kinks' Ray Davies began writing a series of satirical songs that were second only to Bob Dylan in exposing and lampooning social mores.

"I think Ray [Davies] was, without question, *the* social and political commentator for England with songs like 'Dedicated Follower of Fashion,' and 'A Well Respected Man,'" says Shel Talmy, who produced the band from 1964 through 1968. "Ray was incredibly prolific. He'd go home and come back the next day with a dozen songs."

Ruminating over the source of Davies' inspiration, Talmy offers, "I always got the impression that Ray was a fan of British music hall. I'm not sure he was affected by Bob Dylan. I think he liked what Dylan was doing, but I don't think it particularly impacted him one way or the other."

In "A Well Respected Man," Davies casts an acerbic eye on all foibles of British life, keeping his tongue firmly in his cheek with "Dedicated Follower of Fashion," and yearning to emulate "David Watts" in his caustic portrait of the perfect chap who gets straight A's, *"leads his team to victory,"* and, of course, has his pick of the young girls who fawn over him.

Ray Davies always maintained a dry sense of humor throughout his social criticism. It never seemed heavy-handed or dour, which was often the case with Roger Waters' later solo work.

A Kinks fan of the first rank, David Gilmour praised Davies' "Waterloo

Sunset" as "the perfect pop song . . . I would have loved to have written that."
In fact, he nearly did with his own "Fat Old Sun." While the title more closely
resembled "Lazy Old Sun"—another track from the Kinks' fifth studio album,
Something Else—Gilmour's inspiration was sparked by Ray's reverie of the lovers
Terry and Julie and their tryst at Waterloo Station.

"It's one of those songs where the whole thing fell together very easily," David
explained. So easily that Floyd's guitarist wondered if he hadn't "ripped ['Fat Old
Sun'] off from the Kinks or someone," he told *Uncut* magazine in 2015. While
Roger Waters was determined to distance himself from Syd Barrett's whimsical
dreamsongs, Gilmour still seemed to linger under the sway of his "mystical
warblings."

☽

There are few bands in rock history who wholeheartedly admitted to the tedium
of their own work. Pink Floyd claimed to have dropped "Echoes" from their
live shows because, as Nick Mason allowed, the piece was "a bit dull . . . very
repetitive." Whether self-effacing or brutally honest, Waters confessed that he
was "bored" with much of the band's music, to which Mason added the group
was "in acute danger of dying of boredom."

"'Echoes' wasn't built on a typical pop structure," says Matt Piucci, singer
and guitarist with Rain Parade (and an auxiliary member of Neil Young's Crazy
Horse). "They had that textural, mysterious, otherworldly sound. I just love how
the song can go on forever. They were nothing like other prog bands. It wasn't
like, *Okay, now John McLaughlin will play 175 notes in four bars. And then Billy
Cobham will play 175 notes in four bars.* The Floyd never did that. They always
kept it simple."

Keeping things simple was the goal when Pink Floyd converged at Nick
Mason's Camden kitchen, where Roger first presented his ideas for the band's
next album. Inspired by John Lennon's first solo release, *Plastic Ono Band*—
which ruthlessly confronted life's many issues, pressures, and fears—Waters
asked his bandmates to jot down a list of things that disturbed their sleep.
While Rick Wright mentioned his fear of flying and dying on the road, Waters'
concerns were of a more political and philosophical nature. And, of course, there
was collective guilt over Barrett's mental breakdown and their cold-shouldered

abandonment of their friend that remained unspoken and still haunted them. Roger later claimed Syd's mother blamed him for his deterioration, having allegedly introduced her angelic, artistic son to the "fleshpots of London."

Years later, in 1991, Nick Mason told author Nicholas Schaffner that while many considered *Dark Side of the Moon* to be "music of the spheres," the band had actually "been grinding away at very down-to-earth personality disorders." Or, as Rick Wright quipped, "It's more mental ... we've gone mental."

Joking aside, Pink Floyd would soon become a vehicle for Roger Waters' fomenting sociopolitical commentary. For Waters, *Dark Side* marked a clear departure. He claimed the album was "more literal . . . more theatrical than anything we've done before." While *Dark Side* was indeed "dark," the *Metropolis*-inspired "Welcome to the Machine" (from 1975's *Wish You Were Here*) addressed the sense of alienation that has haunted England's citizenry for decades. Then, following the Orwellian vision of 1977's *Animals*, Waters' angst culminated with *The Wall*. In 1983, Pink Floyd signed off with their most bleak and depressing album of all: *The Final Cut* was inspired by Waters' ongoing grief and anger over the death of his father, Eric, a Second Lieutenant killed in Italy during World War II, along with Britain's recent jingoistic skirmish in the Falklands.

"It's difficult telling people to watch out when you're making a million dollars and having a wonderful time," Mason said, addressing the hypocrisy of self-righteous rock stars instilling their songs heavy-handed messages. "But Roger definitely means what he says."

Political views expressed through pop songs often appear trite, simply due to nature of the brief, disposable format in which they are delivered. Few, beyond Bob Dylan and Phil Ochs, with their highly articulate protest songs, and later Bob Marley and the Wailers and the Clash, spoke out against the "shitstem" (as Peter Tosh dubbed it) without smacking of pretense. Clad in fatigues, John Lennon and Yoko Ono helped make revolution fashionable by thrusting their fists in the air and shouting "Power to the People." But the people had to roll their eyes in dismay after realizing they'd been chauffeured to the protest in a Rolls-Royce. While John sincerely meant what he said, walking the walk was another story.

"I have to accept at that point I became a capitalist. I could no longer pretend that I was a true socialist," Roger Waters admitted in 2004. It was not an easy confession for Waters to make, having been raised by his single mother, Mary, a schoolteacher and a staunch communist until November 4, 1956, when Russia invaded Hungary. Roger, the youngest of three sons, had been steeped in left-wing politics and a strong sense of morality.

At a time when music fans fixated on and misconstrued song lyrics to the point of spinning records backward (let alone subscribing to the absurd "Paul Is Dead" hoax triggered by assorted "clues" found on the record sleeve to *Sgt. Pepper*), Gilmour praised Waters' verse in *Rolling Stone* as "very simple, straightforward, and easy to understand."

David, who never considered himself much of a lyricist, was somewhat relieved when Roger took over the band's poetic chores. Waters' greatest strength as a songwriter has always been the economic, haikulike clarity of his words. But Gilmour soon rankled once the bassist began taking charge of the band's musical direction. Band dynamics are often cutthroat. Rick Wright, who allegedly had been bullied by Roger since Pink Floyd's early days, quietly withdrew over the years until finally being given the boot over his lack of enthusiasm for and contribution to Waters' later projects.

◑

Although Wright's harmonies helped carry most of Floyd's songs, his potential as a lead singer and songwriter sadly went unrecognized by his bandmates. While his keyboards were essential to the atmosphere of *A Saucerful of Secrets*, his two contributions to the album seem to drift by like clouds on a spring afternoon. Embroidered by the sharp needle of Syd's searing slide guitar, his "Remember a Day" offers a brief respite of nostalgia, sandwiched between the netherworld excursions of "Let There Be More Light" and "Set the Controls for the Heart of the Sun"; on side two, "See-Saw" features his gentle vocals and cascading piano with a sweeping coda, floating and colorful as Claude Monet's water lilies.

Willie Aron, keyboardist and guitarist with LA's Thee Holy Brothers and former producer for Leonard Cohen, notes that for aspiring keyboard players in the '70s, choices of whom to emulate were plentiful:

> After all, it was the era of caped virtuosos like Rick Wakeman,
> dazzling pyrotechnical showmen like Keith Emerson, Hammond

organ slayers like Jon Lord, Mellotron maestros in bands ranging from Genesis' Tony Banks, and countless Moog mavens.

But what if you eschewed virtuosity? What if the simple act of providing tonal color washes suited the music without all that other technically gymnastic, but emotionally hollow malarkey? That's the kind of keyboard player I wanted to be . . . kind of like the George Harrison of the keyboards. That's how I think of Rick Wright's playing. Others could play rings around him, but few provided exactly what the music required so stately, so elegantly. If I were Pink Floyd's manager, I would've told Rick to drop the "w" from his last name, he was so well-suited to their music.

From Brian Kehew's point of view, Wright is the "centerpiece" of *Saucerful of Secrets*, which he calls "one of the most underrated albums of their career":

On "See-Saw," Rick Wright's beautiful sonic filigree perfectly matches the optics we see on their most psychedelic cover. His textures lead the Floyd into their most popular atmospheric-meets-song era. Rick was already using the organ in unusual ways, offering tonal stacks and textures rather than just the single-note-playing typical of blues or jazz records. But the sounds are more *Star Trek* transporter room than rock band keyboards. It's really his keyboards that took Floyd to that spacey region so effectively.

Wright's Middle Eastern scales and effects instigated a trance feel that began so clearly with *Saucerful of Secrets* and continued through *Meddle* and *Dark Side of the Moon*. "Set the Controls for the Heart of the Sun" is a perfect example of this. Most people would not identify those sounds as an "organ." Rather, Rick was already leaning toward the tones we'd hear a year or so later on their albums. In his expressive hands, a synthesizer was sure to become more of a mood-inducing instrument than just a noisemaker or gimmick.

Having no road map to this new electronic wonderland, Pink Floyd simply followed their collective intuition, while coaxing eerie dark drones from this new, strange black box.

◐

No other member of Pink Floyd possessed the drive of Roger Waters. As he later confessed to journalist, author, and record producer Karl Dallas, "There's something in me that makes me want to kind of dominate people."

In a 1980 *Melody Maker* article, journalist Michael Watts described Roger Waters as "a gloomy, self-obsessed man such as one finds in a [Ingmar] Bergman film." Like the teachers he ridiculed in "Another Brick in the Wall," "Headmaster" Roger was known to stop the music and sternly confront rowdy crowd members for making noise during the band's quieter moments. Bob Ezrin, who co-produced *The Wall* with him, lamented that Pink Floyd had become "Roger Waters Presents" while admonishing Roger's "Teutonic cruelty" toward Rick Wright, who in his modest way described Waters as "an extremely difficult man to work with."

With the release of his first solo album, *The Pros and Cons of Hitchhiking*, in 1984, Waters proclaimed Pink Floyd defunct. Unconvinced by their former bandmate's assessment, Gilmour and Mason decided to carry on; they invited the ousted Wright back into the fold (although not as a full partner), and, just as they had in the past, following Syd Barrett's breakdown, continued recording and touring behind their next release, *A Momentary Lapse of Reason*.

"In the end, it's just a pop group, isn't it?" David Gilmour told Sue Lawley on BBC Radio 4. "And one person leaving. Y'know, it had happened before . . . Syd had left, Roger left, and we carried on. It wasn't a very pleasant period in the early '80s," the understated guitarist added drolly.

A BRIEF CULTURAL
HISTORY OF THE MOON

She is but a mirror hanging in the sky, beautiful and aloof, reflecting our every thought, inspiring our every mood. A shape-changer, constantly fluctuating from one night to the next, like a diva on diet pills, from fat to thin and back again. She is whatever you think she is and none of those things. She is strong. She is pale and wan. She is, as the Mississippi bluesman Howlin' Wolf once croaked, "the cause of it all," alternately praised and blamed for inspiring fools to fall in love. For centuries, poets have struggled to capture her cool, detached charm in verse and song. Tides rise and fall. She causes women to bleed and wolves to howl at her beauty, while the glare of her icy high beam has been known to trigger murder.

Peering through primitive telescopes, early astronomers believed they'd discovered oceans on the moon and drew maps with erroneous names like "Sea of Rains," "Sea of Serenity," and the "Bay of Rainbows."

Wrapped in her silvery dress, she glides from horizon to horizon. Kwakiutl Indians of Northwest Canada held lavish feasts in her honor, fearing the dark monster that swallowed and regurgitated her each month would swoop down from the black sky and do the same to them. No wonder she always wears that weary face, like someone just spilled a drink in her lap.

Before our investigation of the moon continues any further, let's talk with Dr. Matthew Bobrowsky, an astrophysicist who currently teaches at Delaware State University, and who will shed a little light on a few common misconceptions we might have.

JK   Does the moon rotate?

MB   Yes. The time it takes for the moon to rotate once around its axis is equal to the time it takes for it to orbit once around Earth.

This keeps the same side of the moon facing toward Earth throughout the month. If the moon did not rotate on its axis at all, or if it rotated at any other rate, then we would see different sides of the moon throughout the month.

JK   So, to be clear, the moon and the earth rotate in tandem?

MB   While the earth rotates once a day, the moon rotates once every 27.3 days. The earth revolves around the sun in approximately 365¼ days, while the moon revolves around the earth in 27.3 days. Together, the earth and moon revolve around the sun. So, it's not just the earth.

JK   For a layman like myself, could you please explain the difference between rotating and revolving?

MB   When an object spins on its own axis, it is rotating. Revolving means moving in an orbit around another object. So, the earth rotates, spinning on its axis once every 24 hours, while revolving around the sun once a year. While the moon rotates on its axis, once every 27.3 days, it also revolves. Interestingly, because of the additional motion of the earth in its orbit around the sun, the time from one full moon to the next (or from one new moon to the next) is a bit longer than 27.3 days; its 29.5 days. With the time between two full moons being 29.5 days, there are sometimes two full moons in the same month. Except for February, which is too short to have two full moons.

JK   Does the dark side of the moon exist?

MB   The moon has no side that is constantly dark. As the moon rotates, different parts of its surface experience day and night. During a full moon, it is daytime on the side of the moon that faces earth, also called the "near side." During a new moon, it is night on the near side, while it is day on the far side.

JK   So, no one side of the moon is always dark.

MB   The moon rotates, albeit slowly, so, anywhere you are on the moon—except for near its north and south poles—you will experience about two weeks of daytime and two weeks of nighttime. The "dark side of the moon" misconception probably originated from the fact that the moon keeps the same side facing the earth all the time. We never see the far side of the moon from Earth. But the fact that we don't see it doesn't mean it's dark. During the new moon, when the side facing Earth is dark, the far side is fully illuminated. Imagine that you're standing on the moon looking at the earth … from Earth, we see a "dark" new moon, but viewing the earth from the moon, we would see "a full earth." And when people on Earth see a full moon, you, looking at Earth from the moon, would see a dark, "new earth."

JK   Is this why we only see the moon's "face?"

MB   We see the same side or "face" of the moon because the time it takes to rotate once on its axis is the same as the time it takes for it to revolve once around the earth. For instance, after the moon has revolved halfway around the earth, it has also rotated halfway around, so the same side is always facing the earth. So, you see, because of the moon's rotation, there's no one side of the moon that's always in sunlight or always dark.

JK   So then, there is no dark side of the moon?

MB   No … sorry!

JK   Does the moon actually "pull" on the tides?

MB   Yes! Both the sun and moon influence the tides, although the moon's effect is about twice as strong as the sun's. One misconception people have is thinking the tides are specific to water, such as the oceans. But, in fact, the solid part of the earth slightly stretches due to the moon's and sun's tidal forces. The ground on which you stand rises and falls a couple of inches twice a day, and the earth's atmosphere is also affected by tides. The important thing to know is that tidal forces are significant only for large bodies of water, like oceans. The smaller the body, the less the effect it has. So, for example, the water on one side of one of Lake Michigan might rise and fall an inch or so due to tidal forces, but nobody notices because the waves are higher than that. So, tidal forces are totally insignificant for small things like ponds or people. Astrologers, not astronomers, believe it's important where the planets were when you were born. But the tidal forces from the planets when you were born were weaker than the tidal forces from the obstetrician standing next to you! Air currents in the room exert a stronger force on you. So, there's nothing about the moon's gravity or tidal forces that has any effect on people.

JK   So, the moon has no detectable influence over human emotion?

MB   Looking at the moon with a lover can be very romantic and induce feelings of passion, but that's a result of how the moon figures into our culture and what happens in the brain, not anything that the moon is doing or causing through some physical mechanism or force. One other point: the high tides are highest and low tides are lowest at both full moon and new moon. Yet no one ever seems to notice any lunar effect at the new moon—another indication that tidal forces do not cause any changes in human emotion or physiology.

JK   Does the moon have any physiological properties that cause us to assign our superstitions or accusations to it?

MB   As I said, the moon isn't exerting any significant force or causing anything to happen in our brains or bodies, although our minds are easily influenced by suggestion, popular culture, and misconceptions. Astrology falls into the latter two categories. Many people mistakenly think that the moon influences human physiology and behavior. For example, many maternity nurses and moms will swear there's a surge in births during the full moon, but statistics show that that's not true. Hundreds of studies have also looked for a "Transylvania effect"—links between the phases of the moon and other phenomena like suicides, calls to crisis centers, disasters, violent behavior, changes in mood—and found no correlation there either. It's an interesting question as to why such beliefs persist when they've been shown to be false. It has a lot to do with confirmation bias. Say it's a busy night in the maternity ward. Someone might say, "I wonder if there's a full moon tonight." So, then they might check, and if, by coincidence, the moon happens to be full, they say, "Well, that explains it!" It reinforces their beliefs. But if it turns out that the moon isn't full, they tend to forget about it—and all the other busy times when the moon wasn't full. We tend to remember the hits but not the misses.

JK Thank you, Dr. Bobrowsky!

MB You're welcome. My pleasure!

Despite the rationality of scientific logic, Neil Young firmly believed in the effects of the full moon. As he told the *New York Times*' John Rockwell in 1977, "There are certain times to record. For the longest time I only recorded on a full moon, and it always had the same intensity," Young imparted. "Everybody would get crazy."

Few songwriters in modern times have been as obsessed (or perhaps possessed) by the moon as Young. While gleefully "chasing the moonlight" in "Cinnamon Girl," Young's "After the Gold Rush" portrays him strung-out "in a burned-out basement, with the full moon" in his eyes. For Neil, the moon functions like an emotional barometer, from celebrating the glow of love in the lilting "Harvest Moon" to the deep loneliness and despair of the "yellow moon on the rise" in "Helpless," he has written more than twenty-five odes to the enigmatic orb in the sky.

Young was not alone in his fascination with the moon. Apparently, Henry "The Sunflower" Vestine shared Neil's passion. Obsessed with blues lore and collecting records, Vestine was best known for his incendiary "buzz saw" guitar, which he unleashed with Canned Heat, the Mothers of Invention, and free jazz saxophonist Albert Ayler.

Before his death in October 1997, at age fifty-two, of heart failure in a Paris hotel, Henry's last request was to have his ashes transported to and scattered on the dark side of the moon, in a crater named for his father, E. H. Vestine, a distinguished astrophysicist who once headed the Planetary Sciences Department at the Rand Corporation. Unfortunately, Vestine had little money and left no instructions on how this challenging task might accomplished. His ashes remain interned at Oak Hill Cemetery in Eugene, Oregon, to this day.

◗

Long before the release of *Dark Side of the Moon*, artists, poets, musicians filmmakers, and scientists around the globe have all looked longingly toward the sky for inspiration. Galileo Galilei discovered Jupiter and its moons along with the rings of Saturn in 1610, while Mozart completed his 41st symphony, titled "Jupiter," in August 1778.

By the end of the nineteenth century, George Méliès had directed the French silent film *The Astronomer's Dream*. The innovative three-and-a-half-minute movie portrays a frustrated stargazer with a long white beard and a pointed wizard's cap peering through his telescope at a mischievous, big-eyed full moon. Suddenly, the naughty orb swoops down, opens its enormous mouth, and gobbles up all of his equipment. The glowing sphere then transforms into a crescent shape, as a chiffon-draped nymph appears, enticing the astronomer. But the moment he tries to embrace her, she blasts off into outer space. An instant later, the astronomer is found sleeping in his chair, inferring it was all just a dream. As the twentieth century began, Méliès debuted his next film, the fantastic *Le voyage dans la lune (A Trip to the Moon)*, in 1902.

Created by Phillip Francis Nowlan, the space explorer Buck Rogers initially became popular in America through newspapers and magazines until first appearing on the silver screen in 1939. The film adaptation of *Buck Rogers* starred the two-time Olympic swimming champion Larry "Buster" Crabbe, already familiar to audiences for his 1936 role as the hero of the first sci-fi serial, *Flash Gordon*. There were thirteen *Buck Rogers* episodes in all.

After H. G. Wells, Jules Verne, and *Astounding Stories* magazine stoked fantastic visions of a great interplanetary future, Irving Asimov, Arthur C. Clarke, Ray Bradbury, Robert Heinlein, and Phillip K. Dick raised the much-maligned genre of sci-fi to the level of art. There's also never been a shortage of villains trying to conquer outer space, like Nazi rocket scientist Werner von Braun, who gazed at the stars with the mad plan of dominating the galaxy to fulfill his Fuhrer's twisted fantasies of proliferating the master race.

In 1951, rock 'n' roll unofficially entered the space-age with Ike Turner and Jackie Brenston's hit single "Rocket 88." While their song pointed toward the future, enhanced by the enticing new sound of the electric guitar, its lyrics actually refer to "cruising and boozing along" in an Oldsmobile by the same name. A year later, Herman Poole Blount migrated from Birmingham, Alabama, to Chicago and changed his name to Sun Ra. Claiming he'd been abducted by aliens, the eccentric pianist and big-band leader insisted he came from Saturn on a mission to enlighten humanity that "Space Is the Place," and bring earthlings hope for a brighter future in "tomorrow's world."

While the 1956 sci-fi classic *Forbidden Planet* introduced us to Robby the Robot and life on another planet in the twenty-third century (complete with an exotic soundtrack by electronic pioneers Louis and Bebe Barron), the space race officially kicked off with the Soviets' surprise launch of *Sputnik*, their shiny disco-ball satellite, on October 4, 1957. For three months, the pride of Russian engineering orbited the globe, emitting an array of radio signals, before its batteries died and it burned up as it fell back into the earth's atmosphere.

Debuting on September 23, 1962, Hannah/Barbera presented *The Jetsons*, portraying the foibles faced by a space-age cartoon family; a year later, the chilling voice of a faceless narrator alerted you that they now controlled your television set, before stretching the minds of submissive citizens to the far reaches of *The Outer Limits*.

"We choose to go to the moon! Not because it is easy, but because it is hard," President Kennedy exclaimed in his infamous speech at Rice Stadium in Houston, Texas, in September 1962. Assassinated fourteen months later, JFK sadly never lived to see the manifestation of his ambitious dream.

Although the British had no stake in the space race, they understood its entertainment value. The world's longest-running sci-fi TV show, *Dr. Who*, debuted in November 1963, chronicling the adventurers of a time-traveler whose theme song—performed by the "unsung heroine of British electronic music," Delia Derbyshire—apparently inspired the pulsating bass line of "One of These Days," the opening track on Pink Floyd's *Meddle*.

While the Byrds began as a folk trio, they always kept one eye on the stratosphere. In 1965, their leader, Roger McGuinn begged "Mr. Spaceman" (with his "saucer-shaped lights") to "please take me along for a ride," and they then released the first psychedelic song in March 1966. Inspired by Indian ragas and John Coltrane's modal jazz, "Eight Miles High" was banned for its "drug references," despite the band's protests that the song's lyrics recounted their first cross-Atlantic flight for their tour of England. In 1968, McGuinn wrote and sang the innovative, synth-drenched "Space Odyssey," which told of the future discovery of pyramids on the moon "in nineteen and ninety-six."

Beyond their sonic innovations and love for space imagery, the Byrds and Pink Floyd shared a similar dilemma. Neither band's original front man—not Gene Clark nor Syd Barrett, who provided hit songs for their respective groups—possessed the steely nervous systems needed to withstand the demands of the rock 'n' roll lifestyle.

Debuting in September of 1966, the first episode of the classic sci-fi TV series *Star Trek* took viewers on a trip upon the starship *Enterprise*, to, in the words of Captain James T. Kirk (William Shatner), "boldly go where no man has gone before."

●

On July 20, 1969, Pink Floyd were invited to jam live on the BBC, to provide the soundtrack as everyone watched Neil Armstrong's first step on the moon. Gilmour, just twenty-three at the time, later reflected on the event to the *Guardian*: "They were broadcasting the moon landing and they thought that to provide a bit of a break, they would show us jamming."

The excerpt, titled "Moonhead," lasted about five minutes. As David recalled, "It's a nice atmospheric, spacey 12-bar blues." Afterward, at his London flat, Gilmour gazed up at the moon, astonished by the fact that "there are actually people standing up there right now."

That same night in New York City, Silver Apples (comprised of synthesizer pioneer Simeon Coxe and drummer Danny Taylor) performed in Central Park as Neil Armstrong first set foot on the cold, lonely orb. But by the time Pink Floyd and Silver Apples were invited to conjure a lunar soundtrack, they'd already been beaten to the punch by some young strange, obscure bloke named David Bowie.

Following a few failed novelty singles like "The Laughing Gnome," Bowie (still known to his mum at this point as David Jones) wrote and recorded "Space

Oddity," inspired by the forthcoming moonshot and by Stanley Kubrick's majestic *2001: A Space Odyssey*. Uneasy with what seemed like an obvious cash-grab, Bowie's longtime producer and collaborator Tony Visconti balked at the chance to steer the single, leaving the task to Gus Dudgeon, who would soon work with Elton John.

Edited to just under three and a half minutes from its original length of 5:15 (as it appeared on the album), the melodrama of Major Tom's fateful space journey was released on Friday, July 11, 1969, just nine days before Apollo 11 touched down on the moon. While briefly putting Bowie on the pop music map, it would be another three years before *Ziggy Stardust and the Spiders from Mars* fell to Earth and conquered the planet.

Once more, the old saying "It's Sinatra's world, you only live in it" rang true when Buzz Aldrin stepped out of the capsule to the swinging sounds of the "Chairman of the Board" singing Bart Howard's "Fly Me to the Moon."

At the request of astronauts Armstrong, Aldrin, and Michael Collins, record producer Mickey Kapp had whipped up a suitable soundtrack played on Sony's latest invention, the portable cassette machine. In addition to Sinatra, the playlist included Barbra Streisand singing "People"; Blood, Sweat, and Tears' "Spinning Wheel"; and Peggy Lee's cover of "Everyday People," rather than Sly and the Family Stone's original. While Collins chose British singer/songwriter Jonathan King's "Everybody's Gone to the Moon," Armstrong's taste proved a bit hipper than his fellow crewmen's when he asked for Les Baxter's surreal "Lunar Rhapsody," from the 1947 album *Music Out of the Moon*.

Meanwhile, back on Earth, Pink Floyd—much to their chagrin—discovered that they had been scooped to their original title, *Dark Side of the Moon*, by British blues rockers Medicine Head for their 1972 release of the same name. Originally comprised of a pair of multi-instrumentalists—guitarist, keyboardist, and drummer John Fiddler, with Peter Hope-Evans on guitar and harmonica—Medicine Head abruptly changed personnel, substituting the Yardbirds' former front man, Keith Relf, for Hope-Evans. Oddly, the first track on their record was titled "Back to the Wall." But after their *Dark Side of the Moon* went nowhere, Fiddler and Hope-Evans reunited and climbed the British charts to No. 3 with their next single, "One and One Is One."

Ultimately, Pink Floyd, who had for a while decided to change the title of their eighth album to *Eclipse*, had no qualms about reverting to its original title and changing the record's final song, still known at the time as "End," to "Eclipse."*

---

* Oddly enough, a similar dilemma had plagued the Beatles a few years earlier, when they planned on titling their sprawling 1968 double album *A Doll's House*, inspired by the play of the same name by the Norwegian playwright Henrik Ibsen. Upon discovering that Family (whose members included future Blind Faith bassist Ric Grech) had already released their quirky opus *Music in a Doll's House* in July of that year, they redundantly called it *The Beatles* (which, from that moment on, became famous worldwide as *The White Album*).

Pink Floyd, meanwhile, ended up adding a definite article to their original working title, perhaps to differentiate it from Medicine Head's album. Technically speaking, their eighth LP is *The Dark Side of the Moon*, though it is more commonly known simply as *Dark Side*.

SIDE ONE

3

SPEAK TO ME /
BREATHE

The album begins slowly, softly, causing a moment of doubt and wonder in the listener. Is the record even playing? Maybe you twiddle the volume knob. But then, like a star appearing on the distant horizon, the sound begins to rise, softly, gradually. A gentle throb reverberates, as if from below the old floorboards of that Edgar Allen Poe story you read when you were a kid. That steady heartbeat, the relentless pulse . . . boom-ba-boom . . . life's essential electrical charge.

According to David Gilmour, "Roger and Nick tend[ed] to make the tapes of effects like the heartbeat . . . which alludes to the human emotion and sets the mood for the music."

"Speak to Me," the album's opening auditory collage, was initially conceived as an overture, built on the steady of pulse of Mason's modified bass drum. The track undulates with the lunatic laughter of Floyd roadie Roger "The Hat" Manifold and a fragmented soliloquy from Abbey Road doorman Gerry O'Driscoll, who confessed he'd "always been mad."

A sustained piano chord (played backward, of course) and what sounds like fluttering metallic dragonfly wings, or whirring helicopter blades, generated by an EMS VCS3 synthesizer, all add to the track's atmosphere. The grim reminder of rotary wings chopping the air, laced with distant screams whooshing through the speakers, must have triggered nightmarish flashbacks for thousands of jittery soldiers who'd recently returned from Vietnam, sending them ducking for cover beneath the nearest table or behind a sofa or bed.

True to the increasing animosity that had engulfed Pink Floyd by the time Roger Waters left the band in 1985, the bassist and songwriter later groused that

Mason "had nothing to do with 'Speak to Me.'" It was "like a gift," Waters said resentfully, having given Mason sole credit for the album's initial montage. Duly noted, we continue our journey with the song as originally credited.

A moment later, a most welcome "ahh" of relief comes as the ringing chords of "Breathe" fall upon our ears like a gentle avalanche, enveloping the listener in a bright, shimmering sonic cocoon. David Gilmour's chiming guitar and husky voice invites us to "breathe in the air." For, without the breath, we cease to exist. All life depends on it. "Breathing all creatures are," the Incredible String Band's Mike Heron had gently intoned over rolling organ chords in his 1968 tune "Air."

Three years before *Dark Side of the Moon*, pianist and composer Ron Geesin and Roger Waters composed the soundtrack to Roy Battersby's 1970 documentary *The Body*. This intriguing cycle of songs and musical sketches included a tune called "Give Birth to a Smile," which began with the line, "Breathe, breathe in the air." Lightly fingerpicked on an acoustic guitar, the song was delivered by Waters in a soothing, lilting voice, as if trying to lull his children to sleep.

"Breathe, breathe in the *air*," Robbi Robb, Joshua Tree shaman and singer and guitarist with the psychedelic space-rock band the 3rd Ear Experience, sings softly.

> The breath is a symbol of the spirit. Breathing in alludes to "inspiration," literally taking the spirit into your body. *Dark Side of the Moon* is filled with so many little mystical clues. The great anthropologist Joseph Campbell once said all the world's myths tell the same stories. These stories were written by people who gazed into the darkness, into the mystery and were inspired, and stories flowed out from them. Everyone tells the same tale, stories to inspire others to help fellow beings find their own ground. In the song's first verse, Waters tells us, "look around and chose your own ground." All mysticism is based on the principle of "know thyself." Buddhism refers to "the ground of your being." So, we choose our own ground! In the next verse, when David Gilmour tells the rabbit, "Dig that hole—forget the sun," he is speaking to the idea of entering into the darkness, penetrating the deep ground of our being.

Few pop bands at the time, beyond the Zombies (with "She's Not There") and the Beatles ("And I Love Her"), shaded their compositions with the dark mood of minor chords. As singer/songwriter John Prine used to joke, "In folk music, when you play a minor chord, it means that somebody just died." Yet *Dark Side of the Moon* opens with Gilmour's gentle strumming alternating an E minor chord with an A9.

David's hypnotic guitar part is reminiscent of other odyssey songs of the day, including Neil Young's grim tale of a fugitive on the run after shooting his "lady" in "Down by the River," and Traffic's eerie quest for gold in "40,000 Headmen," which the band's drummer and lyricist, Jim Capaldi, claimed to have written while in the depths of "a hash-fueled dream."

"It's the lunar subconscious speaking! It goes below the subconscious and tickles the unconscious," Robbi Robb exclaims. "When Simon and Garfunkel sang 'Hello darkness my old friend' in 'The Sound of Silence,' it was very powerful and intrigued thousands of people. While darkness is the opposite of light, most people don't realize that from the darkness came the light. It makes you stop to wonder, *What was happening on the Tuesday morning before the big bang?*"

Since their wild nights jamming at the UFO's all-night raves, Pink Floyd had routinely conjured up otherworldly soundscapes filled with surprises that leapt out at you like spooks in a sonic funhouse. Among a palette of electronic sound and snippets of recorded voices, an essential part of *Dark Side of the Moon*'s hallucinogenic atmosphere is David Gilmour's unique use of the lap-steel guitar, an instrument with Hawaiian roots but most often associated with country music since its early days, when it sweetened Hank Williams honky-tonk odes.

After discovering a 1962 Fender Duo 1000 double-neck steel guitar in a Seattle pawn shop while on tour with Pink Floyd in October 1970, Gilmour first employed the instrument when recording "One of These Days" on *Meddle*. He later overdubbed the lap-steel guitar on "Breathe" and "The Great Gig in the Sky," stretching the instrument's sonic vocabulary far beyond the clichés commonly heard in country and Hawaiian music.

"David is part of the early wave of modern rock musicians who discovered American roots music secondhand," explains Stan Schneir, bassist and steel guitarist with the latter-day Incredible String Band from 1970 to 1973.

He's from a class of English blues and R&B interpreters, including Jimmy Page, Pete Townsend, Eric Clapton, and Keith Richards, who came to American roots music, having grown up with the Music Hall songs of George Formby [famous for comical tunes strummed on ukulele] and plenty of BBC radio broadcasts of classical music. They took to it with fresh ears and were very original in their approach to playing this "foreign" music. I place Gilmour among them for a couple of reasons. I think he's underrated since he never seared, shredded, or smashed his guitar. Gilmour plays a more sweet, orchestral version of the blues. His lap steel really appeals to me. Most of the guys who play the instrument are either into electric dobro and a hard staccato banjo picking style or a blues feel, since the lap steel can sound beautifully vocal. Gilmour plays clean, with no wide vibrato or country cliches. I really like his tone and tunefulness, that short scale is rough to figure out, and most of all, his economical phrasing, which is not usually associated with lap steel guitar.

Gilmour's level of musicianship and economy is impressive. Every little riff has its place and space. The band members seem to have respect for each other. There is a wonderful sense of who is doing what, between the drums, bass, keys, and guitar, all moving around the vocals, which are always at the center. Gilmour underplays with great taste. Less is more. He's got great tone. There's no showing off here.

The influence of gospel music on *Dark Side of the Moon* can be heard in Rick Wright's keyboard work here, along with the vocal arrangements on "Eclipse." But for Cindy Cashdollar—whose prodigious steel guitar and dobro picking can be heard on albums by Bob Dylan, Van Morrison, and Dave Alvin, and through her membership of the legendary Texas swing band Asleep at the Wheel—that influence comes through strongest via David Gilmour's lap-steel guitar:

It's a whole different thing. I always felt bad for guitar players who think it's so easy to pick up and play lap-steel guitar, but it's not.

It's hard. It's weird. It's a very unforgiving instrument. You have to forget everything you know about the guitar, and think about it as a voice, which is what it is! You're creating a voice with your [tone] bar [which the player slides against the strings to create the instrument's unique weeping sound]. It's a very vocal instrument. I don't sing. I wish I could, but the slide is very much like a voice.

While I've never been a fan of Pink Floyd, Dave Gilmour has such incredible tone. I love his phrasing. He's so different and has a very unconventional way of playing the lap steel. First of all, he uses a flat pick! It's an instrument where you *need* fingerpicks to get the sound out of it. But whatever works! He is his own man on a lap steel. He didn't have an agenda to play "blues," or "country," or "bluegrass." He just sat down and played whatever came to his mind. He plays these soaring notes that go way, way up in the sky and you wonder where is this gonna go? When is it coming back? It's like watching a bird!

The instrument had been so boxed in for years to country and bluegrass and faux blues. Like Daniel Lanois, Gilmour took the sound of the instrument to new places . . . to space! He created something gorgeous. Pink Floyd makes some very dark music, which he made ethereal and pretty. He makes you listen to the melody. His playing sometimes reminds me of the Sacred Steel sect that started in Florida many years ago, which bases their church gospel performances around the steel guitar. The old Sacred Steel guys emulated gospel singers. By the time it migrated up north, the music became more jammy, like the Allman Brothers and Robert Randolph, but the old guys—Willie Eason, Sonny Treadway, and Aubrey Ghent—were the superstar lap-steel players.

For a while, he played a Fender Duo 1000 double-neck. He took off the pedals and two extra strings, making it a six-string instead of eight. But he also played a Jedson lap steel. But it doesn't matter what he played. You could put a fifty-dollar piece-of-crap lap steel in his hands and he could still make it sing! He's got that *tone*!

"He's a much better guitarist than people give him credit for," Pretty Things' lead vocalist Phil May told Richie Unterberger. "Either you're a Floydie and you like Dave Gilmour, or people who aren't Floydies don't see that he's actually an incredibly talented musician. He could play with anybody. He happens to be a really nice bloke ... [and] knows he's been lucky. He appreciates other musicians who he knows, with a bit of luck, would be where he is."

Although Roger Waters was reticent to sing his bandmate's praises for many years, he would eventually allow that "Dave was a fucking good guitar player and a very good singer."

Greg Lisher, guitarist with Camper van Beethoven, enthuses, "Between Rick Wright's sweeping Hammond organ chords that whoosh through a rotating Leslie speaker, and David Gilmour's beautiful clean, delayed slide, played over his swirling, phased, slowly strummed guitar chords, 'Breathe' has an instantly comforting feel to it." Producer and multi-instrumentalist Fernando Perdomo points out that "*Dark Side of the Moon* owes a lot to two sounds: the use of the Leslie cabinet on the guitar, and the UniVibe pedal, which gives David Gilmour's guitar its sound on 'Breathe.'"

●

George Harrison was one of the first people to play guitar through a rotating Leslie speaker, on the Beatles' yearning ballad "It's Only Love," in June 1965. A month later, Brian Wilson followed suit, icing the Beach Boys' "You're So Good to Me" with its unique shimmer. The ethereal wobble of the Leslie helped make John Lennon's vocal on "Tomorrow Never Knows" sound like "the Dalai Lama singing from a mountaintop" (as he instructed the Beatles' producer George Martin), while Harrison reprised the effect to perfection when he played on Cream's 1969 recording of "Badge."

Inspired by the strange swooshing sounds he heard when trying to dial in American radio stations across the Pacific, Japanese audio engineer Fumio Mieda designed the UniVibe pedal, which became an essential component to Jimi Hendrix's sonic toolkit.

"Pink Floyd recorded the majority of 'Breathe' live in the studio, and you can feel its warm, organic quality," says Danny Frankel, drummer with Lou Reed and k. d. lang.

It's got a great feel, like a giant waterbed sailing above the clouds. It was *not* cut to a click track, so there's a real human sense of time there. It sounds like a dialogue between Mason's drums and Doris Troy's voice when the legendary R&B singer starts to wail.

We have to credit Nick Mason with inventing the "shoe-gazer" beat! He only had one set of drums that he used onstage and in the studio, which helped keep the same identity throughout. Nick played Ludwig drums, with a twenty-inch Paiste 2002 for a ride cymbal, which he said was his most important cymbal. He has such a beautiful, even feel on it, especially on the verses, which he breaks up with cascading fills down the drums, sometimes very stately. And he always kept the same tuning on the drums.

Fernando Perdomo concurs:

Nick Mason created magic in his use of space in "Breathe." If the drums didn't have that light, airy feel, the song wouldn't transport you, as a listener, to that other world. Nick's ride cymbal sound is more of a pulse, with a little bit of a pitch to it. It produces a sound wave without overtones. There's no wash. It's more musical sound than the crashy-ride cymbal of Ringo and Keith Moon, or the pingy, big-bell ride cymbal of Neil Peart. There's something very calming about Mason's drumming. His ride-cymbal pattern creates waves of sound, like running water. There must be something special about the bronze that Paiste uses in their cymbals. They have a warmer tone which sits in the mix a certain way.

4

ON THE RUN

"Breathe" floats along, drawing the listener in, leading them on a musical odyssey, until suddenly, at the 2:43 mark, they are pulled down a rabbit hole, ears first, into a new, unexpected dimension of burbling electronic sound. Like a spinning cone employed by a hypnotist to mesmerize their patients, "On the Run" transports us into a strange new realm—an altered state of consciousness.

Pink Floyd's touring schedule for 1972 was a hectic eighty-nine-date grind, but for the first time in their career they took the opportunity to publicly iron out the new batch of songs and instrumental segues that comprised their new album.

The band first presented their new song cycle *Dark Side of the Moon: A Piece for Assorted Lunatics* (as it was originally titled) live, in sequence, at the Brighton Dome on January 20, 1972. As Waters later recalled to *Rolling Stone*, the concert was a disaster, plagued by "severe mechanical and electric horror."

A few weeks later, Pink Floyd kicked off a string of shows at the Rainbow Theatre in Finsbury Park, London, beginning on February 17. A bootleg of the February 20 performance, titled *The Coming of Kohoutek*, began to appear within six weeks of the concert. Well-recorded despite occasional aggravating glitches in "Time," "Us and Them," and "Eclipse," the pirated pressing reveals a warm shower of applause from an audience dazzled by the band's latest musical inventions.

Pink Floyd sound truly inspired as they float through "Breathe" and dive headfirst into "On the Run." An altogether different affair from the song's recorded version, "The Travel Sequence," as the piece was originally called, is built on a jazzy vamp from Gilmour's guitar. Topped with some sonic sugar from Wright's keys and driven by Waters' bass and Mason's tenacious groove, the jam eventually winds down, overtaken again by swirling helicopter sounds.

The audience seems oddly quiet, momentarily mesmerized until roused by the resounding clock chimes from a prerecorded tape. Mason's majestic tom-tom fills tumble, leading the band into "Time." While the tandem vocal delivery from Gilmour and Wright is decidedly more languid than the album version, Dave's guitar and Nick's drums provide a sharper edge to the song.

The spontaneous spirit of making music is all too often lost in the studio during the overdubbing process. For better or worse, the studio polish (whether the work of Alan Parsons, the band, or the combination of all involved) dulled the immediacy of the band's live performance, and *Dark Side of the Moon* became a more formal, calculated affair, every note perfectly in place. Gone is the gulp and growl of Waters' bass while Mason's fills trigger the Floyd's dynamic shifts. Nick's playing on the album might convince people that he never hit his drums very hard. "The difference was like night and day between how Pink Floyd sounded live and in the studio," Robert Musso stresses. "It was almost like two different bands!"

●

Taking the time to develop the songs live was a key component to *Dark Side of the Moon*'s success. The music went through a long organic process of evolution, as arrangements were refined by playing the material night after night. "The differences are unbelievable between the earlier versions of the songs and what wound up on the record," David Gilmour pointed out. "'Time' was [originally], like, half the speed. The vocal was me and Rick in harmony, very low. It sounded terrible!"

An earlier version of "The Great Gig in the Sky," then known as "The Mortality Sequence," was a vehicle for Wright's mercurial organ, laced with murmured voiceovers, sundry gibberish, and occasional passages from the Bible.

A clanking waterfall of coins signals the gangster groove of "Money," and after Waters' bass lays down the song's distinctive riff, doubled by Gilmour's guitar, Wright's keyboard break is lighter and jazzier than the raspy sax solo played by Dick Parry (a member of "the Cambridge mafia," as Nick Mason described their little clique of friends). As always, Gilmour tears the song wide open with a scorching solo.

"Us and Them" features Wright's ethereal organ and Gilmour's lilting vocals, while the power of Mason's drum fills on the live recordings are a revelation when compared to the polished grace of the studio version.

The early live rendition of "Any Colour You Like" (originally known as "Scat," or "Dave's Scat Section") is a slow, swampy, two-chord vamp, recalling Al Kooper and Stephen Stills' groovy cover of Donovan's "Season of the Witch," from their 1968 album *Super Session*. The jam eventually leads to the gossamer fingerpicking of "Brain Damage."

The stripped-down performances of these songs reveal a flesh-and-blood quality that was soon replaced (or lost, as some might argue) by the pristine aura of Abbey Road Studios. As the song cycle ends, the crowd erupts into a fervent ovation before being treated to a string of Pink Floyd "standards," including a mesmeric version of "One of These Days," a ghostly "Careful with that Axe, Eugene," and a blues number that, although spirited, seems somewhat out of place with the rest of the set. Perhaps they were just giving the audience (and themselves) a much-needed breather before diving off the deep end into "Echoes," "A Saucerful of Secrets," and the mystical Arabesque sway of the closing "Set the Controls for the Heart of the Sun."

Beyond their smorgasbord of sound effects and the pure yearning of Gilmour's soaring guitar solos, it was Wright's swelling keyboards and Mason's drums that forged the band's dynamics, while Waters' bass provided a simple, solid foundation that never vied for attention or distracted from his bandmates' musicianship.

Pink Floyd's disembodied music had a way of luring their curious and often stoned crowd down the dark corridors of the human psyche, only to startle them with their own images reflected and distorted in the funhouse mirror of their minds.

●

Bootlegs of *Dark Side of the Moon* recorded at the Rainbow immediately circulated around the UK, selling upward of one hundred thousand copies in the year prior to the album's release. Disheartened by this debacle, Pink Floyd considered abandoning the project altogether when they were unexpectedly invited to France to write and record the soundtrack to Barbet Schroeder's latest film, *La Vallée*.

Released in June 1972, their seventh album, *Obscured by Clouds*, referred to the hidden valley on Papua New Guinea where Schroeder's new movie was shot. By Pink Floyd's standards, the tracks were surprisingly short, stretching to five and a half minutes at most. While the bluesy groove of "Free Four" closely resembles Norman Greenbaum's 1969 chart-topping rocker "Spirit in the Sky," David Gilmour's serene vocals over a gentle descending acoustic guitar riff on "Wot's ... Uh the Deal," achieved new levels of "mellow" (to use a word of the day) for the band. Gilmour later resurrected this number on his 2006 solo tour.

Embroidered by Gilmour's lead guitar, the lilting "Burning Bridges" was one of Waters and Wright's finest collaborations to date. Rick pointed to Steve Miller's "Your Saving Grace" as the inspiration for his keyboard part on the song. The ominous intro to "Childhood's End" creeps in slowly, as unfocused as the album cover's intriguing photograph. A disquieting drone gives way to a rapid heart/drumbeat until breaking into a loping organ-and-guitar groover. You can hear the band's future unfolding in these tracks. "Every album was a step towards *Dark Side of the Moon*," Rick Wright later said. They were clearly "learning all the time."

●

Originally titled "The Travel Sequence," "On the Run" evolved from a repetitive jam built on Rick Wright's keyboards interweaving with David Gilmour's guitar. It was originally meant for the soundtrack to Michelangelo Antonioni's 1970 film *Zabriskie Point*.

"On the Run" went through a major transformation after the band purchased the EMS VCS3 modular analog synthesizer, built by Peter Zinovieff of the BBC's Radiophonic Workshop. Zinovieff's fabulous contraption had already been employed by Tangerine Dream and Brian Eno of Roxy Music over the last few years to conjure fresh, strange sounds. Gilmour described it as a massive, mysterious tangle of wires and components stretching from "floor to ceiling."

"Pete Townshend had been making hit records with his EMS VCS3 since 1970 on *Who's Next*," Brian Kehew reminds us.

> Some of his ideas were unexpectedly creative, like using it to process a traditional organ part on "Won't Get Fooled Again."

Early advertisements for the EMS VCS3 touted it as a "studio." Since earlier electronic-music studios used laboratory oscillators, filters, and other processors to aid in creating "new sounds," the EMS offered all this in one package: hence, the notion of a built-in studio! The more-portable AKS model that Pink Floyd used on *Dark Side* fit into a foldable case which contained the synthesizer electronics on one side, and a touch-plate keyboard with a sequencer on the other.

The built-in sequencer came in handy for the fast ostinato bass line of eight notes, repeating over and over to create the busy-but-trancey backing pattern [for "On the Run"]. But the sequencer was quite limited, with locked-solid timing, which lies in contrast to most of Pink Floyd's traditional hippie-friendly art. Although it functions well here, with just enough tonality-meets-space to push the boundary a bit beyond.

One of the issues with many early synthesizers was their unstable tuning. So, most were used commonly for sound-effects type results, until *Switched-On Bach* proved that "normal" music really could be made with a synthesizer—albeit with some difficulty. The EMS had similar stability issues, so many bands used them for effects only—ideal for things like "On the Run," rather than longer tonal pieces. These issues made it perfect for studio experimentation, but not so great for live. Aside from Brian Eno's wild sonic blasts in early Roxy Music and King Crimson (who used it sparingly), most bands, including Pink Floyd, avoided the EMS live and went for Moog or ARP onstage instead.

"Rick Wright in general, and *Dark Side of the Moon* specifically, was one of the most incredible marriages between technology and popular music in music history," exclaims keyboardist and composer Thollem McDonnas.

Wright had access to instruments that were brand new in that moment. He used a live multichannel control with quadraphonic pan pots during live shows, along with the new EMS Synthi A

105

[with both keyboard and sequencer smartly designed to fit into a briefcase], which had been invented the same year they recorded *Dark Side*. Anyone who was interested in new possibilities of sound—and Pink Floyd was obviously very curious—would also have been aware of the new musical inventions that were suddenly possible, thanks to the esoteric work of the most innovative and experimental electronic composers, like Pauline Oliveros, Clara Rockmore, Delia Derbyshire, Wendy Carlos, Morton Subotnick, Suzanne Ciani, and Karlheinz Stockhausen. One also can't ignore the contributions of the pioneers of Black electronica like Eddie Harris on his [1969 album] *Silver Cycles* and Sun Ra's fearless experimentation; Sly Stone's *There's a Riot Goin' On*.* Les McCann's *Layers* was released the same year as *Dark Side of the Moon*, so that couldn't have been a direct influence. But what an incredible time to have been a keyboardist and a sonic explorer!

---

* Released in 1971, *There's a Riot Goin' On* also employed new synthesizers and was the first album to use a drum machine.

A QUICK HISTORY OF
ELECTRONIC SOUND
BEFORE PINK FLOYD

In 1957, Philips Records released an album titled *Song of the Second Moon* by the Dutch duo Electrosoniks, which would forever change music history. It was the brainchild of Tom Dissevelt and Dick Raaymakers, a.k.a. Kid Baltan, a nickname he devised by reversing his first name, Dick, and the abbreviation for Natlab—the Natuurkundig Laboratorium, the physics lab where Raaymakers worked at the time. The sonic palette of this recording is astonishing, comprised of a series of aural inventions that wobble in your ears like orange and purple Jell-O. Blobs of noise squiggle like mercury, silvery and slippery, and then shatter and crash, inspiring the listener to reconsider everything they previously understood about sound, while striving to invent new language in order to find the words to describe it.

These radical innovations employed elements of echo, delay, tape loops, and sped-up/spliced-up bits of musique concrète—a concept first forged by Pierre Schaeffer in 1948 that was inclusive of all sounds and thereby extended the vocabulary of modern music. Yet Piet Mondrian, whose modern abstract paintings resemble grids of futuristic cities, previously conceived of "neo-plastic-single-color" sounds generated electronically as early as the 1920s!

Hailing from Haight-Ashbury, the Fifty Foot Hose were arguably the world's first electronic rock band. In December 1967, the five-piece group released their first album, *Cauldron*, on Mercury Records. Initially, the album failed to make much of an impression on anyone beyond music critic and *Rolling Stone* publisher Ralph J. Gleason, who drolly wrote, "I don't know if they're immature or premature."

Following in the wake of the Fifty Foot Hose came a flood of electronic and experimental groups, including Silver Apples, the United States of America, and Lothar and the Hand People. "In 1961, Don Buchla saw Sun Ra live in San Francisco and was inspired to build his own electronic instruments," recalls the Hose's bassist and electronic shaman, Cork Marcheschi. "[Guitarist] David Blossom and I had been part of the Mills College Tape Music Center and had access to all of Buchla's innovations."

Marcheschi, who'd been playing bass in North Beach strip joints at the time, built two theremins of his own design and bought another "from a guy down the street who used it to scare neighborhood kids with it on Hallowe'en." He also built homemade audio generators and ring-oscillator circuits, then started experimenting with and attempting to control feedback as a pure sound source by waving a microphone in front of a pair of speakers.

Not everyone worked from the same store-bought palate of sounds. At the time, a more adventurous spirit prevailed—an attitude of, *Let's see what kind of sounds we can create ourselves, without relying on mass-produced instruments.*

The pair of theremins Marcheschi built were from plans he'd found in an article in an old 1957 issue of *Popular Electronics*:

> All of the parts were still available, so I just put it all together. It made a sound unlike any theremin I'd heard. I still have it! Sound is real and lacking any technical finesse I've always played with it, and manipulated it, in its purist form. There's a lot of simple, inventive things you can do, that are readily at hand, like speaking into a fan and have it chop up your voice. As there was no easily available equipment then, what we did with the Fifty Foot Hose was, we got an FM transmitter and put the signal out and would catch it again going into the tape recorder—but use a loop-stick antenna to put it out of phase, which was the basics of a ring modulator. On *Cauldron*, there's a lot of spoken-word poetry. You can hear voices being manipulated simply by moving the loop-stick and changing the phase as the soundwaves travel through space.
>
> It's the same kind of mindset as the guys in the fifties who customized cars. You had to do it yourself. So, you'd take a piece of something, put it on something else, and go down to the drag strip and people would be there, creating their own visions. It was

fantastic. There was a desire, a passion to create. Whether you wanted to go a hundred eighty-five miles an hour, or make louder weird sounds or just get chicks, your brain had to go new places. It wasn't simply, *How much money do I need to buy this*, but *How do I make it?*

At the same time the Fifty Foot Hose were in the thrall of experimentation, Wendy Carlos (then still known as Walter Carlos) recorded *Switched-On Bach*, playing Bach with a new and different set of sounds. Suddenly, one person could create the sound of an entire orchestra with Robert Moog's synthesizer.

> There was also Harry Chamberlin, who created a bizarre instrument which he named after himself. The Chamberlin combined a keyboard with tape loops of every instrument. So, you could play it in every key and have the sound of real instruments, but it involved hundreds of tape loops. It was a real disaster.
>
> There were all these people creating their own sounds and they each had their own specific polish to it. Our approach in the Fifty Foot Hose was to go all the way back to the Italian Futurist Luigi Russolo, with his Intonarumori, a noise instrument so extreme it caused a riot at his *Gran Concerto Futuristico* in 1917.

In 1958, Edgard Varèse composed the eleven-minute "Poème electronique" as an ambient soundtrack to the Philips Pavilion at the Brussels World Fair. The French architect Le Corbusier designed the building with assistance from the Greek composer Iannis Xenakis, known for both orchestral and electronic music. Visitors to the Pavilion were exposed to both Varèse's piece and a "song" by Xenakis entitled "Concret ph," which evoked the sound of burning embers, rain against a windowpane, or rattling chains.

Cork Marcheschi became obsessed with electronic sound in 1962, after hearing the Varèse piece on an album recorded at the Brussels World Fair:

> "Poème electronique" was written with the idea that visitors would walk through Corbusier's sculpture/building in the amount

of time it took for the piece to run. This was the first full-scale exposure of avant-garde music/environmental sculpture and architecture, with projected images that were intentionally *not* matched to the sound.

The Philips Pavilion looked like a cow's stomach turned inside out. They'd built speakers into the walls, which were bowed and elongated, and covered in asbestos! They projected hundreds of images on the walls, chosen to work with the poème, that appeared and disappeared slowly, in time with this amazing piece of electronic music.

Varèse created pure audio sculpture, combining human voices, machine sounds and physically manipulated tapes. We did similar things with the Fifty Foot Hose. I made a lot of those sounds by just simply putting my thumb on the tape reel to slow it down.

While everyone else was in the thrall of Flower Power, Marcheschi found the San Francisco musical scene surprisingly conservative:

In a very short time, everybody was wearing the same clothes, smoking the same dope and listening to the same music. The conformity of the hippie scene was no different than people who worked on Wall Street. Psychedelic people were also parochial in their musical taste. David Blossom and I didn't do drugs. I thought they were boring. I had enough exciting stuff going on in my own head. People who saw us thought, *You must really be out there, man.* . . . Maybe we were, but we were interested in the music. While we were into improvisation, we never reached the level of jazz musicians. We thought about the music more like a combination of avant-garde and classical players than jazz guys. It wasn't that we didn't know we were or wanted to be rock and roll musicians. We were just trying to move the music somewhere else! We had an innocent audacity and were inspired by the concepts of avant-garde composers like Luigi Russolo and John Cage. At live shows we would use silence, stopping the music for sixty seconds, then bang on a giant saw blade, that rang like a gong, and then go right back into the music again, and people would go nuts!

Along with Stockhausen and Varèse, Cork was inspired by the performances and concepts of the Japanese art collective known as Gutai. Formed in Osaka in 1954 by abstract painter, sculptor, and writer Jiro Yoshihara and action painter and sound sculptor Shozo Shimamoto, Gutai presented a series of shocking happenings and created concept art that represented a radical break with the cultural traditions of postwar Japan.

> They did these incredibly aggressive and bizarre performances where three or four people who were covered in mud would scream and holler and take axes and destroy an amplified piano! These artists were the people we'd dropped atomic bombs on! We weren't looking to do anything that intentionally rude or aggressive. We wanted to move rock music ahead, to extend its possibilities, not necessarily to change it. We wanted to add a new electronic dimension to it, taking ideas that Stockhausen had been working with and bring them to a broader arena where people could hear it. We wanted to give it a completely different frame of reference. I thought Jimi Hendrix was very genuine toward sound exploration and experimentation. While I liked Pink Floyd's music, I never thought of them as wholly electronic, like *Switched-On Bach*. They were adventurous on their records and staging, which helped bring a lot of these concepts to a broader arena. They also had some very catchy tunes. I can see why people loved it and went mad for it.

●

No matter how intriguing Pink Floyd's use of electronic effects was, they still had a hard time filling the enormous void left by Syd Barrett's parting. As Barry Miles wrote in his sobering review of *A Saucerful of Secrets* in the August 8, 1968, edition of the *International Times*, "In the same way bad sitar playing is initially attractive, electronic music turns people on at first—then as one hears more, the listener demands that something be made and done with these 'news' sounds, something more than psychedelic mood music."

A Saucerful of Secrets was the first Floyd album to feature all five members of the band. Gilmour had a tough gig indeed. Filling the multicolored, mirrored hobnail boots of the increasingly erratic Syd Barrett was no easy task. "Most of the early stuff embarrassing," he later admitted. "It's all part of growing up … and being British."

Although a lovely dollop of psychedelia, Pink Floyd's fifth single, "Point Me at the Sky," was a futile attempt at preserving Barrett's singular sense of whimsy. Released in the UK (but not in the USA) the week before Christmas 1968, the song was met with indifference and rejection, and Waters considered it a failure. It's interesting to note, though, that the cover photo for the single portrays the band done up in flight suits and goggles, nearly a year before Led Zeppelin donned pilot gear for their second album in October 1969.

"I wasn't crazy about the early Floyd at first," Robert Musso confesses, at the risk of sounding "uncool."

> Syd was okay, but not my favorite songwriter, or guitarist in the band. When I heard "Set the Controls for the Heart of the Sun," I thought these guys might have a chance at getting popular. From there, I got turned on to the craziness of *Ummagumma*. I had really been into the Dead at the time, who were also on the *Zabriskie Point* soundtrack. And even *Meddle* didn't really work for me. Along with Floyd, I listened to Yes, Gentle Giant, and King Crimson, which all came in one swoop, like a second British Invasion. But it wasn't until I got turned onto *Dark Side* by my friends—that record kind of blew me away and really changed things. It was the first real concept album that I was familiar with. It was one of those albums, like *Led Zeppelin IV*, that you didn't have to own, because everybody had it. It was everywhere!

In 1968, a Wisconsin kid named Grant Richter became fascinated with electronic sound and built his first transistor amplifier. "It squealed with feedback, turning into an electronic oscillator by accident," he recalls. "Not to

ABOVE LEFT Pink on the Porch: Pinkney "Pink" Anderson, the South Carolina bluesman who, with Floyd Council, inspired the names Syd Barrett gave to both a pair of cats and his fledgling band. *Photo by Roy Book Binder*

ABOVE RIGHT Grantchester Meadows: a view of the River Cam on a misty winter's morn, where Pan allegedly revealed himself to Syd Barrett, and the inspiration for Roger Waters's lovely ballad of the same name. *Keith Taylor / Alamy Stock Photo*

LEFT Hey! Hey! We're the … Left to right: Roger Waters, Nick Mason, Syd Barrett, and Rick Wright. *PA / Alamy Stock Photo*

RIGHT Pink Floyd's debut single, "Arnold Layne." The B-side, "Candy and a Currant Bun," originally bore the title "Roll Another One." *Vinyls / Alamy Stock Photo*

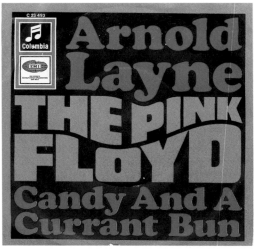

BELOW The shortly lived five-member Floyd. Left to right: Disappearing Syd Barrett; "New Kid" David Gilmour; Rick Wright about to run over Roger Waters (below), while being held back by Nick Mason. *Courtesy Phil Smee / Strange Things Are Happening magazine*

ABOVE Careful with that cymbal, Rog! A fine example of why Pete Townshend feared Roger Waters. Pink Floyd live at Bristol University, March 3, 1969. *Media Punch / Alamy Stock Photo*

LEFT Through a prism brightly: photographer Vic Singh shot the iconic portrait of Pink Floyd that graced the cover of *Piper at the Gates of Dawn* through a prism gifted to him by George Harrison in March 1967. *Vic Singh Studio / Alamy Stock Photo*

THIS PAGE David Gilmour, Nick Mason, and
Roger Waters soundcheck at the Fillmore East,
September 1970. *Photos by Lisa Margolis*

PINK FLOYD
IN CELEBRATION OF THE COMET
THE COMING OF KOHOUTEK

ONE: BREATHE/ON THE RUN/TIME including BREATHE(Reprise)(10:50) TWO: MONEY/US AND THEM/ANY COLOUR YOU LIKE/BRAIN DAMAGE/ECLIPSE (10:10)
TAKRL/1903   STEREO

ABOVE The original shoe-gazers? Pink Floyd during their three-night residence at the Rainbow Theatre, February 1972. *ilpo musto / Alamy Stock Photo*

LEFT *The Coming of Kohoutek*, the bootleg of Pink Floyd's February 20 Rainbow show that sold over 100,000 copies and nearly derailed the release of *Dark Side of the Moon. Courtesy Gunnar Hedman / Record Maven*

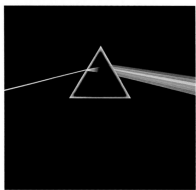

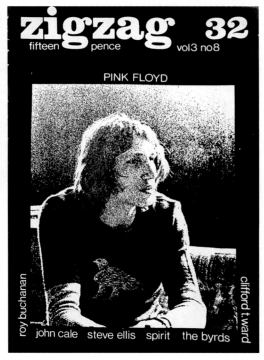

TOP Lost in the fog: the Floyd bring the *Dark Side* to Merriweather Post Pavilion, Columbia, Maryland, June 1973. *The Color Archives / Alamy Stock Photo*

ABOVE LEFT Hipgnosis's simple but stunning design for *Dark Side of the Moon*. *Records / Alamy Stock Photo*

ABOVE RIGHT Rog tells all to *ZigZag*, spring 1973. *Courtesy Gunnar Hedman / Record Maven*

TOP Rick Wright in the keyboard cockpit, Birmingham, England, December 4, 1974. He is playing a Wurlitzer 200A electric piano and a Minimoog model D, among others. *Mick Gold / Redferns / Getty Images*

ABOVE AND LEFT A Korean cassette of *Dark Side* with the wrong running order. *Courtesy Gunnar Hedman / Record Maven*

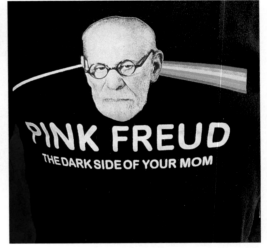

TOP Pink Floyd and Hipgnosis conquer Bogata, Colombia. *Gonzalo Rosendo / Alamy Stock Photo*

ABOVE LEFT The cover of *Not So Bright Side of the Moon*, the Squirrels' hilarious parody of the Floyd masterpiece. *Courtesy Rob Morgan*

ABOVE RIGHT Pink Freud T-Shirt. *Courtesy Gunnar Hedman / Record Maven*

take anything away from Stockhausen, but novelty had a lot to do with the initial appeal of electronic music. In that way, it was similar to abstract art."

Richter eventually "played knobs" in the Milwaukee-based electronic rock band known as F/I, who still remain below the radar despite making thirty albums of "space music" and touring Europe for decades. Their name, he emphasizes, "has no meaning. Don't bother trying to figure it out. It could stand for anything, from *Fuel Injected* to *Fucking Imbeciles*!"

> While the major innovations came from Karlheinz Stockhausen's home studio, Raymond Scott, and WDR Studios, none of this music could ever have happened without "the Wizard of Waukesha," Les Paul, who invented multitrack recording. Once anything is recorded, it becomes electronic music, and you can manipulate it. *Dark Side of the Moon* was a technical achievement—a brilliant confluence of styles that reflected all the advances made from the '40s through the '60s. These experiments in Modernism have been going on for a long time. Jean Dubuffet experimented with two tape recorders to create soundscapes to his living paintings.*

Having studied at the Columbia/Princeton Electronic Center in the 1960s, as well as with Edgard Varèse, Turkish-American electronic musician and composer İlhan Mimaroğlu contributed to the soundtrack of Fellini's *Satyricon* and produced jazz bassist and composer Charles Mingus for Atlantic Records. In 1971 and '72, Mimaroğlu collaborated with jazz trumpeter Freddie Hubbard on a pair of sonically lush albums—*Sing Me a Song of Songmy* and *Wings of a Delirious Demon*—that freely mixed synthesizers with Hubbard's fiery improvisations.

A year later, in May 1973 (just two months after the release of *Dark Side of the Moon*), a Jean Dubuffet retrospective at New York's prestigious Guggenheim Museum presented *Coucou Bazar*, a performance that combined theater, music, and dance, for which the eccentric French painter designed twenty dazzling

---

* The painter Jean Dubuffet was an art-school hero of Syd Barrett's, along with Kurt Schwitters and Robert Rauschenberg.

costumes with interchangeable masks, hats, dresses, coats, and gloves. "The spirit of the whole performance is situated at the opposite pole of realism and rationality," Dubuffet exclaimed. The otherworldly music that accompanied the piece was "composed and realized" by Mimaroğlu and released later that year on the small independent label Finnadar Records.

The avant-garde was not the sole property of a small group of eccentrics and outsiders. Paul McCartney had been enthralled by Stockhausen as well. In April 1966, the Beatles were ensconced at Abbey Road, recording what would become their brilliant seventh album, *Revolver*, which features their first foray into experimental music, "Tomorrow Never Knows." While John Lennon is most often perceived as the "arty" Beatle due to innovative songs like "Strawberry Fields Forever" and "I Am the Walrus" and his collaboration with Japanese conceptual artist Yoko Ono, it was Paul who created a series of homemade tape loops of sounds that were no longer recognizable but evocative of everything from blaring traffic jams to squalling seagulls. When mixed with droning Indian music (George Harrison's latest passion), they created a surreal soundscape for the Beatles' one-chord mantra, in which Lennon enticed listeners to "turn off" their minds with a heady lyric inspired by LSD guru Timothy Leary and *The Tibetan Book of the Dead*.

Beyond the sharing of a studio and engineer/producer Norman Smith, the Beatles' influence on Pink Floyd was inestimable. While they were recording *Piper at the Gates of Dawn* in Studio 3, members of the band were invited to listen to the Beatles' "Lovely Rita." The Fabs' huffs and puffs and grunts and groans on the song's extended tag are said to have influenced the Floyd's feral vocalizations on their psych/jazz instrumental "Pow R. Toc. H."

More obvious examples occur when comparing the lilting fingerpicked guitar figure of "Dear Prudence" with "Brain Damage," or playing the Beatles' dramatic coda to "I Want You" against David Gilmour's guitar figure on "Echoes." While hardly a note-for-note match, both songs build with a sinister tension in a remarkably similar way.

Overflowing with cosmic imagery, "Echoes" also nicks a bit of Lennon's lyric to "I Am the Walrus," as Gilmour and Wright sing in seamless tandem, "I am you, and what I see is me." Leaning on Lennon again for inspiration, Roger lifted the phrase "inviting and inciting me" directly from "Across the Universe."

Was Waters paying tribute to John or simply displaying an enormous amount of cheek? Alan Parsons was of the opinion that "if it hadn't been for the way the Beatles had recorded ... Pink Floyd, who are very much studio-based musicians, would not have turned out the way they did."

Less apparent is the impact the Floyd's sound had on the Beatles. "Wings was in Abbey Road at the same time *Dark Side of the Moon* was being recorded," Fernando Perdomo points out. "There's a track on their 1973 album *Red Rose Speedway* called 'Loup, the First Indian on the Moon,' which sounds, surprisingly, a lot like Pink Floyd."

Listening to this spacey instrumental embellished by liquid electric guitar riffs and Moog synthesizer, floating over Denny Seiwell's lumbering drums, one must wonder if McCartney wasn't intentionally imitating or paying tribute to Pink Floyd. "It was sort of a bit of fun for us. It's pretty experimental," Paul later explained. It's also interesting to note that Alan Parsons mixed the track.

◐

Back in July 1967, Nonesuch Records (Elektra's adventurous "little sister" label, which released everything from electronic soundscapes to Yugoslavian village music) issued Morton Subotnick's mesmerizing *Silver Apples of the Moon*. The album sold surprisingly well, quickly becoming a favorite soundtrack among psychedelic revelers during the heady Summer of Love. Subotnick's evocative title was inspired by the two last lines of William Butler Yeats' poem "The Song of Wandering Aengus" (originally published as "A Mad Song" in 1897), in which the protagonist walks, filled with wonder, "among long dappled grass, [plucking] ... the silver apples of the moon [and] the golden apples of the sun." Inspired by Yeats' classic poem, Judy Collins had earlier sung the entrancing words (set to music by Travis Edmunson of Bud and Travis fame) as the title song on her 1962 Elektra album *Golden Apples of the Sun*.

While early records of electronic music observed few protocols and boundaries, often resembling a menu of random and startling sounds, Subotnick's compositions tended to be more focused, offering melodic themes with dynamics that built toward a sense of resolution. Originally conceiving of *Silver Apples* as a two-part work specifically to fit the LP format, Subotnick employed Donald Buchla's voltage-controlled modular synthesizer as its primary sound source. As composer, keyboardist, and critic Christian Hertzog explains, the "synthesized tone colors" that Subotnick created were striking for their day. Hertzog also admired the composer's "control over pitch that many other contemporary electronic composers had relinquished," while Subotnick's use of counterpoint and "sections marked by very clear pulses" stand "in marked contrast to the simple surfaces of much contemporary electronic music."

More recordings employing the Buchla synthesizer followed. Hertzog describes Subotnick's futuristic chamber music as being "marked by sophisticated timbres, contrapuntal rich textures, and sections of continuous pulse suggesting dance." Finding Subotnick's new and exotic music inspirational, the Stuttgart Ballet and other dance companies around the world would choreograph and present *Silver Apples of the Moon* along with others works of his, including *The Wild Bull* and *A Sky of Cloudless Sulfur*.

Yeats' evocative poetry and Subotnick's otherworldly soundscapes would also inspire Simeon Coxe III and drummer Danny Taylor to form the underground electronic duo Silver Apples in 1967. Before his death in September 2020, Coxe told Austin Matthews of *Shindig!* magazine that the recent flowering of electronic sounds had "sparked the fine-art/intellectual side of my life, that I didn't even know that I had yet." Coxe, who was untrained on keyboards, conjured his unique homebrew of dissonance from an arsenal of vintage oscillators and telegraph keys and pedals, which he played with his hands, feet, and elbows.

Kid Baltan, who had previously studied piano at the Hague's Royal Conservatory, developed the theory of "electroacoustics" for Philips Research Laboratories and would join forces with Jan Boerman to build the premier electronic music studio in Holland. In 1963 came the release of Tom Dissevelt's milestone solo album *Fantasy in Orbit: Round the World with Electronic Music*, a sonic stew comprised of a series of "tropicolours and woomerangs"—whooshes and washes that evoked everything from the reverberation of rockets blasting off for galaxies unknown to deep-sea rumblings, to snarling electronic leopards.

While Cork Marcheschi's Fifty Foot Hose remained below the public's radar, Lothar and the Hand People and Joe Byrd's short-lived ensemble the United States of America (both of whom recorded for major labels—Capitol and Columbia, respectively) left a few exotic ripples in people's ears before nosediving into the deep end of rock 'n' roll oblivion.

Peter Stampfel recalls Paul Conly of Lothar and the Hand People stopping by to meet the Holy Modal Rounders, who were living in Hollywood and recording for Elektra Records at the time. The group had recently expanded from their original duo format (Stampfel and singer/guitarist Steve Weber) to a five-piece that included drummer and aspiring playwright Sam Shepard, then working on the script of Antonioni's fragmented depiction of the counterculture, *Zabriskie Point*.

"You've got to see Lothar! They're going to be huge!" Peter recalls raving to Shepard. He continues:

> Coming from Denver, Lothar and the Hand People deliberated between going to New York or San Francisco. If they'd gone to the West Coast they would have made it there. It was a smaller scene. They were somewhat like the Lovin' Spoonful, only influenced by R&B instead of folk. Sam went to see them and was knocked out. Around the same time, *Newsweek* ran a feature on Sam. When they asked him about New York's off-off-Broadway theatre scene, he said he found bands like the Mothers of Invention and Lothar and the Hand People were much more interesting.
>
> But Lothar and the Hand People were up against something more than bad contracts and crooked managers. For the first time ever, the music scene had hit a critical mass and there just wasn't enough room at the top for all the great bands.

In 1970, Shepard asked Paul Conly and Rusty Ford, Lothar's bassist, to perform with him during the intermission between his plays *Forensic and the Navigators* and *The Unseen Hand*, which premiered at the off-off-Broadway theater La Mama on December 26, 1969. Conly played a prototype ARP loaned to him by the manufacturer. "It was probably the first synthesizer used in a play," Stampfel stresses. "He improvised a different part for each performance, accompanying a prepared tape that he created for the play."

◑

Electronic music was not solely the domain of white European composers, eccentric university professors, or stoned hippie visionaries. In 1969, soul/jazz saxophonist Eddie Harris "went electronic" with the release of his innovative album *Silver Cycles*.

"Eddie Harris was very modern," Atlantic Records producer and arranger Arif Mardin told me, shortly before his death in 2006. "He used a device called the Echoplex, which at the time was state of the art. It created the reverb on *Silver Cycles*. He'd play one line and the machine would reply, so he would play these licks responding to the machine repeated lines. It was beautiful. He also had a special mouthpiece built for his tenor sax, that made it sound like a trombone."

"A lot of people thought Eddie's music was weird," says Harris' former partner, soul/jazz pianist and vocalist Les McCann. "And it was! Because he was tryin' everything. But he knew what he was doin'! Eddie simply was a genius. He played everything. He was crazy, you know. Mentally ill!" McCann laughs. "He was completely the only one like him. The source of where his music came from was one that nobody had ever heard before. Musicians will use whatever is out there. They don't necessarily think about electronics. They think in terms of music," Les notes, referring to Harris' electric sax.

McCann would soon delve into the seductive tonal pallet of ARP synthesizers, creating the auditory equivalent of a lava lamp for his 1974 album, *Layers*. "Certain guys can take electronics and play it and make it come out sounding like music," Les says. His *Layers* remains a milestone of electronica and a revelation, particularly for those previously only familiar with *Switched-On Bach* or *Silver Apples of the Moon*. "We made some real innovations with *Layers*," he recalls. "The engineer on that session, Bob Lifton hooked up two sixteen-track recorders and made it work as the first thirty-two track machine, I believe."

Before *Layers*, McCann's brand of soul/jazz was built on his irresistibly funky piano vamps. The new album represented a new direction as he expanded his sound by employing an ARP Odyssey, Moog modular, and the Prophet 5. Les had been at New York's Atlantic Studios when he first heard Joe Zawinul of Miles Davis' electric band and Weather Report playing a Fender Rhodes. "I've never put it down since!" he exclaims. "After that, my whole career jumped about two and a half notches higher. Once I found the electronics, I could make the sounds I'd been lookin' for. But at the same time, it's not the instrument, it's the musician that creates the feeling. It's still *me*, whether I'm playing piano or electronics. Anybody can play it, but you gotta know how to *use* it."

"There's an understandable tendency when meeting an exciting new technology, whether a synthesizer or sampler, that one becomes obsessed with it and wants to use as much of it as possible," says Brian Kehew.

> Sadly, many early synthesizer/electronic records are examples of someone just beginning to learn their instrument. There are cartoony noises, over-the-top sounds, and "look at me," attention-grabbing moments using that new technology.
>
> But Wright followed in the style of the Beatles, who were always a fine example, and used the synthesizer as just another instrument. They always integrated musical sounds into a song rather than use them just as icing on the cake. No one thinks of *Abbey Road* as a "synthesizer album" any more than *Dark Side* fits that description.* Largely because the sounds and choices made are completely in line with the other parts of the concept. While they helped broaden the pallet and sometimes aided that spacey feeling, many listeners might not even notice that a synthesizer has entered the fray at all.

On June 15, 1971, Malcolm Cecil and Robert Margouleff, a pair of electronic pioneers who became known as Tonto's Expanding Head Band, released *Zero Time*. Technologically groundbreaking, the album offered a cornucopia of new sounds and textures, while most of the music within reflected more traditional song structures. "Cybernaut" is essentially a minor blues built off a keyboard-driven fuzz bass riff and highlighted with "brass" arrangements, while "Tama," a meditative ballad played on "flute," is drenched in a variety of "natural" wind and sea effects.

TONTO, in the case of Cecil and Margouleff, had nothing to do with the Lone Ranger's long-suffering Native American sidekick but was an acronym standing for "The Original New Timbral Orchestra." Designed and constructed by Malcolm Cecil, TONTO was the world's first and largest multitimbral (based

---

* George Harrison added electronic touches to four tracks on *Abbey Road*: "Because," "Here Comes the Sun," "I Want You (She's So Heavy)," and "Maxwell's Silver Hammer."

on Cecil's concept that each note has a different tonal quality) polyphonic analog synthesizer. Cecil's formidable "Wall of Sound" stood six feet tall and twenty feet wide, arranged in a semicircle of huge curved wooden cabinets.

Beyond their own unique recordings, Malcolm Cecil and Robert Margouleff would collaborate with Stevie Wonder in the early '70s, adding their electronic innovations to four of his best albums, from 1972's *Music of My Mind* through *Fullfillingness' First Finale* in 1974. The following year, TONTO could be heard on Weather Report's *Tale Spinnin'.*

In November 1971, critic Michael Watts wrote a smarmy review in *Melody Maker* titled "Pink's Muddled *Meddle*," claiming the band's "use of electronics and spacey atmospherics" on their recent album, *Meddle*, "is not as adventurous as it may seem … especially when compared to Tonto's Expanding Head Band." Describing "One of These Days" as "a throwback to 'Telstar' by the Tornados," Watts disparaged the Floyd for being "so much sound and fury and signifying nothing."

"In the early seventies, England turned to art rock, while music had gone soft in the States, with people listening to Crosby, Stills, Nash, and Young," John Frankovic points out. "But at the same time there was all this great electronica coming out of Germany. The best-known bands were Kraftwerk from Düsseldorf and Tangerine Dream out of Berlin, whose album *Atem* was 100 percent experimental electronic music.* You could just feel this surge of creativity coming from from Guru Guru, Amon Düül, Ash Ra Tempel, and the uncategorizable Can."

Before forming Tangerine Dream in 1967, Edgar Froese led a psychedelic band called the Ones. His greatest influences at the time were Syd Barrett and Salvador Dalí, who invited Froese and his group to perform at his villa in Cadaqués, Spain. Froese cited "Interstellar Overdrive" as a major influence on Tangerine Dream's approach to improvisation. But while their 2007 album *Madcap's Flaming Duty* was dedicated to the memory of Syd, who'd died of pancreatic cancer a year earlier, on July 7, 2006, the sonic palette and slick production shared little with Barrett's daring spirit or esthetic.

---

* *Atem* was released simultaneously with *Dark Side of the Moon* in March 1973.

5

TIME / THE GREAT
GIG IN THE SKY

"The mass of men lead lives of quiet desperation."
—Henry David Thoreau, *Civil Disobedience*

Whether inspired by the Kinks' "Big Black Smoke," or the opening of Black Sabbath's eponymously named debut album, or John Lennon's "Mother," the presence of bells, either chiming brightly or tolling dolefully, have loaned a sense of mystery to pop records.

Time is intrinsic to music. "It don't mean a thing if it ain't got that swing," the great bandleader and composer Duke Ellington taught us. Red Garland's perky celeste on the introduction to Miles Davis' 1956 swinging take on "If I Were a Bell" from *Guys and Dolls* demarks time with syncopated block chords, while the Chambers Brothers evoked the tick-tock of a grandfather clock with the heavily reverbed spank of a cowbell on their 1968 smash "Time Has Come Today."

"The tick-tock pulse which begins 'Time' is not synthetic-sounding at all, but a fairly decent replica of a traditional clock sound," Brian Kehew points out. "The synthesizer bass and Freeman String Symphonizer they used had fairly organic-sounding tones that blended perfectly with the other band instruments."

In October 1972, Alan Parsons was charged with lugging a portable reel-to-reel down to a nearby antique-clock repair shop in St. John's Wood to capture the various vibrations of mechanical time as a test recording for Pink Floyd's new quadraphonic sound system.

In his 2004 memoir *Inside Out: A Personal History of Pink Floyd*, Nick Mason recalls how the mad flurry of clocks on "Time" came about after the band "ran riot in the EMI sound effects library." Whether Parsons was dispatched by EMI Studios or by the band to record the clocks specifically is unclear. Either way, it achieved the same goal.

Mason's drums seem like a natural extension of the tick-tocking grandfather clock in the song's intro. As Danny Frankel explains, "It sounds as if Mason is randomly hitting his [tunable] Rototoms until he enters with a stately fill on the drum kit. He's got an authoritative but relaxed feel, while Waters' bass playing is very open, tagging the Pink Floyd groove. 'Time' is another example of how it's not just Nick but the combined elements of the band that make him sound so great."

Saturated in reverb, the sizzling, sparse notes from Gilmour's guitar evoke an Ennio Morricone soundtrack. "I love the spaghetti-western sound of the song's intro combined with Rick Wright's gently played electric piano," says Greg Lisher. "Wright's funky keyboard contrasts with David Gilmour's cutting, acerbic, in-your-face guitar fills in the verses, followed by his long delayed, distorted guitar solo as they return to 'Breathe' once more for the outro."

Waters' lyrics speak a powerful truth to those lost in a no-man's-land, whether disaffected teenagers waiting for life to begin or the hordes of middle-aged people stuck in meaningless jobs and marriages, leading lives of "quiet desperation." All too soon, they come to realize "the time is gone, the song is over," and they've tragically spent their lives caught up in meaningless routines.

Reprising the easy groove of "Breathe," Gilmour's husky voice cuts through a flood of gorgeous, honey-laden "ahh's" rolling off the tongues of the backup choir. Rick Wright's gentle, funky keyboard lays a solid foundation as Gilmour's Stratocaster takes flight. "Home . . . home again," he sings wistfully, with a sense of resignation and exhaustion, yet glad to be "warming my bones before the fire," while Wright's organ softly washes up on the shore of the album's next track.

◐

Originally referred to as "The Religious Section" or "The Mortality Sequence," "The Great Gig in the Sky" was inspired by Rick Wright's fear of dying while on tour, whether in a plane crash or "on the motorways of America and Europe," as he explained.

Early bootleg recordings from Pink Floyd's live shows reveal that "Great Gig" was once a very different piece of music from the track that closes side one of *Dark Side of the Moon*. First conceived as a dreamy organ fugue for Antonioni's *Zabriskie Point* but rejected by the finicky director, "The Mortality Sequence" provided a much-needed respite from Pink Floyd's sonic onslaught during their live shows, while shining the spotlight on Wright's ethereal organ playing for a few minutes.

Pink Floyd's creative quest was always in a state of flux. Like jazz musicians, their mode of composing often relied on their ability to improvise together as a unit, although the Floyd's method was more laborious and costly than that of artists like Miles Davis and John Coltrane, whose extraordinary musicianship allowed them to spontaneously compose onstage and in the studio.

"As a guitarist, it's a constant question I face," Robert Musso muses. "Am I going to improvise—do one or two takes and play free—or am I going to get compositional and create parts? Am I harmonically and rhythmically correct and serving the composition? I always try to do both."

Pink Floyd often arrived at Abbey Road with little more than a foggy notion of what their next album might be. "Basically, we're the laziest group ever," Gilmour quipped, unabashedly unapologetic for wasting expensive studio time and burning through record company budgets.

Eventually, the Floyd's crazy quilt of half-finished lyrics, riffs, and rhythms would take the shape of songs, as in the case of "Echoes," which initially began as a few vague ideas first dubbed "Nothing," then growing into "The Son of Nothing" and finally "The Return of the Son of Nothing," before blossoming into the side-length track that became their most significant post-Barrett recording to date.

Similarly undefined was the role of their young engineer/producer Alan Parsons, who'd previously worked on *Atom Heat Mother*, the Beatles' *Let It Be* and *Abbey Road*, and Paul McCartney's debut solo album, *McCartney*. While he is credited on the album sleeve as "engineer," Parsons helped expand that role by "making criticisms or suggestions that would normally be made by a producer," as he later recalled.

"Sometimes I did and sometimes I didn't (keep my big mouth shut)," Parsons admitted. One of his brainstorms of a lesser magnitude was to mix recorded fragments of the 1969 moon landing throughout the album—an idea that was quickly (and wisely) dismissed by the band, as it would have forever linked *Dark Side of the Moon* to that historic event, rather than leaving the work open to listener's interpretation.

While Pink Floyd often had "no idea of what they were going to do," Parsons was relieved to find that, with *Dark Side*, rather than enduring the band's usual process of endless jamming and stumbling along until finding a melodic figure to hang a new song on, there was "an excellent piece of music to see coming together."

Despite making a variety of innovative contributions to *Dark Side of the Moon*, Alan Parsons, who worked "ridiculously long hours," was never given a production point on the album (which would've continued to pad his bank account for years to come). "I still wake up occasionally, frustrated about the fact that they made untold millions and a lot of the people involved in the record didn't," he pointed out. But while he received no further financial reward from either Pink Floyd or Capitol Records for his role in creating on one of the greatest-selling albums of all time, the "engineer" credit worked wonders for his burgeoning career.

Oddly, Parsons is best known in America for "Sirius," a 1:48 instrumental track from his band the Alan Parsons Project's 1982 album *Eye in the Sky*. While "Sirius" is regularly used for everything from wrestling matches to commercials, to background music for sitcoms, it is a staple of NBA games, used to rev up the crowd when the Chicago Bulls, Phoenix Suns, and Milwaukee Bucks introduce their starting lineups.

○

"Great Gig" begins with a sparse keyboard meditation reminiscent of an etude by Chopin or Beethoven, which Wright modestly referred to as a "really nice piece of music."

"Despite Pink Floyd's more progressive leanings, it always seemed that Rick Wright wasn't afraid to ground things to a solid chord progression, a simple part that forms a backbone for all that happens around it," Brian Kehew imparts. "The power of notes, on any instrument, is real composition, and Rick used synthesis and electronic organs and effects just like he did an acoustic instrument. He wasn't gimmicky or showy at all."

John Leckie, who had previously engineered *Meddle* and recorded John Lennon's blistering *Plastic Ono Band* album at Abbey Road (which Roger Waters claimed inspired him to write more emotionally honest lyrics), believed Wright's piano playing was one of the key components of Pink Floyd's albums.

Willie Aron concurs:

> What distinguishes Rick Wright's piano playing from his more florid, technically flashy peers, like Rick Wakeman and Keith Emerson, is that unlike their aspirations towards virtuosity, Wright's playing is simple and evocative. The intro to "Great Gig" is a series of rolling eighth-note chords similar to the way Lennon or McCartney might start a piece before giving way to lovely major-seventh voicings not unlike something Burt Bacharach or Brian Wilson might base an entire song around. There are no dazzling runs or knotty time-signatures; just a beautifully conceived and executed little fugue before the drums announce the wailing, majestic coda. It's masterful in every sense.

"I absolutely love Rick Wright's piano playing and chord progression on this song," Greg Lisher enthuses. "It's kind of jazzy but filled with classical flourishes. There's just so much emotion on display here."

Ruminating over who might bring the strongest vocal performance to the piece, Alan Parsons called veteran session singer Clare Torry. Torry had tickets to see Chuck Berry with her boyfriend at the Hammersmith Ballroom on the night Parsons suggested, so they rescheduled the session for Sunday, January 21. Besides, as she later admitted, she just "wasn't much of a fan," of Pink Floyd.

Upon arriving at Abbey Road studios, Torry discovered the song had "no words, no melody line, just a chord sequence."

"See what you can do with it," Parsons suggested.

The session lasted "only a couple of hours," Torry later recollected. "They didn't know what they wanted, just said it was a birth and death concept," which she deemed "rather pretentious." Rick Wright's only instruction was to "just go in and improvise." Rather baffled, the singer followed her intuition and "just sang something off the top of my head."

Experimenting with a variety of ideas, Torry combined tones with words but was quickly instructed to drop all identifiable language. Her instinct was to "sound like an instrument, a guitar or whatever, and not to think like a vocalist." She quickly laid down three or four tracks, which were met with measured approval by both Parsons and the Floyd.

"It was left totally up to me," Torry recalled. The band said, "Thank you very much," and sent her on her way. Beyond David Gilmour, Clare had the distinct impression they were "infinitely bored with the whole thing," and she was certain her contribution would "never see the light of day."

By Alan Parsons' recollection, the session went down pretty quickly, with Torry recording "two or three tracks" from which he then "assembled the best bits" to create the stunning piece.

In hindsight, Torry realized she should have demanded a partial songwriting credit. "I would be a wealthy woman now," she said. Her session fee in 1973 was a paltry fifteen pounds. Since the session fell on a Sunday, she brazenly charged double rate, for a grand total of thirty pounds (approximately $320 today). Clare felt she'd been "very daring" when she billed EMI for "twice the going rate." She was quite surprised when the album was released, and "Great Gig" "became a massive hit."

For the mesmerizing New York chanteuse Carol Lipnik, "The Great Gig in the Sky" is "such a powerful track—a wordless primal scream personified":

> This is music to be played through headphones alone at night, a soundtrack to comfort as you drift through life in quiet desperation. After a male voice proclaims his resigned fearlessness towards death, Clare Torry begins her explosive, orgasmic shrieking, a climbing improvised wailing that runs the gamut of shifting raw emotions and color, over Hammond organ and chiming piano chords. "La petite mort" is a French phrase for orgasm, meaning "a little death," and "Great Gig" is indeed *the* most fabulous shrieking death! In the aftermath of the climax, a voice [belonging to Gerry O'Driscoll] mumbles, "I am not frightened of dying; any time will do. I don't mind. Why should I be frightened of dying? There's no reason for it. You gotta go sometime ..." while Torry softly, sweetly

moans, her voice drifting off, way up and out into the unknown. Of course, there are no words in the afterlife.

○

The gig of great divas—whether opera, jazz, or blues singers—is to mine the depths of their emotion and transform blood and breath into a passionate sound. Clare Torry's voice resembles the cry of a wounded angel, or one of the mythical sirens (said to be half woman, half bird) who lured sailors with their seductive songs, causing them to smash their ships against the rocky coast of their Mediterranean island. Their ethereal melodies continue to reverberate through the ages, in the mercurial scat of Ella Fitzgerald to the bursting fountain of pure sound that was Abbey Lincoln, to the kooky angular abstraction of Annie Ross of Lambert, Hendricks, and Ross (the champions of jazz vocalese who sang "Twisted" years before Joni Mitchell donned a beret).

Jazz singer Judi Silvano is a more recent link in that chain. "I was a big fan of *Dark Side of the Moon* when I was in college, and revisiting it again now, all these years later in 2021, I can see why!" she enthuses. "At that time, I was studying and performing classical vocal music, along with contemporary modern dance, so their sound created a soundstage for my imagination!"

Judi found Rick Wright's chord progression on "The Great Gig in the Sky" "rhythmically comforting," pointing to the "modulation which gives the song a dreamy feeling rather than just plodding along." Noting the spoken-word snippets that appear and vanish throughout the album, she continues:

> Curiously, you hear voices muttering periodically in the background, but it's not always clear what they are saying. A few words poke through, but they're not "front and center," as in most rock and pop songs. It's quite mysterious! Listening now I get how bravely and philosophically Pink Floyd spoke of the taboo of death. The energy picks up when the voice suddenly enters at one minute, eight seconds into the piece, taking flight with the pure emotion of long, legato lines, swooping and soaring with abandon. The effect really carries you along from the lowest to the highest points in her melody! I really connect with this kind of voice,

expressing our deepest humanity through color and feeling and movement in the most universal sense. Most songs are focused on lyrics and the stories they tell. They are a form of literally sharing a time and a place through "word painting" that people can relate to, helping them to recall or feel their own experiences and desires. Beyond the spoken words at the beginning of the piece, the story is open to individual interpretation since there is no lyric. Clare Torry's singing has enormous power, and has captured so many people's imaginations, becoming an international icon since its release in 1973.

While studying Western classical music at Temple University in Philadelphia in her twenties, Judi discovered a similarly powerful composition titled "Vocalise" by the Russian composer and pianist Sergei Rachmaninoff.* It was written in 1912 for a soprano woman's voice, Silvano explains:

The entire piece was sung with the single vowel sound of "ah," and yet the poignant melody conveys much emotional color.

The quest among improvising musicians to find the perfect balance between deep spiritual expression through seemingly effortless is endless. A most important ingredient to this wonderful international and universal music is an almost telepathic connection that envelops both the listener and musician in a cloud of juicy and amorphous sound expression.

From all accounts, Clare Torrey improvised her vocal to a prerecorded instrumental track. This is a great example of an artist spontaneously tapping into some unknown source of inspiration. Whatever genre you classify this music, it is palpable the improvised human vocal line speaks to a very deep connection among us and provides inspiration to the millions who've heard

---

* Be sure to check out opera diva Anna Moffo's radiant 1964 recording of "Vocalise," conducted by Leopold Stokowski, who was famous for conducting the score to Disney's *Fantasia*.

it, of a shared humanity. We surely need this confirmation in our time as we have through all time, as we are indeed all related!

"The Great Gig in the Sky" is a truly cathartic listening experience. By the end of the piece, you feel as if you have been through something that is both gentle and fierce. These four minutes and forty-four seconds of music evoke the soul's transmigration through the bardo—what Tibetan Buddhists describe as the transitory state a human being passes through between death and rebirth. Filled with unspeakably frightening visions (as due per one's karma), this trip through the "fun house of the soul" (which is said to last approximately forty-nine days) is designed for the soul's spiritual growth and to help in creating a better life next time around.

In 1987, Durga McBroom and her sister, Lorelei, joined the recently reformed Pink Floyd for their *Momentary Lapse of Reason* tour. She recalls, with a laugh:

As David put it in his very chill way, they wanted to "add some color" to their sound. They kept me on all the way to their last show in 1995. Pink Floyd was part of the fabric of my early teen years, and I loved *Dark Side of the Moon*. I grew up mostly listening to musicals like *Funny Girl*, *Oliver*, and *Cabaret*. But the person who really shaped me as a musician more than anyone was Joni Mitchell. I went to a very interesting alternative school in Los Angeles, and my teacher, who was a former Haight-Ashbury Beat poet, played *Dark Side* on an 8-track stereo, along with Jethro Tull's *Thick as a Brick*. And that's when I *really* got into prog!

"Great Gig" wasn't originally in the set when they started the tour in November 1987. We took a break for Christmas, and then in January we toured Australia and Japan and performed it live at Budokan. We had to learn the piece note-for-note, which was really hard. Not only had the original been an ad-lib, but it was built from several pieces of ad-libs put together in the studio. I've seen Clare perform it since then, and even she doesn't do it the same as she did on the recording.

Richard told me that the song is about dying. It was originally called "The Mortality Sequence." It's split into three movements. The first part, where you're really wailing, represents when you learn that you're dying and you're raging at God with unbelievable anger, like, *Why me? Why me? This isn't fair.* Anger is the second step in Dr. Kübler-Ross' theory of the "Five Stages of Dying."* So, the second section is when the sadness hits you and you want to cry, "I'm not ready to go yet!" But there's nothing you can do to stop it. You're going to die, and you feel regret over all the things you haven't done. The third and last part is about acceptance, making peace with the fact that you're going to die.

I don't need to win a Grammy . . . but it would be nice! I have already received the highest accolade I could ever receive. When Richard knew he was dying, he put the money aside for a celebration of his life and asked that I sing that song at his memorial service. They flew me over to London, and John Lord started out with a classical piece, and then Jeff Beck got up and made his guitar literally weep. And I had to follow fuckin' Jeff Beck! Excuse my language . . .

I'm an alto and Clare is a mezzosoprano, and I had to sing "Great Gig" in its original key, as I was singing to the recording of Richard's piano. No pressure! In the audience was David and Nick and Jeff Beck, who had just come offstage. But I nailed it. I did it for Richard. It was the biggest honor of my life to sing the song he wrote about dying at his memorial service.

A key aspect of "Great Gig" is the run of graceful fills that Nick Mason plays, leading Wright's meditative piano comping as Clare Torry's torrential vocals explode. "Mason plays these cascading drum fills, sometimes in every bar, but it never sounds busy, because it's so fluid and seamless," Danny Frankel enthuses.

"At the transition to the second section of 'Great Gig,' it's as if Mason opens the door to let us in," says Michael Blair, percussionist and drummer with

---

* Denial, anger, bargaining, depression, acceptance.

130

Lou Reed, Tom Waits, and Elvis Costello. "He and Clare Torry create a lovely, majestic duet. Nick on the drums is the only band member who matches Torry riff-for-riff. They improvise together, weaving in and out as she literally opens up the heavens."

Before forming the Fifty Foot Hose, Cork Marcheschi recorded a single called "Bad Trip," which he recalls with a chuckle as "my very first effort at experimental or what some might call 'psychotic music.'" A home recording made in 1966, the song (if it can be classified as such) featured Marcheschi playing bass in his kitchen while Bob Noto played guitar in the bathroom and Bob Gibson (no, not the folksinger, nor the St. Louis Cardinal MVP pitcher of the same name) stood in a closet and relentlessly screamed his head off.

"I hollered 'one, two, three, play!' and watched the clock," Cork recalls. "When two and a half minutes was up, the music abruptly ended." Not only was the track atonal but, as a "Dada gesture," Cork requested that no rpm speed be assigned to the disc, encouraging DJs and fans to spin it at whatever speed they chose. "I think humans respond on a precognitive and prelinguistic level to sounds that are made by the voice," he points out. "It doesn't matter what language, or where or how. A parent can tell if a baby is hungry or hurt purely by the tenor of its voice, a non-verbal scream or holler."

○

While we're on the topic of screaming babies ... this might sound like another crazy "urban myth," but a woman I interviewed who we'll call "Suzanne," as she prefers to remain anonymous in these pages, was an International Ultimate Frisbee champion in her youth. Still in terrific shape, Suzanne gave birth to her son while standing up in the kitchen of her off-the-grid New England cabin.

"Nothing can prepare you for giving birth," she laughs. On the brink of bringing a child into this world, Suzanne reached over and flipped on the CD player. As *Dark Side of the Moon* began to play, she noticed her heartbeat was perfectly in sync with the album's opening pulse. "Breathe," David Gilmour's voice coaxed, and she began breathing along.

"Vocalization is such an important part of childbirth," Suzanne imparts. "It's a common and ancient practice to sing through labor. If you can allow the air to flow from your lips, through your windpipe and lungs, and reverberate, then the blood flow that comes from that creates the mirror image along your birth canal. You soften into the feeling and the emotion, and your pelvis softens and makes way for the baby to come through."

Suzanne's timing was impeccable. About fifteen minutes into the first side, Rick Wright began to play the serene opening chords to "The Great Gig in the Sky." Just as the infant's head emerged, Clare Torry started her torrid vocal performance, and Suzanne began to scream along, her voice, rising and falling, shrieking and sighing, until, at last, the child appeared, baptized in blood, lungs filling with his first breath. "He cried too, unrestrained as well," Suzanne says proudly.

○

As Robbi Robb points out, in the writings of the famous occultist Aleister Crowley there is "a goddess known as Nu, Nut, or Nuit in Ancient Egypt."

Her body is composed of infinite space. She is filled with infinite stars. Her hair is the tree of eternity. She claims she is divided for love's sake. "I am above you, and within you. My ecstasy is in your ecstasy. My joy is to see your joy," she says. Can you imagine having grown up in a religion like that? From Nut we get the word "naught" and "not." She is the symbol of the infinite—she is the ground of our being. To unite with her is to truly come "home." And so, *The Dark Side of the Moon* leads us unto none other than the great sky goddess herself in "The Great Gig in the Sky"! What joy to hear Clare Torry channeling the goddess as she longs, loves, and cries. This track contains my most favorite lyrics on the album—the lyrics with no words!

A BRIEF HISTORY OF
THE CONCEPT ALBUM
FROM 1940 TO 1973

Tom "Big Daddy" Donohue, as he was known for both his size and reputation, was a respected local San Francisco DJ who also produced the Seattle band the Beau Brummels for his Autumn Records label. Along with his partner Bobby Tripp, Big Daddy also produced the Beatles' legendary farewell concert at Candlestick Park on August 29, 1966. Perplexed as to why radio stations refused to play the Doors' debut album, Donohue approached the owner of the foreign-language station KMPX, Leon Crosby, with his fresh concept of freeform, album-based rock music, promising no yammering DJs, obnoxious commercials, or Top 40 singles. Support and advertising revenue, he assured Crosby, would come from the local community of hippies and businesses of Haight-Ashbury.

On April 7, 1967, from 8 p.m. to midnight, Big Daddy Donahue and his wife, Raechel, broadcast their debut show on KMPX-FM. Donohue backed up his crusade for more tasteful and intelligent broadcasting with an article (or more accurately a manifesto) for the new counterculture paper *Rolling Stone* with the scathing title, "AM Radio Is Dead and Its Rotting Corpse Is Stinking Up the Airwaves." Along with a smart mix of blues and jazz, Big Daddy featured an assortment of fresh tracks by a new breed of rock bands, including the Jefferson Airplane, the Grateful Dead, Jimi Hendrix, plus an interrupted premiere of the Beatles' masterpiece, *Sgt. Pepper's Lonely Hearts Club Band*, heralding the birth of freeform/underground FM radio.

In early 1967, the BBC had a firm grip on England's national airwaves, with programming that allowed for only the occasional rock 'n' roll song. Pirate radio stations began to pop up offshore, offering an alternative playlist, and immediately began drawing a large listening audience.

Upon returning from a visit in the States, a bloke by the name of John Ravenscroft became known as John Peel, joined the rebels of Radio London, and began hosting a new late-night show, *The Perfumed Garden*, spinning platters by happening American bands like the Velvet Underground, Jefferson Airplane, Moby Grape, Captain Beefheart, Love, and Big Brother and the Holding Company, while also championing under-the-radar English acid-folk rockers the Incredible String Band and Tyrannosaurus Rex. Producer Shel Talmy praises Peel for spinning "really oddball stuff that nobody else would play."

It should also be noted that John Peel was the first DJ to play Pink Floyd's *Dark Side of the Moon* in its entirety on British airwaves. Alan Parsons considered *Dark Side* "very programable ... perfect fodder for AOR/FM radio." DJs could "play two or three tracks, one right after the other," he told me, adding that their work was already done for them, "because all the segues were carefully worked out" within the album's grooves.

"FM radio is where everything started to change," the late, great producer Hal Willner told me in an interview shortly before his death in 2020. "They played cool stuff like King Crimson, Pink Floyd, the Doors, Led Zeppelin, and Frank Zappa. Stuff that lonely guys with acne and no girlfriends mostly listened to. Growing up in Philadelphia, I used to listen to this disc jockey called Hy Lit, who played kazoo along to the Mothers' 'You're Probably Wondering Why I'm Here.' That really turned my head around, as I hadn't heard Spike Jones giving raspberries to the audience yet."

The sequencing of songs on new albums of the mid-to-late sixties seemed to directly reflect the free-form stream of consciousness programming of FM disc jockeys who would cross-fade from one song into the next, creating an amazing flow—a cathartic journey for listeners wanting to, in the words of John Lennon, "turn off your mind, relax, and float downstream."

"The real beginning of the album era started in 1965, with *Rubber Soul*, which was the first Beatles album without a single on it," says Michael Tearson, the former late-night host on WMMR 93.3 in Philadelphia from 1970 to 1976.

> Then came the more experimental *Revolver*, an album of discovery, followed by *Sgt. Pepper*, an album of application, which used all of the tricks they learned while making *Revolver*. FM was a totally new

form of radio at that time. FM disc jockeys even spoke differently, not with that forced insincerity of Top 40 style but more like they were having a one-to-one conversation with you. In addition to busting the three-minute barrier [the typical length of singles of the day], the FM format allowed for songs of whatever length, which helped bands with concepts that needed more time to deliver what their music intended. FM went deep into albums, particularly if they had a sequence of songs, rather than just individual tracks. Those kinds of records were absolutely supported by the FM format. But sometimes the [album's built-in] segues would create problems for DJs who only wanted to play one song. It made it tricky to cross fade. I always strove from day one to make my segues musically coherent—to create a continuity, from note to note, whether it was about the sound or the storytelling. Today, the care in album sequencing is nearly a lost art, as is our shortened attention spans, which have sadly made albums irrelevant.

Released on September 26, 1969, the Beatles' *Abbey Road* featured a sixteen-minute medley comprised of eight songs, artfully woven together into one seamless, continuous flow punctuated by Paul McCartney's finale, a tongue-in-cheek valentine to "Her Majesty."

Released a month later (and knocking *Abbey Road* out of the first-place slot that December), *Led Zeppelin II* kicks off with the lusty powerhouse "Whole Lotta Love," built on a grungy, swaggering guitar riff nicked from Chicago bluesman Willie Dixon's "You Need Love." But then, one minute and twenty seconds into the song, it suddenly dissolves into an atmospheric soundscape driven by John Bonham's whooshing hi-hat, bongo beats, and chiming cymbals that evoke the midnight hour in an antique clock shop (oddly like the opening sequence of "Time"). The listener is swept up into a tsunami of sound emanating from Jimmy Page's slide guitar and a swooping theremin, as Robert Plant screams and screeches a series of feverish "ooh's" and "ahh's" from the depths of a psycho/sexual nightmare. His feral howl does a free-fall through space, boomeranging from speaker to speaker, until Bonham's snare shatters the delirium, followed by a series of scorching blues licks from Page's guitar that return mesmerized listeners to the song's monster groove once more, with no rhyme or reason given for the sonic detour they've just experienced.

Despite Led Zep's initial protestations, Atlantic Records was determined to cut all that "weird stuff" out from the song's middle section. The label released an edited version of "Whole Lotta Love" as the band's new single, ready for airplay on AM radio stations across America. No further complaints were heard from Led Zeppelin after "Whole Lotta Love" shot to No. 4 on the *Billboard* charts.

○

The term "concept album" has always seemed hazy. What differentiates a concept album from a "song cycle" or a "rock opera" is a subjective decision, best left to the composer, or maybe the critic. But the notion of the concept album had been around long before the release of *Dark Side of the Moon* on March 1, 1973. In fact, Pink Floyd's masterpiece was one of the last of its kind.

While rock fans tend to view the Beatles' *Sgt. Pepper's Lonely Hearts Club Band* as the original concept album, or perhaps the Who's *Tommy* (more accurately, a "rock opera," as it follows a narrative from start to finish, no matter how strange or fragmented it gets at times), the concept album had already been around for years.

Whether its roots lay in the opera halls of Europe, or the Grand Ol' Opry, the idea of a song cycle comprised of a thread of tunes that convey a mood or tell a story is as old as the hills. Folk and country singers conceived and released themed albums years before the trend caught on with Frank Sinatra (an unacknowledged master of the genre) and was then adopted by a generation of longhairs.

Frustrated by the constraints of the three-minute pop tune, songwriters have long sought ways to create works of a grander sophistication and scale. Time after time, we've seen good pop songs lose their impact and soul when fettered by heavy orchestration and laborious arrangements. Where "conceptual art" tends to give more credence to the idea that inspired the work than the finished piece itself, the concept album is usually a high-budget, more polished, and "formal" work that yearns to be taken more seriously. But the first concept album began humbly, as a series of stirring songs from an Okie hobo who portrayed American life just the way he encountered it. Here are a few classics of the genre that set the tone for *Dark Side of the Moon.*

DUST BOWL BALLADS (1940)

Chronicling the catastrophic conditions migrant farmers faced during the Great Depression, Woody Guthrie's *Dust Bowl Ballads, Vol. 1* and *Vol. 2* (originally released as two sets of 78s) are often considered the original concept album, a two-part sonic novel on par with John Steinbeck's *Grapes of Wrath*. While concept albums tend to be elaborate multitracked affairs, Guthrie recorded this striking portfolio of songs in a single day—April 26, 1940—at RCA Victor studios in Camden, New Jersey.

Facing hunger and foreclosure in the wake of severe drought conditions, Guthrie left his hometown of Okemah, Oklahoma, in 1935 and rode the rails west from the Great Plains to California. But, lacking the necessary "Do Re Mi," Woody soon discovered the new Eden was far from welcoming.

While "I Ain't Got No Home in This World Anymore" portrays a man at his wits end, trapped by desperate times, Guthrie still manages to maintain his sense of dignity and humor. In "Dust Pneumonia Blues," he quips that no matter how he tried, he couldn't manage to yodel due to the dust "rattling" in his lungs. As haunting a portrait of America as Dorothea Lange or Walker Evan's stark black-and-white photographs, *Dust Bowl Ballads* remains as fresh and true as the day Guthrie recorded it.

Woody's music would inspire a generation of War Baby songwriters, including Bob Dylan and Roger Waters, who once said, "I learned my lessons from Huddie Ledbetter [a.k.a. Lead Belly] and Bessie Smith. And I listened to a lot of jazz and Woody Guthrie. I learned a lot from all of that protest music when I was a very young teenager."

LUKE THE DRIFTER (1954)

Hank Williams was in trouble, again. This time it wasn't just his usual problems with women and drinking. It was something more worrisome and profound. At age twenty-nine, Williams sensed his race on this earth was run and he was headed straight for hell. He'd been rambling down that stark "Lost Highway" long enough, wandering that lonesome valley from honky-tonk to honky-tonk and woman to woman. It was time to get right with his maker before the final curtain fell. Determined to share his tale of caution and warn fellow sinners of the pitfalls of iniquity, Williams—at the height of his popularity and against the better judgment of his manager, Fred Rose—forged an alter ego known as Luke the Drifter.

Hank would be found dead in the backseat of his baby-blue Cadillac on January 1, 1953. Released a year later, this four-record, 78-rpm box set is comprised of a stark series of songs and sermons that don't exactly follow a linear narrative as much as create a song cycle. Bob Dylan, in his memoir *Chronicles: Volume One*, claims to have nearly "wore out" the records: "I could listen to the *Luke the Drifter* record all day and drift away myself and become totally convinced in the goodness of man."

IN THE WEE SMALL HOURS (1955)

Love him or loathe him, one can never underestimate the artistry and staying power of Frank Sinatra. While a generation of baby boomers swooned to *A Hard Day's Night*, their parents were already hip to the onscreen antics and undeniable charisma of the Rat Pack. Comprised of Sinatra, Dean Martin, Sammy Davis, Jr., Joey Bishop, and Peter Lawford, this swaggering bunch boasted just one token WASP (Lawford) among its ethnic mix of Italians, an African American, and two Jews (if you count Sammy Davis, Jr.'s conversion).

Long before integrated rock bands like Booker T. and the MG's, Love, and Sly and the Family Stone toured the country and topped the charts, Sinatra swung hard with Count Basie's band and sang with Ella Fitzgerald and Louis Armstrong. And, unlike most rockers, Sinatra could act—check out *The Man with the Golden Arm*, *Pal Joey*, and *The Manchurian Candidate*, to name a few.

Released in April 1955, with lush arrangements by Nelson Riddle, *In the Wee Small Hours* was Sinatra's ninth studio album and represented his great comeback. The album cover depicts Frank in a fedora, holding a cigarette, drenched in a blue streetlight, setting the melancholy mood for a portfolio of late-night laments (thanks to his recent breakup with Ava Gardner) that sparkle to this day like ice cubes in a glass of scotch.

Sinatra continued to crank out concept albums over the next couple of decades. In 1970, he released the bleak *Watertown*, written by Bob Gaudio (of the Four Seasons) and Jake Holmes (responsible for "Dazed and Confused," the shoe-gazing blues pilfered by Led Zeppelin on their debut album).

The worst-selling album of his career, *Watertown* alienated most of Frank's fans. Sad and blue as he was on *Wee Small Hours*, his streetlight aura still revealed a ray of glamour. *Watertown* was a mood swing that few could swing with. Ol' Blue Eyes sounds one drink away from clinically depressed. Though it was out of print for years, a new generation of Sinatra connoisseurs now recognize the "genius" within its gloomy grooves.

SATAN IS REAL (1959)

While the Louvin Brothers sang of sin and preached salvation, Ira Louvin, the duo's mandolin player, led a notoriously wild and reckless life. The Alabama duo delivered their stark message of fire and brimstone in a seamless high/lonesome two-part harmony that inspired everyone from the Everly Brothers to the Byrds. Their albums, produced by Chet Atkins, always featured plenty of hot picking, whether from Ira on mandolin or "Mr. Guitar," as Chet was known.

Not only did the Louvins warn of the pitfalls of human desire, they spelled out certain doom for the planet, dreading "the mushroom of destruction" in "The Great Atomic Power." Considered a classic of country music, the album photo for *Satan Is Real* depicts American surrealism at its best. Dressed in white suits with their arms extended, the Louvin Brothers beckon us to their homemade vision of Hell. Staged at the Nashville dump, the photograph has them standing beside a cross-eyed devil, crudely cut from a sheet of plywood and painted red. After soaking a pile of tires in gasoline, they lit a match. The flames rose higher and higher until Ira, according to his brother Charlie, somehow caught on fire during the photo shoot.

SGT. PEPPER'S LONELY HEARTS CLUB BAND (1967)

Following their August 1966 performance at Candlestick Park in San Francisco, the Beatles were through with being fab. The mayhem of their concerts had prevented them from progressing any further as a live act, and now the refuge of Abbey Road offered a much-needed haven from struggling to play the hits over the din of screaming teenagers. A creative, heady atmosphere soon emerged as new songs and sounds arose, thanks in part to their fondness for pot and LSD, and new technological leaps in overdubbing with 4-track tape.

Having recently visited a slew of new San Francisco bands who sported longer hair and longer names, like the Jefferson Airplane, the Grateful Dead, and

Quicksilver Messenger Service, Paul began to feel like the Beatles were "old hat." In search of a new identity, he pondered the idea of an alter ego to free the band from the tight corner they found themselves stuck in. Stories vary as to how he came up with the legendary name. Some claim Paul was inspired by Dr. Pepper, a favorite soda unavailable in the UK at the time, which British movie and rock stars had shipped across the Atlantic by the caseful. But years later, McCartney said he'd misheard the band's roadie, Mal Evans, say "Sergeant Pepper" when he'd actually asked if he could pass the "salt 'n' pepper."

In many ways, the Beatles seemed profoundly out of touch with the time when the album was recorded. Amid the '60s sexual revolution, they were happily proposing marriage to the sound of old-timey clarinets on "When I'm Sixty-Four." In "Lovely Rita," McCartney invites a cute meter maid over for tea and winds up "sitting on a sofa with a sister or two." It's all very quaint compared to the Doors, who incited us to "break on through to the other side," while Hendrix had an overwhelming, itching desire to "stand next to your fire."

Oddly, too, very little rock can be found within the tracks of "rock's greatest masterpiece," as a variety of reeds, brass, sitars, harpsichords, organs and, at times, McCartney's bass replace the usual lead guitar. "She's Leaving Home" features a cascading harp and shimmering string section, over which McCartney addresses parental heartbreak about a runaway teenage daughter.

As the spring of 1967 blossomed into the Summer of Love, hordes of middle-class refugees across America headed for San Francisco (with or without flowers in their hair) to dig the free dope and free love to be found on the streets of Haight-Ashbury. Few gave a damn about their parents, as they were just part of the Establishment.

In comparison to the sloppy psychedelic deluge of Big Brother and the Holding Company, *Sgt. Pepper's Lonely Hearts Club Band* hardly seemed radical. But within the grooves of "A Day in the Life" (and the double A-side single "Penny Lane" and "Strawberry Fields Forever," released earlier that February), a new realm of consciousness could be found brewing in the "marmalade skies," as John sings in "Lucy in the Sky with Diamonds."

George Harrison's lone contribution to the album, "Within You Without You," was a stunning piece of work, unlike anything else on *Sgt. Pepper*—or anywhere else for that matter. Having picked up the sitar in 1965, while on the set of their second film, *Help!*, the "Quiet Beatle" became enamored of all things Eastern, spirituality in particular. He soon devoted himself to sitar lessons with Pandit Ravi Shankar, and he sat cross-legged in bliss at the feet of gurus Maharishi Mahesh Yogi and Srila Prabhupada, inspiring fans and friends worldwide to take up their own divine practice.

In a 1970 interview with *Rolling Stone*, David Crosby addressed the naiveté that lay beneath the era's idealism when he confessed, "I would've thought *Sgt. Pepper* could've stopped the [Vietnam] war, just by putting too many good vibes in the air for anybody to have a war around. Somehow it didn't work. Somebody isn't listening. I'm not saying stop trying, but the inertia we're up against, I think everybody's kind of underestimated it."

Pepper was nothing if not extravagant. Being the most expensive record cover in the history of pop music (£3,000, at a time when the norm was £50), it sported an inner gatefold photo of the band, plus a fun insert of cardboard-cutout pictures of the group, a mustache, and sergeant stripes (designed by the Fool), along with another first: the song lyrics, printed as a libretto on the album's back sleeve. Not even rock's poet laureate, Bob Dylan, had published his verse for his fans to painstakingly analyze.

SMILE / SMILEY SMILE (1967)

Finding little support from his band, record company, or family after writing and arranging the brilliant *Pet Sounds* (released in May 1966), Brian Wilson soldiered on, attempting to top the Beatles' latest artistic triumph, *Revolver*.

The original *Smile* was an ambitious affair—a "teenage symphony to God," as Brian described it—that included the Beach Boys' most imaginative tracks to date, "Good Vibrations" along with the enigmatic "Cabinessence." While Wilson's aspirations drove him to create greater, more elaborate works, the conflict brewing within the band's ranks exploded after an exasperated Mike Love claimed he couldn't understand Brian's new lyricist, the enigmatic Van Dyke Parks' free-associative poetry. Meanwhile, Brian, teetering on the edge of a nervous breakdown, plunged into the deep end of drugs, depression, and delusion from which he never fully returned. Instead of a second Wilson masterpiece, the Beach Boys released the watered-down (yet not without its delights) *Smiley Smile* in September 1967.

Fleeing the quagmire of the Wilson brothers' dysfunctional family band, Van Dyke Parks went on to compose and arrange his own brilliant (yet maligned at the time of its release) album, *Song Cycle*, while the original session tapes for *Smile* became rock's most revered and bootlegged lost masterwork, until Brian Wilson re-imagined, re-recorded, and released it as an eighteen-track CD in 2004.

THEIR SATANIC MAJESTIES REQUEST (1967)

Between the haze of drugs and the abrupt departure of the Stones' original manager and producer, Andrew Loog Oldham, who was fed up with his band's lack of focus, *Their Satanic Majesties Request* was a mess, albeit a glorious mess. The public were confused and disappointed by the band's delightful psychedelic misadventure, which was mercilessly skewered by the press, and even John Lennon slagged the album, complaining, "*Satanic Majesties* was just *Pepper*." While the Stones' inspiration sprang from a darker corner of the musical galaxy, John had a point. There, hidden within the mounds of flowers engulfing the band on the album's fabulous 3-D cover, photographed by Michael Cooper (the same chap who'd also recently shot *Sgt. Pepper*) one could find images of all four Fabs, while hearing John and Paul's soaring harmonies on their recent single "We Love You."

The Stones were no longer just serving up a batch of songs spiced with various auditory delights from their resident multi-instrumental genius, Brian Jones. For one brief album, they created a series of sonic dreamscapes that transported listeners from their familiar environs to "Another Land."

Hounded by the police in 1967, Mick Jagger, Keith Richards, and Brian Jones were routinely hauled before the courts and into prison in a series of sensationalized drug busts intended to destroy the band. By the time of the album's delayed release in December of that year, the spirit of Flower Power had already withered and died on the vine. Besides, the Stones, despite their shaggy hair and exotic togs, made lousy hippies. If they were any sort of "Flowers," they were Venus Flytraps.

Listening back, years later, to *Their Satanic Majesties Request* remains a rewarding and frustrating experience. The hits: "She's a Rainbow," with its elegant string arrangement by Led Zeppelin's John Paul Jones, is nothing short of radiant; "2000 Light Years from Home" is the song that, along with the Byrds' "Eight Miles High" and the Floyd's "Interstellar Overdrive" and "Astronomy

Domine," helped create the new genre of "space rock," and leads you down into the dark dungeon of despair and alienation that Jones, Jagger, and Richards undoubtedly felt after having being thrown into the dreaded Wormwood Scrubs Prison on drugs charges. It features a classic Keith Richards grungy guitar hook and rumbling drums from Charlie Watts, while Brian Jones conjures up a mystical swirling atmosphere with the help of some backward piano and a meandering Moog.

Not to be overlooked is Bill Wyman's one brief moment in the spotlight, "In Another Land." Over a sinister harpsichord, Wyman delivers the tune's loopy lyric, his voice drenched in vibrato (beating Tommy James and the Shondells to the psychedelic punchbowl, with their trippy, tremolo-soaked anthem, "Crimson and Clover," released nearly a year later in November 1968).

Side one ends with a reprise of "Sing This All Together—See What Happens," which sounds like a home recording of a strange late-night shamanic ritual taking place in Keith's basement. "The Lantern" offers a gloriously mystical moment, while pop-music scholars can argue whether the fluttering flute, swirling organ, and tabla-driven jam of "Gomper" invented "world music." (Or was it George Harrison's sitar on "Norwegian Wood" ... or, as Donovan claims, the conga/flute island groove of his "First There Is a Mountain"?)

No one was more brutal in their assessment of the Stones' brief dalliance with psychedelia than Keith Richards, who, years later, sadly dismissed the album as "a load of crap." Even Charlie Watts' mother, Lilian, took a shot at the record, claiming, "It was at least two weeks ahead of its time."

OGDEN'S NUT GONE FLAKE (1968)

Following their troubled tour of Australia and New Zealand in January '68, the Small Faces, needing some relaxation, took a boat ride down the River Thames. Bassist, singer, and songwriter Ronnie Laine was filled with wonder and inspiration as he gazed up at the moon "in the heavenly abode." Brainstorming with his bandmate, guitarist Steve Marriott, they soon concocted the strange and fantastic saga of "Happiness Stan." Peppered with whimsical narrations by comic actor "Professor" Stanley Unwin (a.k.a. the Master of Gobbledygook, as he was dubbed by the BBC), the Small Faces' fanciful "mini-opera" comprised six songs and filled the second side of the third and final album by the original group.

A gumbo of sci-fi, Beat poetry, and fairytale, the story unfolds like this: Puzzled by the waning of the moon, Stan, unfamiliar with physics, wonders where half of the silver orb has disappeared to. He soon meets a fly (a.k.a. the Hungry Intruder), with whom he generously shares a bit of his lunch; in return, the grateful insect, possessing superpowers, transports him on his back to a distant cave, where he meets a hermit by the name of Mad John. The all-knowing recluse reassures Stan that all is well, and during the time he's spent worrying about the moon, it has grown back again to its original shape! Moved to song, everybody (as in a musical) spontaneously breaks into the rousing "HappyDaysToyTown."

Whether inspired by the moon, J. R. R. Tolkien's tales, childhood bedtime stories, or hash-induced dreams, the Small Faces' farfetched adventures of "Happiness Stan" eventually climbed to No. 1 after the album's UK release in May 1968. The LP also came wrapped in one of rock's most distinctive album covers: a round replica of Ogden's Nut-Brown Flake tobacco tin.

As they sang in their hit single "Itchycoo Park," it was "all too beautiful."

S. F. SORROW (1968)

Rock's first "opera," *S. F. Sorrow* by the Pretty Things recounts the story of Sebastian F. Sorrow, born (to the sound of chiming guitars and driving drums) at the beginning of the twentieth century in an ordinary small town and raised in row house "Number Three." All seems well until Sebastian's childhood ends abruptly and he is forced to join his father, slaving away at the local "Misery Factory." Not surprisingly, Sorrow's saving grace arrives in the form of a young girl's love, depicted in "She Says Good Morning."

Lead singer Phil May's vision originated as a short story titled *Cutting Up Sergeant Time.* But when the Beatles' masterpiece featured a protagonist of the same rank, May demoted his leading man to the more fitting "Private Sorrow." Drafted into the army to fight in the muddy trenches of World War I, Sorrow suffers shellshock but manages to survive the bloody fray. He then emigrates to "Amerik" and finds work in another factory, awaiting the arrival of his fiancé from across the sea on the *Windenberg.* But all hope is dashed as he watches the doomed airship burst into a "bright orange flame," as described in the rocking "Balloon Burning," followed by a minor-keyed dirge simply titled "Death."

Deeply depressed, Sebastian stumbles upon a shamanic healer named "Baron Saturday" (inspired by the Haitian Voodoo spirit of death, Baron Samedi). Saturday takes Sorrow on a grueling journey to the underworld. As he flies through the sky, he's amazed to see the moon, whose face strangely resembles that of our hero.

As in the French silent film *The Astronomer's Dream*, the moon opens its enormous mouth and gobbles up Sorrow, who then finds himself standing before row of oak doors, which, thrown open by Saturday, lead our protagonist into a room full of mirrors. May seems to have been inspired by Dickens' moralistic tale *A Christmas Carol*, in which Ebenezer Scrooge—led by spirits past, present, and future—is forced to face the repercussions of his greed and arrogance.

The generation of war babies born during the Blitzkrieg not only shared the traumatic experience of the death of parents and loved ones as well as hiding in bomb shelters, and witnessing the decimation of their hometowns, but also had a great need to express their pent-up pain in some meaningful way. It's not unusual to find commonalities in the art that later blossomed from their mutual distress. Yet the parallels between Pete Townshend's *Tommy* and Phil May's *S. F. Sorrow* are startling. Both "operas" are set in the early twentieth century, with World War I as their backdrop. Both protagonists experience trauma and are then subjected to the strange healing practices of Baron Saturday and the Acid Queen, respectively. Townshend also employed a mirror as the key to his hero Tommy Walker's transformation. After Tommy's frustrated mother smashes the mirror, the deaf, dumb, and blind boy is suddenly healed of all afflictions; Sebastian's mirror simply reflects his grim reality. And in both May's song "The Journey" and Townshend's "The Amazing Journey," the hero's odyssey ends in despair and loneliness.

S. F. Sorrow differs from other rock-opera concept albums, like *Tommy* and Pink Floyd's *The Wall*, which tell their story through song lyrics. In addition to their well-crafted songs, the Pretty Things included brief narrative passages in the liner notes of the LP to flesh out the tale.

While ridiculed by Pink Floyd for his work on *Piper at the Gates of Dawn*, producer Norman "Hurricane" Smith was integral to the creation of *S. F. Sorrow* and was considered, for all intents and purposes, a "sixth member" of the band.

Hamstrung by poor record sales in the States, the album languished for six months until it was finally released on Motown's subsidiary rock label, Rare Earth. By that time, the Pretty Things' most ambitious effort was all but lost to history. To add insult to injury, the blusterous but brilliant critic Lester Bangs slammed the album as "pretentious" and an obvious imitation of Townshend's *Tommy*.

While some complained that the storyline of *S. F. Sorrow* was too whimsical and vague, May felt the album should be viewed subjectively and refrained from any further explanation. "I always believe the listener's right to interpret the lyrics and narrative as they feel it," he said.

Although virtually ignored in America, the Pretty Things—once rivals of the Rolling Stones and the Kinks in the early '60s—remained cult favorites in England. In September 1998, thirty years after the album's release, they returned to Abbey Road Studios to perform a live, letter-perfect reading of *S. F. Sorrow*, with David Gilmour guesting on lead guitar and Arthur Brown narrating the excerpts which linked the song cycle.

"I loved the Pretty Things since I was ten years old," declares Plasticland's vocalist, guitarist, and organist, Glenn Rehse. "I first saw *S. F. Sorrow* at Woolworths about six months after it first came out. It changed my life's path. From that point on, I tried to get people to listen to it. AM radio would never play them. I guess there just wasn't enough room for all the great music coming out at the time."

TOMMY (1969)

Pete Townshend had an axe to grind with rock's "masterpiece," *Sgt. Pepper's Lonely Hearts Club Band*: "The Beatles copied us!" he told *Rolling Stone* in 2021. "Paul McCartney came up to me at the [the Soho London club] Bag O'Nails [and said] he really loved our mini opera, which was called 'A Quick One, While He's Away.'"

The nine-minute track appeared at the close of their 1966 album, *A Quick One* (released with an altered track listing as *Happy Jack* several months later in the US), and Paul, Townshend added, "told me they were thinking about doing similar things." Hoping to avoid a row with McCartney, Pete backpedaled a bit, adding, "I think anybody that was even a little bit 'art school' back then, a little bit adventurous—and, of course, the Beatles were encouraged to experiment to the max in the studio—would have thought about doing something which was a concept."

Townshend, who has been consistently inconsistent in his opinions over the years, has also said, "On the Herman's Hermits tour, we were listening to *Sgt. Pepper*, and I was enchanted by it. I think we all were. We thought it really was an amazing piece of studio craftsmanship."

Pepper may have started out as a concept album, but it quickly lost its focus. With Brian Epstein rushing the release of the single of Lennon's "Strawberry Fields Forever," backed with McCartney's "Penny Lane," the album lost its original theme of a nostalgic look back at the band's early years in Liverpool. So it became a concert, of sorts, by this strange band ...

Whatever it was, *Pepper* wasn't rock. In fact, the album barely rocked at all, except for those few moments when McCartney unleashed a flurry of stinging lead guitar riffs on the album's title song, and Lennon's "Good Morning, Good Morning."

"Rock 'n' roll music has got to have that bounce," Townshend told *Rolling Stone* in 1968. "It's got to have that thing to make you swing. ... It's got to have a rhythm which undulates. ... It doesn't have to be physical because when you think of a lot of Beatles music, it's very non-physical. Like *Sgt. Pepper* is an incredibly non-physical album."

Nonetheless, *Pepper* captured the world's collective imagination by creating "a sense of place" in their fans' imaginations by opening the album with the sounds of a crowded concert hall while the orchestra tuned up and reprising the album's title song and audience's cheers again on its B-side. The intriguing record jacket—a gatefold that featured the lyrics printed on the back—resembled a timeless photograph of the band, with an odd group of concert attendees posing on the village green (although some claimed the Beatles' name and McCartney's bass pictured in flowers depicted a funeral scene). But whatever "concept" the album was allegedly built on seemed to fall apart after just a few songs.

With its free-form radio format, complete with fake ads, *The Who Sell Out* was just too weird for most people, despite containing a bona fide Who classic single, "I Can See for Miles." Released in December 1967, the album quickly met with a harsh fate in the States after Joe Bogart, the program director of WMCA, New

York's leading AM station, denigrated it as "disgusting." Undoubtedly, Bogart took offense at the record's hilarious Warholian cover, which has Townshend swiping his armpit with a jumbo stick of deodorant while singer Roger Daltrey bathed in a tub of Heinz baked beans. Bogart discouraged his disc jockeys from giving the album any further airtime.

Just by size alone, double albums demand the gravitas of being hailed a "masterpiece." And while *Tommy* is probably closer to an actual rock opera than any other work of that description, it is built on a peculiar, farfetched narrative.

In his 2012 autobiography, *Who I Am*, Pete Townshend claims to have composed *Tommy* out of "pure desperation." Following a recent trip to California, he began the enormous task of composing "a self-contained song cycle with spiritual themes." Townshend's personal spiritual search had led him to the lotus feet of a "genuine master," Meher Baba, the smiling, mustachioed Indian guru who had adhered to a forty-four-year vow of silence, using a hand-held blackboard ad hand signals to communicate. His simple pop philosophy, "Don't Worry—Be Happy!" soon spread worldwide.

Yet *Tommy* revealed little joy. Released in May 1969, Townshend's rock opera was neither the first nor only of its kind. Recorded throughout 1967 and into the fall of 1968, the Pretty Things' *S. F. Sorrow* was released in December 1968. Lacking decent publicity and distribution, the album soon fell into obscurity, while *Tommy* was hailed as a rock milestone. The Kinks' brilliant but obscure *Arthur (Or the Decline and Fall of the British Empire)*, soon followed, released in October 1969.

While the war in Vietnam continued to escalate, it's interesting to note that all three albums were infused with strong antiwar statements. The Pretty Things' "Private Sorrow" becomes somewhat unhinged on the frontlines of World War I, while Tommy's father, Captain Walker, is presumed dead or at least "missing with a number of men," and Ray Davies' "Yes Sir, No Sir," reveals the hapless predicament of infantry men forced to follow orders, no matter how absurd they seem. The album also includes a pair of strong antiwar statements from Mr. Davies, "Mr. Churchill Says" and "Tin Soldier Man."

While *Arthur* failed to move the public (beyond its lead-off single, "Victoria"), *Rolling Stone*'s formidable critic Greil Marcus judged the Kinks' first foray into a long run of "Koncept" records, "by all odds the best British album of 1969. It shows that Pete Townshend still has worlds to conquer and that the Beatles have a lot of catching up to do."

Townshend likened the concept of rock opera to something in the air, like "guitar feedback—many others had the same idea at the same time." While some immediately took offense at the protagonist of "Pinball Wizard" being deaf, dumb, and blind, Pete explained to Jann Wenner in a *Rolling Stone* interview, that Tommy simply existed "in a world of vibrations."

Pete Townshend unveiled his next double-album song cycle, the Who's *Quadrophenia*, in October 1973, before inventing "the rock novel" on 2019's *The Age of Anxiety*.

AQUALUNG (1971)

In January 1968, Ian Anderson left his hometown of Blackpool, England, and met up with his old mate Jeffrey Hammond, who was attending art school in London at the time. Crashing at Hammond's tiny one-room flat, Ian rifled through his friend's record collection, discovering albums by Ornette Coleman, Captain Beefheart, and Roland Kirk, whose snarling, bluesy flute style would set him on his path to fame.

Anderson had first picked up the flute a year earlier, but he hadn't gotten very far with it. "When I heard Roland Kirk it was right at the point when I learned to make a noise on the flute," he told me in a 2000 interview.

> It immediately created a point of reference for me, to try and develop that into an all-out assault on the ears.
>
> I was absolutely penniless at the time. I had no lessons or instruction book. I didn't know where to put my fingers or how to make an embouchure. I had to figure it out for myself. I found the scat-singing approach—singing along with the notes you're playing—a good way to fire up a note. It allowed me to produce a more aggressive and rougher-edged sound. I could actually get a sound by doing that, where it was very difficult for me to get a clean, clear tone. From not playing the flute at all in 1967 to being the main featured instrument in Jethro Tull in the summer of 1968, it was a pretty short six months.

Things indeed happened fast for Tull, whether due to Anderson's freaked-out stage antics (he was known to occasionally hold the flute between his legs and stroke it like a gleaming phallus) or their "heavy" prog-rock sound, or the novelty of the flute in a hard-rock band.

Beyond the beatnik cool of Herbie Mann's *Live at the Village Gate*, the instrument could be heard adding an introspective touch to the Beatles' 1965 Dylan knockoff "You've Got to Hide Your Love Away," and, a year later, providing the haunting solo to "California Dreamin'" by the Mamas and the Papas. The flute was also a prime ingredient of Traffic's rock 'n' roll stew.

Nick Mason's first wife, Lindy, would also overdub a clutch of lilting medieval flutes to the array of drums, percussion, and sound effects provided by her husband on the meandering soundscape "The Grand Vizier's Garden Party (Entrance)," from Pink Floyd's *Ummagumma*.

While most bands still maintained some semblance of hygiene and style, Jethro Tull, on the front cover of their debut release, 1968's *This Was*, posed as gnarly forest dwellers, complete with pipes, hats, and canes, with a pack of mangy dogs. Whether described as "a stork with St. Vitus' dance" or "a mad dog Fagin with a lecherous point of view," Anderson strongly resembled the greasy codger hunched in the doorway portrayed on the record sleeve of *Aqualung*.

Critics deemed Tull's fourth album either "boring and pretentious" or "extremely profound," with little leeway in between. Love it or loathe it, Ian Anderson's opus to the "poor old sod" remains one of rock's classic *themed*, "never a concept!" albums, as the band's front man stressed. To Anderson, *Aqualung* was "just a bunch of songs."

Beyond the title number and "Cross-Eyed Mary," which calls out the protagonist by name, there are few clues to prove otherwise. Yet the record's second side offers a religious tirade comprised of "My God," "Hymn 43," and "Wind-Up."

With Martin Barre's sinister minor chords on "My God," Anderson lambasts the "Bloody Church of England." "He is the God of nothing, if that's all that you can see," Tull's front man snarls. In "Hymn 43," the protagonist begs Jesus for redemption, then boldly demands answers from God, to which the heavenly Father famously replies, "I'm not the kind you wind up on Sundays." And with "Wind-Up," the protagonist abruptly returns to his "old headmaster," informing him that he "had the whole damn thing all wrong," certain that excommunication is forthcoming for his insolence.

THE RISE AND FALL OF ZIGGY STARDUST AND THE SPIDERS FROM MARS (1972)

Following the harrowing events of 1968—which included the back-to-back assassinations of Dr. Martin Luther King, Jr., and Bobby Kennedy, the riots at the Democratic Convention, and the ensuing election of Richard Nixon— disillusioned counterculture refugees, seeking escape, began moving to the country, to "live naturally."

A year later, the Rolling Stones' disastrous Altamont concert and the Bianca/Tate murders by Charlie Manson's ghoulish gang cast a grim pall over the '60s dream. The Vietnam War continued to escalate, and disenfranchised youth found solace in the proliferation of harder drugs like coke, speed, and barbiturates. "It was a mighty time," Peter Stampfel recollects. "But by 1969, the party was definitely over. Things had gotten very shitty."

Indeed, it seemed like the whole world was still reeling under the spell of the dollar-a-hit brown acid that caused a thousand bad trips among the mud-covered masses of Woodstock. After the Beatles' *Magical Mystery Tour* failed to take them away, and unable to find the secret cove where their Yellow Submarine was docked, a generation of aging children needed the soul-soothing deep blue lullabies of "Sweet Baby" James Taylor, or a bit of happy-go-lucky sightseeing on Crosby, Stills, and Nash's hash-fueled "Marrakech Express." Or, better yet, a strange bisexual savior from outer space. Despite John Lennon wearily crying "the dream is over" on his 1970 solo album *Plastic Ono Band*, those unable to cope with the ex-Beatle's harsh message turned to the first bit of magic they could find: David Bowie's *Ziggy Stardust and the Spiders from Mars*.

Bowie's romance with the spheres had previously inspired the mini-musical-melodramas "Space Oddity" and "Life on Mars?" So, when he came along with a new "screwed-down hairdo" and the Spiders' deliciously edgy sound (Mick Ronson's crunchy power chords on "Hang on to Yourself" throwing down a new level of heavy five years before punk hit), it felt both fresh and familiar.

Borrowing Marc Bolan's special sonic sauce of one part fuzz with one part crisply strummed acoustic guitar, gently tossed with conga drums, a bit of sax, and a killer rhythm section that any sod reading the *NME* would die for, Bowie and producer Ken Scott forged an album for the ages. The songs flow flawlessly, from the opening gloom and doom of "Five Years" to the blue-eyed soul of "Stone Love," to the giddy sense of liberation that only a kick-ass rock 'n' roller like "Suffragette City" can bring.

While the music was innovative, Bowie's lyrics were peppered with clichés of hippie vernacular: "Far out!" he exclaims in "Moonage Daydream," while he fears the "Starman" waiting in the sky might "blow our minds." Yet *Ziggy Stardust* was a gorgeous game-changer. With one blast of the record (and perhaps a chaser of Lou Reed's *Transformer*, produced by Bowie and Ronson) you knew the '70s had officially begun.

With one eye on the future, Bowie's concept drew heavily on the past. Inspired by sci-fi films of the 1950s like *The Day the Earth Stood Still*, he created Ziggy, a disaffected alien who (much like Sun Ra with his space-jazz ensemble) struggles to improve the lives of us pathetic Earth inhabitants with help from a wild haircut, some crazy makeup, and irresistible music. The song cycle mostly follows an arc, while making a few unexplained detours along the way, until Ziggy, the rock 'n' roll savior, commits suicide rather than face another day on this doomed planet.

Perhaps the album could have ended on a gentler note had Ziggy only climbed into his spacecraft and vanished into the stratosphere, but David (who left his body in January 2016 for the outer realms) understood the staying power of heartbreak.

BERLIN (1973)

Released in July 1973, hot on the heels of *Dark Side of the Moon*, came Lou Reed's third and most ambitious album to date, *Berlin*. Teeming with the sort of dark stuff we came to expect from the man who unleashed "Heroin" on teenage America, the album chronicles the crumbling relationship of a couple of amphetamine freaks named Jim and Caroline. Inspired by the failure of Reed's brief marriage to Bettye Kronstad, *Berlin* is a voyeur's holiday, filled with drugs, promiscuity, and suicide.

More than any other artist of his time beside John Lennon, Lou Reed's life was open book. Reed's "life as art" style of songwriting (like Lennon's on *Plastic*

Ono Band) was bold and brutal, sparing no detail, no matter how damning or disturbing.

The hype was heavy following Reed's stellar *Transformer*, which included such perennials as "Walk on the Wild Side," "Perfect Day," and "Satellite of Love." Author and journalist Larry "Ratso" Sloman showered *Berlin* with high praise in *Rolling Stone*, boldly claiming, "It's not an overstatement to say that *Berlin* will be the *Sgt. Pepper* of the seventies."

"Nobody captured the zeitgeist of the time like Lou," Sloman told me in 2021. "While *Pepper* personified the '60s, Lou defined the '70s with his songs about sex and amphetamine. RCA made posters with my quote on them and when the album tanked, Lou blamed me! He wouldn't talk to me! He hated *Sgt. Pepper!*"

Reed's biographer, Anthony DeCurtis, deemed Ratso's burst of enthusiasm "an absurdity"; *Billboard*, one of the few publications to praise *Berlin*, called it "a top notch set from one of the most creative artists on the pop scene today."

In 2003, *Berlin* experienced a renaissance when Lou toured Europe performing the album. "I felt vindicated!" Ratso crowed.

Originally, the concept for the album came about from Lou's interaction with his producer, Bob Ezrin (who later co-produced *The Wall*, as well as the post-Waters Pink Floyd albums *A Momentary Lapse of Reason* and *The Division Bell*). *Berlin* took shape after Ezrin suggested that Lou expound on some of his earlier songs and ideas to create a "rock opera." Reed reworked the song "Berlin," from his eponymous debut album, and morphed the Velvet Underground classic "Stephanie Says" into "Caroline Says" to better fit the narrative.

INNERVISIONS (1973)

With sonic valentines like "Baby Love," "Where Did Our Love Go," and "I Hear a Symphony," no one could imagine the Supremes would lead the revolt against Motown Records' strict regimen of romantic love songs to say something real about life in Black America. So, when "Love Child" was released in September 1968, it came as something of a pleasant shock. Motown founder and producer Berry Gordy, who dressed his bands in classy fashions and schooled them in smooth harmonies and slick dance moves, could never have predicted a song about a fatherless child raised in poverty would top the charts. On top of that, Diana Ross was lauded for her candor after claiming the song was autobiographical.

A year later, the Supremes' "I'm Livin' in Shame" shot to No. 10, ensuring the reign of girl-boy love songs had come to an end at Motown. The Temptations soon followed suit with a pair of message songs, "Cloud Nine" and "Runaway Child, Running Wild," which addressed the struggle with and consequences of drug addiction. The extended versions of both songs, released years later, revealed jams by the fabulous Funk Brothers rhythm section (heavy on the Fender Rhodes, Fender bass and congas) that still sound fresh to this day.

On his 1971 masterpiece *What's Goin' On*, Marvin Gaye stretched beyond previously taboo subjects like poverty and drugs to address other issues, including the escalating Vietnam War and the deteriorating state of our environment. The steady groove of a conga drum and a lyrical soprano saxophone evoking jazz giant John Coltrane brought a new level of cool to the otherwise typically slick Motown production.

Inspired by Marvin's giant steps, Stevie Wonder released *Music of My Mind* the following year. The first of his socially conscious albums, *Music of My Mind* revealed a new, hipper Stevie, making political statements, delving into mysticism, and, as always, exploring love in all its complexities. Stevie's revolutionary new sound sprang from a combination of multitrack overdubbing and collaborating with synth wizards Malcolm Cecil and Robert Margouleff of Tonto's Expanding Head Band.

Talking Book quickly followed and included a pair of No. 1 hits: the irresistible funky, clavinet-driven "Superstition," and the groovy bossa-nova "You Are the Sunshine of My Life." Stevie soon found himself opening for the Rolling Stones on their legendary STP tour. When he found the time to write and record his brilliant song cycle *Innervisions* (released in August 1973) it's hard to know. But Wonder was determined to sing truth to power in songs like "Living for the City" and "Higher Ground," despite the tight leash Berry Gordy struggled to keep his artists on.

SIDE TWO

6

MONEY / US
AND THEM

There's something literally odd about Roger Water's catchy bass riff that lays the groove to *Dark Side of the Moon*'s single. With its 7/4 feel, "Money" is one of rock's rare hit songs—along with Jethro Tull's "Living in the Past," Cream's "White Room" (in the introduction and bridge sections), and "Solsbury Hill" by Peter Gabriel—to employ an odd time signature. While 7/4 is commonly used in Arabic music, whose rhythms were initially defined by and designed to support Quranic verse, there is no trace of Middle Eastern tonalities in the song's melody. Its syncopated bass line sounds immediately familiar, as if Waters was inspired by Led Zeppelin's "How Many More Times," which they'd lifted from (and eventually settled a plagiarism suit with) Chicago blues bassist and songwriter extraordinaire Willie Dixon.

"It is not easy to get rockers to stumble along to a song in an odd time signature, but 'Money' is a seductive and cool way of doing it," Brian Ritchie says. "The subconscious tension generated by the 7/4 feel is released dramatically when the band shifts into to the 4/4 section. Of course, the audience doesn't know what hit them because they're not sitting there counting beats."

"Rock Math Nerd Alert!" Danny Frankel declares.

"Money" is in 7/4 meter, which means there are seven beats to a bar, with each beat having the value of a quarter note. At the end of the verses, it begins to "walk" like it is in 4/4, and it is ... but there's fourteen quarter notes, which is two bars of seven, so it's still locked in to 7! During the "big jam" section, the song changes from 7/4 to 4/4. It's a nice relief. They didn't use a click track, which gives the arrangement a more organic, human feel. When the song returns to the 7/4 groove again, it's like the strobe light was suddenly flipped back on!

Fernando Perdomo points out:

"Money" is the most successful rock song in an odd time signature. It doesn't feel like seven—you can actually groove to it. On tour, the backup singers had no trouble doing their dance moves to it, because the song grooves so hard. Nick Mason always held down a great groove but was never a very technical player. I think he is very underrated compared to Bill Bruford, Neil Peart, or Phil Collins, but that's because he plays simple parts, especially in the world of prog. What makes prog different from all other styles is that it's always changing, not just in meter but in feel, constantly switching from half-time to double time. But Mason always played the perfect parts for the songs.

"'Money' is such a great earful," says Robert Musso.

It goes through so many musical, engineering, and production elements and changes. If you listen closely, when the song changes from 7/4 to 4/4, you'll notice Gilmour is actually playing two solos on the song. One guitar is panned left while the other is on the right. They are almost identical, note-for-note. He's playing the exact solo twice, with same guitar, amps, and effects, twice. It's actually two different takes. He nearly nailed it note-for-note for the whole solo, until the end, when he messed up a couple of notes, timing-wise, and that's when you can decipher there are actually two different solos. It shows how great Gilmour really is! He's used that technique repeatedly over the years.

There are lots of production tricks on that song worth noting. In the middle section, between the two guitar solos there is a breakdown where, producers and engineers would usually add lots of effects to make it special. But Floyd and Parsons took the opposite approach and removed all the delay and reverb to create the break. If you listen very closely to what Nick Mason played on the drums in that section, it sounds like he suddenly grew a second pair of arms. He not only played the hi-hat through the entire section: you also hear tom fills while he was doing all that. Mason was very subtle and conscious of what he played. Like Ringo Starr, he always played the right thing at the right moment. If he'd played like Neal Peart, he wouldn't have been in that band!

While the Abbey Road sound-effects library supplied the bright, ringing "cha-ching" of cash registers, Nick drilled "holes in old pennies" and strung them together like a necklace, using their clank and jangle, which he recorded for a homemade tape loop, to accent the song's odd-metered rhythm. Meanwhile, Roger recorded the sound of tearing paper and coins swirling centrifugally in a mixing bowl to add to the soundscape.

"The opening cash register loop sets up the song so well," says Michael Blair.

Nick marks the two-two-three phrasing of the 7/4 riff the song is built on, while Gilmour and Wright's accents stab the backbeat as Waters' bass plays continuously through it all, repeating the entire phrase and turnaround. They are all swinging, implying what could be described as a 21/8 beat! In the fill leading to the first guitar solo, Nick and Dave play all those triplets together, pulling the listener out of the previous trance-like riff [into the hard-driving solo section]. Later, Mason keeps to his toms for the second round of guitar solos, creating another sonic texture. Nick played to the song, up until his big fill into Gilmour's blues guitar solo blast-off. It's all very impressive.

"Rick Wright used a Fender Rhodes and a Wurly [Wurlitzer EP-200]," says Kenny Margolis, keyboardist with Mink Deville, Smithereens, and Cracker. "But on 'Money,' he comps the chords on his Wurly. From the sax solo on out to the end, he also employs the Mu-tron Wah pedal, which was new in 1972. That sound was popular in many Blaxploitation soundtracks at the time. Wright also turned on an Echoplex, that's reminiscent [of] albeit a simplified version of the dark funk played by Herbie Hancock a couple years before, on his *Mwandishi* album."

Years later, David Gilmour revealed the enormous impact Booker T. and the MG's' 1962 hit "Green Onions" had on *Dark Side of the Moon*, recalling how, in his early days with Joker's Wild, he'd "done a fair bit of that [Memphis soul] stuff. It was something I thought we could incorporate into our sound without anyone spotting where the influence had come from. And to me, it worked. Nice white English architecture students getting funky is a bit of an odd thought ... and isn't as funky as all that," he said, self-effacingly.

○

"Money" is so unlike Roger Waters' other songs that it might have been born out of a happy accident. He may have fumbled the bass riff, liked what he heard, and kept the results.

"Bass players come in two flavors for me," says Victor Krummenacher, bassist with Camper van Beethoven. "Lateral players and box players."

> Lateral players use scales and passing tones and bring great harmonic motion to their bass lines, which add harmonic complexity, such as Paul McCartney, John Paul Jones, and Brian Wilson. Box players lean on the use of the notes in the box: the fourth, fifth, flat seventh, and the octave. The groove is always the key. These are pattern players. John Entwistle [of the Who] is a box guy but a sophisticated box guy. He knows all the lateral moves, but he's also about leading tones, groove, fancy fills, and energy. Roger Waters is a rudimentary box player, thoroughly utilitarian. To some degree, he's like a classical musician, reading the chart, especially on the studio recording of *Dark Side of the Moon*, while Waters' playing on live versions of *Dark Side* was looser, funkier, and edgy. That great edgy tone, provided by his Hiwatt amps, was not at all the sound that Alan Parsons engineered in the studio.

The energy of the live performance and the edge of the tone are missing on the album. As a bass player, it doesn't thrill me, but it does serve the album well, which is the point.

It's a sticky issue that continues to fuel disagreement and ignite tempers among Pink Floyd fans to this day. In 1992, David Gilmour aired a bit of dirty laundry regarding his former bandmate's musical ability: Waters' bass playing, he groused, was both "limited" and "simple." Frustrated by Roger's lack of improvement on the instrument over the years, Gilmour took the matter into his own hands. "Half the time I would play bass on the records, because I would tend to do it quicker," he told the UK monthly magazine *RCD* (*Rock Compact Disc*). "At least half the bass on all recorded output is me," he claimed. "It's certainly not something we go around advertising," he added. According to Gilmour, Roger would acknowledge his musicianship and thank him whenever he was voted best rock bassist in the polls.

While Gilmour is credited with playing bass on "Narrow Way" from *Ummagumma*, followed by "Fat Old Sun" from *Atom Heart Mother*, as well as "Pigs (Three Different Ones)" and "Sheep" from *Animals* and 1979's "Hey You," if we are to judge by album cover notes (just ask Ron Geesin about *Atom Heart Mother* sometime), this is certainly not "half" of "all recorded output."

Having played bass with David Bowie and Robert Palmer, Guy Pratt was picked to handle the low-end chores for the post–Roger Waters era of Pink Floyd, beginning with 1987's *A Momentary Lapse of Reason*. "David played half the bass on those records," Pratt told *Rolling Stone*. "I never thought of Roger as a bass player. He was this sort of grand conceptualist."

There is more than a little truth in Brian Ritchie's dressing down of the Floyd's bassist:

> Roger Waters is an amazing musician. He was the best songwriter in Pink Floyd, except for Syd Barrett. The best singer, except for Barrett, David Gilmour, and Rick Wright. And he was the best bass player in Floyd, except for Gilmour. ... Waters took advantage of a lot of talent around him, especially Syd and Gilmour. When I saw Roger Waters' solo show, there was a second singer (I think

it was Andy Fairweather-Low) who was doubling *all of his parts*, and it was obvious the sound man mixed him in, especially for the high notes. Likewise, there was a second bassist who played the real parts. It was weird, as if Waters was a figurehead in his own band.

○

"None of the members of Pink Floyd gave many interviews," Thollem McDonnas points out. "I never really heard Rick Wright talk about his influences, other than Miles Davis and John Coltrane." Although Wright lauded Bill Evans' lyrical piano stylings on Davis' classic 1959 album *Kind of Blue*, he never publicly praised Miles' funk/fusion work of the late '60s and early '70s. And yet, McDonnas emphasizes, "It's the influence of Miles' electric band that really comes through in Wright's playing on 'Money,' whether he was inspired by Herbie Hancock, Joe Zawinul, or Chick Corea. *Dark Side of the Moon* was recorded following Miles' *In A Silent Way*, *Bitches Brew*, *Live-Evil*, and *A Tribute to Jack Johnson*."

While Wright was not a jazz musician, improvisation was integral to his approach and the band's live performances. To improvise well, one must maintain a clear mind and be fully present in the moment. "For me, playing music is like meditating," he once said. "I just play and don't really think about what I'm doing, I just let it happen."

"I love Rick's funky, rhythmic Wurlitzer played through the wah-wah pedal on 'Money,'" Greg Lisher enthuses. "Dick Parry's sax solo is also pretty bad-ass and bluesy, leading up to the rhythm section breaking into a double time groove for Gilmour's big guitar solo, which definitely swings. I love the breakdown where the rhythm section gets quiet, and the guitar is really dry and in-your-face."

Accented by Wright's swooshing Wurlitzer and Parry's scorching tenor sax, "Money" grooves down and dirty with a slur of blues, until Mason's fills pound upside your head and Gilmour's guitar rips the song open with a rapid burst of staccato, machine-gun notes. Once again, Pink Floyd's mastery of dynamics takes their music to another level.

Gary Lucas offers a somewhat more sobering view:

On "Money," Gilmour plays a decent albeit by-the-numbers blues guitar solo, which is more about the overall sound of his guitar than what he's actually playing, especially in the initial heavily echoplexed section. Beyond a smidgeon of exciting noise-guitar skronk on "Breathe," there's only a handful of moments where there's any breakout guitar playing on the album. There's nothing too adventurous or ballsy conceptually about his playing, beyond his "tasty fills." It's not like he couldn't go there if he wanted to. I'm sure Gilmour had the chops, if he chose, to stretch out. But that quotidian averageness of playing may have also been the key piece in the puzzle of Roger's grand design scheme that eventually put the group over to the masses with this album. It seems Gilmour's playing was meant to fit the grand architectural schema of *Dark Side of the Moon*. Maybe that's just the way Rog planned it.

O

Lyrically, Roger may have found inspiration in old blues and folk songs, drawing on Woody Guthrie, who once warned those migrating west during the Depression, seeking a brighter future, that they wouldn't find the promised land of California "so hot" if they lacked the necessary "Do Re Mi." Soon after, there's Hoyt Axton and Ken Ramsey's "Greenback Dollar," which became a standard in the folk world. Popularized by the Kingston Trio, the song portrays a hapless protagonist who foolishly spent all his money as quickly as he made it.

The Beatles' cover of Barrett Strong's "Money" (released on 1963's *With the Beatles*) revealed what a great rock 'n' roll singer John Lennon was, as he shreds his larynx, screaming, "Money don't get everything its true, what it can't get I can't use!" While never shy about the Beatles' career ambition to make it to "the Toppermost of the Poppermost," Lennon's contempt for the upper classes was barely concealed when he invited the queen and company to "just rattle your jewelry" before the Fabs performed "Twist and Shout" at the Royal Command Performance on November 4, 1963.

Upon the band's arrival in New York City on February 7, 1964, a throng of journalists besieged the Beatles at the newly renamed Kennedy Airport, firing off questions about the length of their hair, and what future plans lay in store after their popularity faded. Hoping to puncture the Beatles' jocularity, one reporter, skeptical of their talent, asked them to sing.

"No," Lennon shot back. "We need money first!"

The veneration of money, materialism, and "the people who gain the world and lose their soul," as George Harrison sings in "Within You Without You," became increasingly frowned upon as 1960s counterculture attitudes became mainstream. As the war in Vietnam escalated, and the assassinations of Martin Luther King, Jr. and Robert Kennedy robbed a generation of hope for a brighter future, an escapist, back-to-nature/off-the-grid trend was quickly adopted by thousands of disillusioned baby boomers who'd recently made the pilgrimage to Woodstock.

Nobody personified the hippie idealist philosophy more than Robin Williamson of the Incredible String Band. "I thought it was the beginning of a new era," he told me, "and I think that people at the time thought that everything would change at that point—that money would break down, that we'd go back to a barter economy, that the world was forever going to go back to a more idyllic state. Everyone was very optimistic about it, and it was very disheartening to find out that this did not occur. A lot of people got cynical. And then you had the cynical and self-seeking '70s."

There were plenty of signs along the way to indicate "the new boss" was "same as the old boss," as Pete Townshend sang in "Won't Get Fooled Again." Even the whimsical Donovan tried to warn everybody of the rapacious ambition of rock stars when he crowed "stoned beatniks are out to make it rich," in his song "Season of the Witch." While John Lennon's yellow Rolls-Royce, painted by artist Steve Weaver to resemble a Romany caravan, was a bold statement of hippie nouveau riche, Marc Bolan crowing "I got a Rolls-Royce, 'cause it's good for my voice" in T. Rex's "Children of the Revolution" caused some fans to wonder what kind of revolution he had in mind.

From the gatefold photograph that graced the interior of the May 1969 release of *Crosby, Stills, and Nash*, it was apparent this new breed of counterculture "superstars," swaddled in their fur coats, were hardly, as Pink Floyd sang "ordinary men."

Another revealing portrait appeared on the cover of *Stephen Stills 2* in 1971: Stills posing beside a jet window with a hefty bag of cocaine at his elbow (later edited out of the picture). "Detestable, the ultimate rich hippie—arrogant, self-pitying, sexist [and] shallow," Robert Christgau ranted in his *Village Voice* review of the album. The "Dean of American Rock Critics" lambasted Stills not only for his extravagant rock-star appetites but for a highly indulgent album of lackluster music as well.

While Syd Barrett sang whimsical ditties of gnomes and unicorns, the Roger Waters–led Pink Floyd never harbored such naïve beliefs. Whether the "Woodstock Nation" wanted to hear it or not, it was hard to argue with Joel Grey when he sang about "that clinking clanking sound" that "makes the world go 'round" in Bob Fosse's 1972 film *Cabaret*.

Waters, a great admirer of Bob Dylan's starkly honest lyrics, might have found inspiration in "It's Alright Ma, I'm Only Bleeding," when the bard from the North Country sings, "Money doesn't talk, it swears / Obscenity, who really cares?"

O

In 1931, Florence Reece, the wife of a Kentucky miner, boldly begged the age-old question, "Which Side Are You On?" Still sung to this day, her stark song was inspired by the time her husband and family were threatened in their home by mining company thugs. Whether based on a Baptist hymn named "Lay the Lily Low" or the traditional folk tune "Jack Munro," the song became the rallying cry of Harlan County miners to form a union or be controlled by the mine's owners.

Recorded in 1941 by the Almanac Singers (which included the "radical" banjo-picking folksinger Pete Seeger), "Which Side Are You On?" has served as a protest anthem for various causes over the years, prompting those within earshot of its powerful lyric to stand up for what they believe—whether braving McCarthyites during the dark days of the "Red Scare," or to bolster souls struggling for civil rights, or as a reveille for an entire generation unwilling to participate in the unjust Vietnam war.

While it was never the intention of its author, "Which Side Are You On?" perfectly addressed the disparity and dividing lines firmly drawn between the counterculture and the Establishment. In the mid-eighties, punk troubadour Billy Bragg's rendition of Reece's song helped spark disenfranchised workers in their battle against British prime minister Margaret Thatcher's union-busting policies. Hailing from Quincy, Massachusetts, Irish pub/punk rockers the

Dropkick Murphys played the song with grunge guitars and a thunderous rhythm, while Talib Kweli reworked it with a hip-hop beat to deliver his message on the National Day of Protest to Stop Police Brutality in October 2015.

In recent years, presidential candidate Bernie Sanders employed "Which Side Are You On?" on his campaign to emphasize the worldwide struggle for human rights over the prevailing policies of corporate greed. Most recently, disabled activists defending the Independent Living Fund, which had been snatched away from them, sang Reece's song in solidarity as they were physically removed during a protest at the British parliament.

○

"In order to understand life's mysteries, we must eliminate all unnecessary baggage," Robbi Robb theorizes.

> As we've been taught for centuries, the wealthy man cannot enter the temple, because he either carries too much baggage or too much intellect. Perhaps he relies on language too much, and can't reach a place of stillness, which is necessary to gaze into the darkness and intimately connect with the divine—the supreme erotic union known as the "alchemical wedding."
>
> It was falsely believed that alchemists tried to make gold from lead. But this is not true. Pink Floyd's "Money" points to materialism and the trap of materialist consciousness. The Tarot card of the sphere of Malkuth represents the tenth sphere of manifestation, called the Kingdom, also known as "the disks or the coins." The materialistic plane of wealth is measured by money, and herein lies the trap that leads to division. "Money" is then followed by "Us and Them." The light splinters as our psychological minds scatter and fragment into duality, which is a fractal of madness. Every day we are surrounded by the madness of duality—the bitter struggle between democrats and republicans, vaxxers and anti-vaxxers, et cetera, et cetera . . .
>
> We tried to build a tower to the heavens, but we cannot understand each other because our spiritualty has become "a battle

of words," as in "Us and Them"! The song is a beautiful mournful prayer, so sad yet so compassionate.

Pairing Rick Wright's ethereal melody with lyrics by Roger Waters, "Us and Them" was the first song Pink Floyd recorded, on June 1, 1972, for their new album. According to Waters, the opening verse represents "going to war" and the lack of communication between the soldiers risking their lives in battle. The second verse delves into "civil liberties, racism, and color prejudice," while the final couplet evokes the experience of "passing a tramp in the street (a homeless vet, perhaps one of the soldiers mentioned earlier in the song) and not helping [them out]."

Like the old joke about chop suey, Pink Floyd never threw anything away. They frequently concocted new recipes from whatever leftovers they had lying about. In need of inspiration, they regularly returned to their scrapheap of abandoned ideas and songs.

Rick originally wrote "Us and Them," then titled "The Violent Sequence," to accompany a scene of student riots in Antonioni's *Zabriskie Point*. Although they had been chosen to the create the film's soundtrack, in the end Pink Floyd contributed just three songs after the director repeatedly rejected their efforts.

While *Zabriskie Point* was panned by critics at the time of its release, in part due to its director's apparent lack of focus, now, with the passing of decades, it is hailed as a "cult classic." Not only did Antonioni repeatedly dismiss Pink Floyd's musical efforts, he also couldn't decide on a suitable screenplay: he employed four writers, including our old friend Sam Shepard.

◗

In October 1972, Dick Parry received a call from his old Cambridge mates, asking him to overdub sax solos on "Money" and "Us and Them." Later that month, a choir comprised of Doris Troy, Lesley Duncan, Liza Strike, and Barry St. John added their volcanic vocals to "Us and Them," "Brain Damage," and "Eclipse."

According to Duncan (previously heard on tracks by Donovan and Dave Clark Five), the atmosphere at Abbey Road ranged from tense to hostile. She found the group "cold" and "rather clinical . . . there were no smiles. They didn't

emanate any kind of warmth. They just said what they wanted, and we did it. ...
We were all quite relieved to get out [of the studio]."

The Floyd weren't known to be a very demonstrative bunch. They rarely,
if ever, complimented each other, let alone the sidemen and technicians who
quickly came to realize if they were looking for a slap on the back from the band,
they might have had better luck finding a bottle of milk in a hardware store.

They may have been a bunch of sulky British blokes, but "Us and Them," as
Carol Lipnik points out, is

> a grand testament to human emotion! It is an almost unbearably
> moody delight of a track. The delay echoes the last word of each
> line in a deep space that lacks gravity. Roger Waters has written a
> resoundingly resigned sermon on the futility of life, with human
> nature doomed to the boredom of repeating the same mistakes
> over and over and over ... of hatred and war, propelled by a wild
> pulsating gospel choir that blazes the darkness with glowing hot
> red embers of extreme dynamics. And then it just ends, like life,
> and melds into the next track.

For Michael Blair, "Us and Them" "emanates beauty on many levels":

> It's one of my favorite Floyd numbers. I fondly remember the
> beautiful, clear, floating eighth note movement in Nick Mason's
> cymbals. But when I listened back again, to my surprise and
> delight, they aren't there! There is no discernible eighth-note
> motion in the cymbal track! Mason is not playing a backbeat to
> drive the track. Nor is he using the cymbals to delineate time.
> Perhaps he did actually play clear cymbal beats on the original
> recording session. I've heard him often from afar and even quite
> up close, and he's not a particularly heavy hitter. The drum mix
> on this song is very much in the fog, as it should be. He's a very
> expressive player, indeed, a real song interpreter, like Ringo. The
> cymbals combine with the guitar shimmers, vocal delays, and the
> white noise from the organ, to create a floating feeling that is *so*

perfect for this track, that creates an emotional storytelling sum greater than the individual parts. At that point, Pink Floyd was very much a real band.

"The intro to 'Us and Them' is sublime," Kenny Margolis says. "Wright's slow-speed rotating Leslie speaker creates a glorious sound and was recorded to perfection by Alan Parsons."

"Rick's piano playing is beautiful," Greg Lisher concurs. "The band leaves so much space between the vocal lines. The B section of the song turns so dramatic and tragic with Gilmour's guitar part, the Hammond organ and the women's vocals boosting all of it. When they return again to the A section, there's a real sense of release."

"The album is so controlled, theatrical, and full of space," Victor Krummenacher muses.

> More than an album of individual songs, it's like a classical piece, a song cycle, or an opera. It still sounds astoundingly good to my ears. The arrangements, the mixes, the guitar tones, the electronic music, the keyboard playing ... Rick Wright is clearly the unsung hero here. Objectively, it's simply a great piece of work. But objectivity isn't easy for me, as I was psychologically pummeled by the ubiquity of this album for years. Though I have a love of Pink Floyd, this for me, is where things started to go badly. But it is where they made money, and good for them. Personal bias shouldn't get in the way of appreciating great work. I don't love *Dark Side of the Moon*, but I do think it's a great work.

"I think 'Us and Them' in particular illustrates Richard Wright's genius more than anything else Pink Floyd did," Durga McBroom emphasizes.

> His contribution to the band's sound remains so underrated! Among all the photos, rare stuff, and equipment at Their Mortal Remains [the traveling Pink Floyd exhibition], I remember seeing this film clip of Richard talking about the end of "Us and

Them," when it returns to the reprise of "Breathe." There's a really bizarre chord progression he plays that every tribute band pretty much gets wrong. He would deliberately make things a bit more dissident and unpredictable. That's the genius of Richard.

The dreamy quality he created in the verses captures everyman going through everyday life in a haze, a bit numb to what's going on around them, while the chorus is the desperation that lives underneath. The verses show how people present their mask to the world, but underneath there's this, "*Ahhh!*"

◑

The notes tumble from Rick's intergalactic cocktail-lounge piano, leading to the album's oddest segue as his ethereal keyboards combine with Gilmour phased, stinging guitar jabs over a two-chord vamp reminiscent of Neil Young's odyssey "Down by the River." Live, the song transformed into another beast altogether, with Wright's menacing synthesizer providing a dark, brooding foundation for David, who wrenched leads from his guitar with a fiery passion rarely captured on their records.

"Us and Them" is said to be Nick Mason's favorite tune on the record. "There's a nice lingering elasticity in the drum feel," Danny Frankel points out. "His lush ride cymbal has a slight shuffle, giving it the feeling of a gigantic Waterbed floating above the clouds."

A prime example of Pink Floyd's masterful use of dynamics, Nick Mason's drum fills throw open the door to a choir of gushing voices before the band returns once more to the song's gorgeous, gentle pulse. David Gilmour's very white, very British voice stands in contrast to Doris Troy's gospel soul soar.

The daughter of a Pentecostal preacher who sang in church choirs, Doris "Just One Look" Troy grew up loving R&B and rock 'n' roll, despite her parents' desperate attempts to save her from the Devil's music. Discovered by James Brown while working at the Apollo Theater in Harlem, Doris joined Cissy Houston and sisters Dionne and Dee-Dee Warwick in the Sweet Inspirations, whose vocals sweetened dozens of tracks for Atlantic Records. Her voice also appeared on Van Morrison's "Brown Eyed-Girl," Jimi Hendrix's "Burning of the Midnight Lamp," and the Rolling Stones' "You Can't Always Get What You

Want," to name a few. After she was signed by the Beatles in 1970, her self-titled debut album was co-produced by George Harrison. But like so many well-intentioned but bungled projects on Apple Records, it was poorly marketed and quickly fell through the cracks into obscurity.

Floating atop the cumulonimbus of Rick Wright's keyboards, Dick Parry's sax enters, smooth and breathy with smoky, soulful, Lester Young–like phrases, until a choir of soaring voices parts the sea. A fellow Cantabrigian, Parry originally played around Pink Floyd's former hometown in a group called Phuzz. His sax also brought a rough, brassy edge to songs by the Who and Irish blues guitarist and singer Rory Gallagher. Parry, along with backup vocals from a pair of Black soul sisters, "the Blackberries," Vanetta Fields and Carlena Williams, joined the newly expanded Pink Floyd on their 1973 North American tour, which began in Madison, Wisconsin.

A little over a decade later, Parry joined Wisconsin's Violent Femmes and led their revolving-door horn section, known as the Horns of Dilemma. "His tone was electrifying," bassist Brian Ritchie recalls. "It provoked a Pavlovian response in me, having been weaned on Pink Floyd from the moment I started listening to music. Several times we heard him warming up, quoting bits of 'Us and Them' and other Floyd classics. It was uncanny. Dick also had tragicomic reminiscences about Syd Barrett. Despite being in different Floyd lineups, they shared an apartment for some time. Mostly, I remember Dick as a self-effacing and humble English gentleman who blew the sax like a possessed madman. Those were some great times."

"He didn't care to be thought of as Pink Floyd's sax player," Violent Femmes auxiliary multi-instrumentalist and sometime producer Jeff Hamilton points out. "Dick's typical reply, whenever someone complimented him on his playing on *Dark Side of the Moon*, was, 'Piss off! I've done a lot more than that over the past forty years!'"

"Every night on the European tour, Brian would introduce Dick 'from Pink Floyd,'" Femmes road manager Darren Brown chuckles. "Dick hated that and tried to charge the band more pounds for each 'offense.'"

THE STRANGE SAGA OF
"LOUIE LOUIE" AND THE
MOTHERS OF PREVENTION

Profanity, whether real or imagined, has remained a sore spot with radio programmers since the Kingsmen's subversive cover of Richard Berry's "Louie Louie" in 1963. Not so much sung as sprayed by a braces-wearing lad named Jack Ely, the song's indecipherable lyrics tantalized adolescents from coast to coast, while rocketing an obscure Seattle garage band up the *Billboard* singles chart to No. 2 for six weeks.

"Louie Louie" had been part of Pink Floyd's early repertoire, and they were known to sometimes stretch it out for ten to fifteen minutes. Roger Waters confessed that the band's inability "to play covers forced us to come up with our own direction." In this way they were not unique.

As performed and recorded by over two thousand bands, including the Kinks, the Mothers of Invention, and Iggy Pop, the vulgarity of this jubilant three-chord anthem of teen bravado was first brought to the attention of then attorney general Robert Kennedy. Bobby then handed the matter to the FBI, prompting a two-year investigation, whose repeated listening (at various speeds) ultimately concluded . . . nothing. Ask any red-blooded American boy of the day to decode the slurred verse, chances are they'd tell you, "Tonight at ten, I lay her again."

But, as is often the case, those in charge of the problem were looking for answers in all the wrong places. Upon closer scrutiny, one hears the alleged offense fifty-six seconds into the song—not in the subversive lyrics, but when the drummer Lynn Easton shouts "Fuck!" after dropping his stick.

Although the Federal Communications Commission found neither Wand Records nor the Kingsmen guilty of any crime, they were nonetheless accused of "improper motivation" for deliberately recording "lyrics so unintelligible as to give rise to rumors that they were obscene." Wand Records laughed all the way to the bank; Ely quit the Kingsmen in the thick of controversy and sought redemption as a Christian rocker, taking the mystery of the lascivious lyrics to his grave in April 2015.

Following the absurd "Louie Louie" controversy, the Beatles topped the *Billboard* charts with "I Want to Hold Your Hand." FCC watchdogs, now on the prowl for any possible drug reference, imagined they heard the Fabs repeatedly cheering "I get high," rather than the more innocuous "I can't hide."

In 1973, most radio stations remedied Roger Waters' "offensive" lyric in "Money," "goody, goody bullshit," by masking the dirty word with a momentary audio dropout. Over the years, rock 'n' roll (itself a euphemism for copulation) has faced more than its fair share zealous censors, with radio stations bleeping Warren Zevon's "Lawyers, Guns, and Money," Steve Miller's "Jet Liner," "Life in the Fast Lane" by the Eagles, the Who's "Who Are You," and even "The Devil Went Down to Georgia" by Charlie Daniels, who was pressured by his record company into replacing the offensive "son of a bitch" with the less offensive "son of a gun."

In September 1985, Frank Zappa cut his long scraggly hair, donned a suit, and flew to Washington, D.C., to confront the "Washington Wives," led by Tipper Gore, the wife of then-senator and soon-to-be vice president Al Gore. This crew of prim and proper culture cops was known as the Parents Music Resource Center (or PMRC) and funded by Mike Love of the Beach Boys and beer magnate Joseph Coors, who seemed determined to instate Pat Boone as the "King of Rock 'n' Roll." Zappa was not alone in standing up to these vigilantes of vulgarism. He was joined by Twisted Sister's Dee Snider and wholesome singer/songwriter John Denver, who were also appalled by the PMRC and its "goody, goody bullshit." Its mission was to clean up rock 'n' roll by slapping warning stickers on any recording alluding to sex, violence, drugs, alcohol, and the occult. Tipper's committee singled out songs by Prince, Cyndi Lauper, Black Sabbath, and a dozen more, branding them "The Filthy Fifteen." A total of nineteen record companies immediately folded under the pressure and invited the committee to judge their music according to its moral standards.

Zappa pointed out that the PMRC's desperate attempt at control was "an ill-conceived piece of nonsense which fail[ed] to deliver any real benefits to children, infringes on the civil liberties of people," both in and out of the music industry, and was bound to tie up the courts indefinitely.

Fierce and adroit as Zappa was, John Denver's testimony packed a wallop when he equated the PMRC's censorship agenda to Nazi book burnings. Denver had previously faced censorship charges after his joyful anthem "Rocky Mountain High" was absurdly accused of containing drug references.

Released in November 1985, *Frank Zappa Meets the Mothers of Prevention* featured the powerful track "Porn Wars," a collage of tape recordings of the hearings (played at various speeds) over an ominous composition, punctuated by a variety of snorts, sound effects, and idiotic comments made by members of congress, repeated to create a nightmarish soundtrack of the times. Zappa also included a warning sticker of his own, stating, "WARNING/GUARANTEE: This album contains material which a truly free society would neither fear nor suppress. In some socially retarded areas, religious fanatics and ultra-conservative political organizations violate your First Amendment Rights by attempting to censor rock & roll albums. We feel that this is un-Constitutional and un-American."

Following Janet Jackson's Super Bowl "wardrobe malfunction" in 2004, Clear Channel, in its crusade to whitewash American popular culture, bought up every possible radio station on the dial. In the end, hip-hop would triumph in the war over obscenity, along with the internet, which opened the door to whole new assortment of previously unimagined issues.

The first and only Frank/Floyd fusion took place at the Actuel Festival, on October 25, 1969, in Amougies, Belgium, when Zappa sat in on a lumbering fifteen-minute version of "Interstellar Overdrive." Comprised of between fifteen and twenty thousand "European hippies," the audience, as Frank recalled, "brought their sleeping bags" and camped out in freezing temperatures "in the middle of a turnip field."

"Our music, and the way we behave onstage, makes it very hard to improvise with us," Nick Mason pointed out. But the Floyd's mustachioed drummer considered Frank Zappa, "the exception ... one of those rare musicians that can play with us. The little he did in Amougies was terribly correct."

Pink Floyd appeared sweat-soaked and wide-eyed (many claim they were high on LSD at the time), while Zappa, who shunned all intoxicants (except cigarettes and coffee), ironically claimed to have no memory of the occasion. This brand of free-form sonic marmalade was closer to the organic San Francisco school of acid-fueled jamming than Frank's approach to improvisation, which drew its inspiration from jazz, blues, and the sudden outrageous outbursts of experimental theater. The Floyd's slow rowing toward nirvana was clearly not Zappa's cup of tea.

While Frank appeared frustrated, jabbing at the neck of his Telecaster, trying to cut through the sonic morass, the reporter from *Melody Maker* took a more positive view of this strange meeting, exclaiming, "a few new galaxies were discovered."

"They don't look too happy being up there together, do they?" Gary Lucas observes, offering a blunt assessment of the scenario after reviewing the videotape, fifty-three years later.

Maybe it was the literally frosty atmosphere on the ground in Amougies . . . or maybe not. . . . After launching into the shuffling cosmic space-jam section from their Gilmour-inflected version of "Interstellar Overdrive," Nick Mason finally cues Frank at 4:39. They both seem to have hateful looks on their faces, like, *I really don't want to be up here with this guy/these guys.* Frank launched into his typical modal guitar-solo improv style, as perhaps best exemplified on *Uncle Meat's* "Nine Types of Industrial Pollution" (although his improv on that tune was sped up on the final mix). Essentially, he played a series of short triplets and extended curlicues—basic modal jazz noodling, phrases that circle back on themselves while staying safely "in the mode." A couple of minutes into this clip, Frank is suddenly *taken out of the mix* and supplanted mainly by Gilmour's slide/Echoplex noodling, which doesn't really make it when compared to Syd's playing.

Frank got paid $10,000 to emcee the festival, and, to his credit, he brought Captain Beefheart and his current lineup with him. There's no doubt he would he rather have jammed with Beefheart than this sorry tepid bowl o' noodles. No wonder Frank later claimed to have no memory of this experience! Some things are best left forgotten.

7

ANY COLOUR
YOU LIKE

Like their West Coast counterparts the Grateful Dead, the early Pink Floyd jammed relentlessly, seeking new sonic horizons known to few, beyond John Coltrane and Karlheinz Stockhausen. But by the early '70s, both bands began taking a more formal approach to the recording studio, the Dead with *American Beauty* and Pink Floyd with *Dark Side*.

While the Dead's albums eventually replaced their electric extrapolations with buttery acoustic guitars, warm-heart harmony vocals, and polished production values, they still continued to improvise at live shows, while the Floyd, under Roger Waters' dominance, eventually lost their desire to conjure fresh soundscapes from the unknown.

By the mid-'60s, rock musicians had begun to embrace a new level of discipline (some even learned to read and write music) in order to create large scale, "serious" works, beyond churning out three-minute singles for the hit-parade conveyor belt. Concept albums and themed song cycles seemed like a more legitimate, "respectable" form of expression. But all too often, the outcome led to paramount conceptual buffoonery of the like perfectly lampooned by director Rob Reiner and the members of Spinal Tap.

In November 1972, Pink Floyd took a hiatus from their relentless recording schedule at Abbey Road to collaborate with the Ballet of Marseille's choreographer Roland Petit and featured dancers Danielle Jossi and Rudy Bryans. The project's outcome lay awkwardly somewhere between "art" and *Spinal Tap*'s "Creation" scene, in which bassist Derek Smalls finds himself trapped inside an oversized malfunctioning plastic pod.

Divided into three sections, the ballet opened with "Allume les etoiles" ("Light the Stars"), inspired by events of the Russian revolution with music by Mussorgsky and Prokofiev, followed by an interpretation of William Blake's symbolic poem "The Sick Rose." Part three featured "The Pink Floyd Ballet," comprised of a playlist of the band's songs: "One of These Days," "Careful with That Axe, Eugene," "Obscured by Clouds," the hard-rocking "When You're In," and a somewhat menacing finale of "Echoes," as the blueprint for the dancer's movement.

The majority of Floyd fans found the ballet's opening segments boring and became increasingly restless and agitated. At one point, Roland Petit confronted the crowd and implored them to go to the lobby and get a drink until their heroes took the stage, rather than remain in their seats, grumbling through the performance. More problems arose when Pink Floyd's jams extended beyond the choreographer's original plans, creating a few awkward unscripted moments for the dancers. The collaboration was not an easy fit for anyone, whether they came to see Pink Floyd or the ballet. And then there was the rest of the crowd, who seemed to have little idea what was happening or why they were there in the first place.

"All these people prancing around in tights didn't mesh" with Pink Floyd and their audience, David Gilmour confessed. Luckily, they were spared any further embarrassment after plans to perform the ballet in Canada fell through when the Commonwealth refused to allow the company to fly the dreaded red Communist flag in the opening scene, thus canceling the second half of the tour.

The final recording sessions for *Dark Side of the Moon* took place in late January 1973, when Pink Floyd gathered once more at Abbey Road Studio 2 to finish "Brain Damage," "Eclipse," and "Any Colour You Like."

"We used to do very long extended jamming onstage—indeterminable, many people would say, and probably rightly," David Gilmour mused. "And that's what ['Any Colour You Like'] came out of."

A quick listen back to the slow (and not so funky) groove of "Funky Dung" from *Atom Heart Mother* reveals the two-chord motif that Pink Floyd used repeatedly, whether in "Echoes" (coming in at approximately the seven-minute mark) or to propel "Any Colour You Like." A brilliant waterfall of color spills from Rick Wright's keyboards, evoking the rainbow that streaks across the album's cover, until Gilmour's "extraordinary" (as described by Nick Mason) guitar enters, slicing through the buoyant mood like a hot jagged blade.

"'Any Colour You Like' begins like a funky, Black soul tune," Greg Lisher points out. "It's kind of refreshing, like Pink Floyd are driving down a different musical street. It sounds like Gilmour was experimenting with the notes he's choosing. The guitar seems to be going through a Leslie simulator. In one section it sounds like the guitar was having a conversation with itself, talking back and forth, from the left channel to the right."

"'Any Colour You Like' is probably the least-popular piece on *Dark Side*," Brian Kehew opines. "Though it avoids the gimmicky synthesizer tricks of other groups, the material itself is the issue, rather than the instruments. It's barely a jam, even by Floyd's looser standards, but the synthesizer work does lend an air of the spacey and progressive to what would otherwise be a standard bar-band jam moment."

Meanwhile, Waters' determined and dependable bass stays the course, pushing the jam forward toward the album's final chapter.

MEDITATIONS ON A PRISM, OR FOUR SIDES OF THE ETERNAL TRIANGLE

Following the release of the Beatles' *Sgt. Pepper's Lonely Hearts Club Band* in June 1967, the album was no longer perceived as a mere collection of songs but was suddenly considered "a work of art." Sculpture and paintings adorning gallery and museum walls had already begun to lose their preciousness by the 1950s with the emergence of abstract expressionist painters like Jackson Pollock (a.k.a. "Jack the Dripper") and John Chamberlain, who made modern sculpture from crushed cars. But this trend (which empowered viewers to believe that they or their children could make art, whether by sloshing paint around on a canvas, or imaginatively welding scraps of steel together) can be traced all the way back to the late nineteenth century, when photography first made portraiture accessible to the masses, who no longer had to sit still for long hours and pay an artist's exorbitant fee to fashion a reasonable likeness.

In 1914, Dadaist Marcel Duchamp challenged the public's understanding of art with a series of tongue-in-cheek pieces he dubbed "Readymades"—manufactured objects like bottle racks and snow shovels, on which he bestowed names with intriguing titles. This puzzling, poetic portfolio included *Fountain*, a porcelain urinal signed by one "R. Mutt" and positioned to leak back on the user; as well as a bicycle wheel turned upside-down and built into a stool, rendering it useless while creating a visually compelling sculpture.

While his concepts appeared highly intellectualized, Duchamp was, at heart, a provocateur and a prankster who killed all vestiges of elitism associated with art. The basic materials with which fine art was made for centuries—like marble and oil paint—no longer had to be precious or costly and were replaced with everyday objects found in junk shops.

Duchamp's ideas were soon adopted by Joseph Cornell, who fashioned his series of "Dream Boxes," while Robert Rauschenberg painted his bed in lieu of a canvas and hung it on a wall. Rauschenberg's *Monogram*, which combined a painted canvas with a three-dimensional taxidermized Angora goat with a tire around its waist, remains one of modern art's most radical and compelling works.

By the early '60s, Andy Warhol delivered the knock-out punch with his series of Brillo boxes and Campbell's Soup cans, making icons out of everyday objects while raising the mundane to the status of art.*

Until Warhol's enormous popularity, silk-screen printing had been primarily employed for low-end commercial work, like printing signs for grocery stores advertising sales on tomatoes and hamburgers, not as a medium for portraits of the rich and famous. Art was no longer defined by curators' tastes, collectors' purse strings, or critics' opinions, but by whatever the artist proclaimed it was. As Warhol boldly declared, "Art is what you can get away with."

These ideas eventually spilled over into the realm of pop music. Readymade sounds from "store-bought" synthesizers, drum machines, and the multitude of effect pedals (a.k.a. stomp-boxes) became the norm, regularly employed by guitarists and keyboardists around the globe. Unlike Duchamp's inventiveness, this palette of readymade sounds ultimately led to a dull homogeneity and conformity among musicians rather than facilitating their individuality.

For a brief time in the mid-sixties, rock 'n' roll musicians were no longer just the flavor of the moment for the teen market but were elevated to the status of "recording artists." Their albums, which once contained maybe one or two hits and a couple of B-sides at best, became vehicles for a variety of complex and intriguing concepts, while record jackets, once no more esthetically pleasing than cereal boxes, were suddenly the new canvas for a generation of innovative artists and designers.

Integral to Pink Floyd's sonic explorations were Hipgnosis' striking, surrealistic album covers, which never failed to ignite the imagination of their fans, from the

---

* This concept was later employed by television host David Letterman, whose "Stupid Pet Tricks" elevated mundane aspects of everyday life to that of entertainment on his network TV show *Late Night with David Letterman*. Letterman would also redefine acts of destruction as entertainment by crushing objects in a hydraulic press and throwing objects off office building rooftops to the delight of his viewers.

hall of mirrors on *Ummagumma*, to the majestic Holstein grazing on the jacket of *Atom Heart Mother*, to the pair of businessmen engulfed in flames while shaking hands (which perfectly illustrated the sort of record-company hustlers Roger Waters skewered with "Have a Cigar") on *Wish You Were Here*.

"Roger Waters particularly had quite a cynical view about life and about the business and about how things should be," Aubrey Powell told journalist Craig Bailey of *Floydian Slip*. "He wasn't about to kowtow to the feelings of a record company or what they wanted."

According to Powell, all the members of Pink Floyd were in agreement. "They would never want something that was obvious," he stressed. "Actually, it worked phenomenally well," he said, recalling the cover to *Atom Heart Mother*. "It was the first Pink Floyd No. 1 record [in the UK]. When people saw this image of a cow in *Billboard* or *Rolling Stone*, or saw it in a record shop, or saw it on a billboard on Sunset Strip, they immediately said, 'Who's that? What's happening?' It had the reverse psychology ... the reverse effect. It wasn't a lack of interest; it was all interest, and this album helped tremendously to sell Pink Floyd."

Hipgnosis' unique brand of surrealism revealed the influence of European surrealists like René Magritte, Salvador Dalí, and Max Ernst, rather than their San Francisco counterparts, Rick Griffin, Alton Kelly, and Stanley Mouse, who were known for their flowing designs on Grateful Dead album covers and posters advertising concerts at the Family Dog, Avalon Ballroom, and Fillmore West.

Graphic designer and author Norman Hathaway, known for his captivating album covers for Paul McCartney, Peter Gabriel, and Brian Eno (as well as his tome to psychedelic art, *Electrical Banana*), provides some insight on the prevailing style of the day:

> The appeal of the San Francisco style is that it's a hand done home-brew art. It's a little bit Victorian but wasn't all the same. There is a huge difference between Rick Griffin and Victor Moscoso's posters. Victor rarely used line.* He put pure colors next to each other in a more successful way. His posters have a less designed quality.
>
> There was nothing special about the print quality of the

---

* His bold sense of esthetics was passed on to him by his father, a Spanish painter.

Fillmore posters. They were produced by quick commercial printers. That wasn't so much the case in England . . . everybody had been hugely influenced by a recent rediscovery exhibition of Aubrey Beardsley [which ran from May through September 1966]. All the stuff by the Fool was based on Beardsley!

Beardsley's burgeoning Art Nouveau style also influenced Klaus Voormann, whose pen-and-ink line drawings adorned the Beatles' August '66 release, *Revolver*. But while the young, doomed artist (Beardsley died at age twenty-five of tuberculosis) resonated with a new generation of artists and musicians, not "everybody" was so taken by the collection of his fine-line decadent prints. That July, the Beardsley retrospective at the Victoria and Albert Museum became a hotbed of scandal, facing prosecution for what Oscar Wilde once described as "the naughty scribbles of a precocious boy."

Hathaway continues:

Hipgnosis was hugely influential on all the designers of the seventies. Aubrey and Storm were very bright people. They were unusual as their work was not decorative. They made great conceptual work, which no one had really done. Plus, coming from Cambridge, they had long-time relationships with Pink Floyd, which was really unusual because, in the music industry, most designers work for the record label and not the band, which makes a huge difference. When you have the band on board with you, you have a lot more power, as the label generally wants to make the band happy. So, when you're hanging out together, listening to the record, talking esthetics, you're gonna do a better job. And in England they tend to be more respectful of the designer's ideas and what they bring to the project.

Hipgnosis were definitely influenced by what was going on in the fine art world. They were very conceptual but did a lot of understated things. We were just coming out of the psychedelic era. Everything was in your face, like Martin Sharp's album covers for Cream [*Disraeli Gears* and *Wheels of Fire*]. People were taking LSD, going to India, but eventually the trend changed. Hipgnosis wasn't flashy in that way. They were a bit more quiet. They didn't always have type on their covers. They were mysterious and usually beautiful. They would make you look and wonder, *What is this?* Back then, a lot of designers would look at their work and have no idea how they achieved their results. Their standards of craftsmanship were about as high as it got. Exquisite. No one was doing that sort of high-quality retouching, airbrushing, or dye transfers. I have to point out that it was George Hardie, with his tremendous airbrush technique, who was really responsible for manifesting Thor and Po's concepts.

Minimalism was very big at the time, and Richard Hamilton's *White Album* (a.k.a. *The Beatles*) reflected that. I was stunned by the cover to *Dark Side of the Moon*. It was beautiful! When I first saw it in the record store it was like there was a spotlight on it compared to everything else. It wasn't glamorous or fashionable or trying to be hip. It was closer, in some ways, to something you might have seen in a school textbook. It made you curious and wonder, *What is this?* It was dark and different from anything Hipgnosis had done in the past. The cover was smooth and perfect in every way. It was sleek, closer to automotive design than most graphic work of the time. The black was *really* black. And remember, British printing was also better at that time than in America. And when you opened the gatefold . . . it was like, *Wow!* It was beautiful. The cover matched the recording perfectly. In some ways it was like they'd designed a monument to the record, even before they knew how huge the album would be! Usually record album covers are unique to the time when they're released and then they fade a bit. When *Sgt. Pepper's* came out, it had such depth to it, but even that cover has become dated over the years.

Originally, Storm Thorgerson wanted to use Marvel Comics' popular character the Silver Surfer on the cover of *Dark Side of the Moon*. Bold and shiny as a hood ornament on black limousine, Jack Kirby's superhero cuts a striking image as he flies through space on his cosmic surfboard. But getting a consensus from the members of Pink Floyd was no easy task.

While Waters and Gilmour squabbled over the album's final mixes, the band could unanimously agree on the bold, simple image of the prism on the record jacket. Rick Wright felt the album cover should be "clean and elegant" and not "photographic" in any way. Waters suggested the rainbow should continue inside the gatefold and morph into a cardiograph image of a heartbeat (the sound that bookends the album). But the idea of adding additional stickers and posters was immediately (and predictably) shot down by EMI as too costly and extravagant.

●

Speaking of artistic rejection, the Beatles' *Revolver* originally had a number of working titles, including *Abracadabra, Magical Circles, After Geography* (Ringo's spoof on the Rolling Stones' recently released *Aftermath*), and, worst of all, *Beatles on Safari*. One of Lennon's ideas, rejected by the band, was *Four Sides of the Eternal Triangle*.

When holding the album or CD cover of *Dark Side of the Moon*, we see "the eternal triangle" positioned in the center of the four sides that John, the self-proclaimed "dreamweaver," had once imagined. Lennon, whose earthly mission was to ultimately help unite mankind through peace and music, might have appreciated the power of this simple symbol.

As Westerners, we read from left to right. So, we see the beam of white light on the album cover entering the prism from the left side; and, as it exits, the ray of white light splinters into a rainbow. But if you read from right to left, as in Hebrew, Arabic, or Japanese, then all the colors of the rainbow, after striking the prism, become one—a shaft of white light—symbolizing diversity and multiplicity becoming all one.

"There are plenty of incorrect prism illustrations out there," Dr. Matthew Bobrowsky reminds us.

> But the one gracing the album cover to *Dark Side of the Moon* accurately depicts a side view of a three-dimensional prism. White light is actually composed of numerous colors. The angles are correct, refracting the different colors, as well as the order of the colors. There is a lot of speculation regarding the symbolism.

One interpretation might be that if you examine any person, their personality will resolve into the different emotions addressed in the songs, much in the same way that white light is revealed to be composed of numerous colors. Although I doubt this is what the album cover designer or Pink Floyd were thinking when they agreed on the image.

Also, the cover image shows distinct colors with sudden transitions from one color to the next. A real visible light spectrum, to use the correct scientific terminology, would show the smooth transition of color, going from red to violet. The red then gradually becomes more orange, as the orange turns to yellow, and the yellow blends into green, et cetera. It's a smooth continuum of millions of colors, and the human eye is capable of perceiving millions of colors.

There's a popular misconception that a light spectrum or rainbow consists of seven colors. People ask why the cover image used six colors instead of seven. It's not the case that there are only seven colors, as you can plainly see by observing a color wheel.

Dr. Matt now explains why colors separate in a prism:

Light bends, or "refracts," when it travels from one medium to another as a result of its speed changing. The area on the left shows light moving through air, then entering the prism, where the colors first separate (not shown in the illustration), and then exiting the prism and separating more. This second color separation is what's depicted on the album cover. If the cover illustration were scientifically accurate, you'd see colors within the prism, as well as coming out of it.

More about the color separation . . . shorter wavelength light (e.g., blue, violet) travels slower in the glass than the longer wavelength light (e.g., red, orange). Therefore, the shorter wavelengths bend more than the longer wavelengths. That's why the colors separate, or, as physicists say, disperse.

"It's the mystery of the rainbow in the darkness, because the dark absorbs all!" guitarist and shaman of the high desert Robbi Robb emphasizes, in contrast to Dr. Bobrowsky's scientific explanation.

The cover image of the prism would morph into images of pyramids, which appear on the album's insert (as well as on various posters and stickers), based on a glowing, greenish infrared photo of the Giza pyramids shot by Storm Thorgerson.

"The refracting glass prism referred to Floyd light shows [and their] consummate use of light in the concert setting," Thorgerson once said, shedding light on the iconic image. "Its outline is triangular, and triangles are symbols of ambition, and are redolent of pyramids, both cosmic and mad in equal measure, all these ideas touching on themes in the lyrics."

The power of the pyramid is credited with everything from improving health to preserving food, sharpening razor blades, and triggering sexual desire. In 1978, the Alan Parsons Project recorded a concept album titled *Pyramid*, which features the song "Pyramania." Sung by Jack Harris, the song's lyrics take the piss out of New Age devotees, reducing their belief in the mystical symbols of ancient Egypt to nothing but "yap, yap, yap."

Two years later, Tom Robbins' 1980 novel *Still Life with Woodpecker*—subtitled "Mediations on a pack of Camel Cigarettes"—fixated not only on redheads but on pyramids (as depicted on the Camel pack) and the moon as well. And then there's the pyramid on the flipside of the almighty Yankee dollar bill. The stalwart purveyor of American normalcy, *Reader's Digest*, claims that when forefathers Ben Franklin, Thomas Jefferson, and John Adams first powwowed over what the new nation's currency should look like, pyramids were not in the running. But that eerie, all-seeing eye (said to be a Masonic ... symbol), floating above the unfinished Egyptian tomb that many have speculated belonged to King Tut, was said to be "an ancient symbol of divinity."

"The pyramid in the mystical arts represents the highest point, or infinity, dividing into male and female, from nothingness to infinite luminous light," Robbi Robb points out. "The prism on the *Dark Side* cover represents nothingness, which contains all within it. The rainbow comes into the prism, from the right side, and becomes a single point of light—which is what each of us is!"

8

BRAIN DAMAGE / ECLIPSE

A woman I interviewed who prefers to go by the alias of "Trixie Dane" in these pages has been a top surgery nurse at a New York City hospital over the last couple of decades, assisting a leading brain surgeon who must also go unnamed here. The good doctor is fond of blasting loud music while slicing open craniums and removing tumors. Ludwig van Beethoven, Led Zeppelin, Richard Wagner, and *Dark Side of the Moon* are among his favorite soundtracks.

Beyond helping him to put aside his terror to focus at the job at hand, this surgeon finds a strange thrill in listening to "Brain Damage" while he works, giving the lyrics, "You raise the blade, you make the change," a somewhat different, unexpected meaning. Trixie claims the surgeon's movements seem, at times, to be synchronized to the music, transforming the operating theater into a strange ballet as she hands him the scalpel, the drill, the suction, the irrigating bipolar forceps.

Patients must be kept awake during a craniometry, to make sure their cognitive abilities remain intact. "The drugs they're given break down all inhibitions, making them relax and sometimes they say some pretty weird things," Trixie says. "One patient began speaking what sounded like gibberish. We realized it was Russian once we got a translator in the operating room. He had been describing his childhood years ago in the USSR. Another guy was really poetic, claiming he felt 'mental tentacles' and a 'crater' in his brain."

Originally known as "The Lunatic Song" at early live performances and in the first phases of recording, "Brain Damage" was written in entirety by Roger Waters at his Cambridge home, during the *Meddle* sessions, but for whatever reason was left off that album.

Explaining his intent behind the song and its enduring lyric, which contains the famous album's title, Waters clarified, "The line, 'See you on the dark side of the moon,' is me speaking to the listener, saying, 'I know you have these feelings and impulses, because I do too, and one of the ways I can make direct contact with you, is to share the fact that I feel bad sometimes.'"

As the Czech author Franz Kafka once wrote, "Everyone carries a room inside them." *Dark Side*, despite all its sonic accoutrements, offers a stark view of Roger Waters' interior life at the time, aloof as he and his bandmates often appeared.

In 2003, Waters told *Uncut* magazine that the album characterized "a general catch-all of the downside of the human condition" (a theme he continued to explore and expand on for the duration of his time with Pink Floyd and into his solo career). Yet, as Waters pointed out, "There's a camaraderie involved in the idea of people who are prepared to walk the dark places alone."

"We were all committed to the mood," David Gilmour told Sue Lawley of BBC Radio 4's *Desert Island Discs*. "We all found that melancholy or the very down words about madness and alienation coupled with uplifting music made a very interesting mix."

"Not a barrel of laughs, being in Pink Floyd, then?" Lawley prodded.

"No, being in Pink Floyd there were lots of laughs," Gilmour gently explained. "But they're not overly evident on the records. We had many, many years of artistic satisfaction, great joy and a lot of pleasure in each other's company. But, you know, there comes a time when things get a little sticky, differences of opinion become insurmountable . . . and things change, but that's pretty common in all walks of life."

Waters, like Kafka, also believed, "We need books [or in this case, records] that affect us as a disaster, that grieve us deeply, like the death of someone we loved more than ourselves, like being banished into forests far from everyone. . . . A book," Kafka declared, "must be the axe for the frozen sea inside us." Or, as the Scottish bard Robin Williamson once said, "There is a music that will melt blood and bone, that will wash away the rock of the mind."

A flash of inspiration can happen anywhere at any time, springing from anything—from the most mundane aspects of day-to-day life to a wistful memory. Beyond the prevailing sense of alienation that runs through this *Dark Side*, there is a deep feeling of nostalgia and yearning, despite whatever remaining pain and disappointment still lingers. "The grass" on which the madcap sat, laughing, raging out of his head, Waters told *Louder Sound*, "was the square in between the River Cam and King's College chapel, [while] the lunatic was Syd... he was obviously in my mind."

"'Brain Damage' is built on a simple, arpeggiated guitar riff that signifies the mind-numbing churning of conformity disguised as sanity," Carol Lipnik points out. "The song's narrator, Roger Waters, is another weary inmate, trying to survive in a reverse insane asylum where carefree child-souls are groomed by the society's establishment to walk down a mind-numbing path.

"As in 'Us and Them,' the dark chorus lights the song ablaze with a tremulous gospel 'choir in a tremendous sudden shift of dynamics, while the message 'I'll see you on the dark side of the moon' remains as prescient as ever."

●

The sonic dynamics of "Brain Damage" are key to the song's emotional impact. The melancholy lullaby gently begins with just voice and acoustic guitar until it is suddenly whisked away by Rick Wright's sweeping organ, sparking the gospel choir to sing, "I'll see you on the dark side of the moon."

Despite the innovations of jazz, rock, and funk musicians, the organ will forever remain linked to Christianity in people's minds, whether reverberating the walls of majestic cathedrals or driving the rhythm to a holy rolling gospel rave at a neighborhood church.

"The organ horrifies me," Miles Davis once said. "[It] reminds me of religion. It's fear that makes people religious, and the sound of the organ reminds them of that fear." Davis recalled his mother taking him to church as a child, where he wondered why he "was treated as a sinner" despite having done nothing wrong. After his mother failed to provide "a satisfying response," Davis "stopped going to church. Today I believe in nothing but myself."

Weighing in again on Nick Mason's majestic drum fills on the song, fellow drummer Danny Frankel remarks, "'Brain Damage' is a good example of Mason's very patient, minimalist playing, with just the pedals on the verses and until crashing into these big ass fills. His half-time playing is bliss during the choruses. The song then morphs into 'Eclipse,' which is a world of waltz time, with stately fills."

Having found himself exiled from Pink Floyd, Syd Barrett experienced a crushing sense of alienation, which Water's lyric addresses as he knowingly sings, "If the band you're in starts playing different tunes." The discordant sentiment evokes George Harrison's "Only a Northern Song." "You may think the chords are going wrong," George mocked, suggesting Syd's "Have You Got It Yet?"—the mutating riddle that befuddled his bandmates. Dropped from *Sgt. Pepper* only to later wind up as filler on their soundtrack to *Yellow Submarine*, "Northern Song" sadly illustrates Harrison's second-class stature in the Beatles.

"At the song's end comes an invitation to the greater conversation," Robbi Robb exclaims.

> When Roger Waters sings, "I'll meet you on the dark side of the moon," he is speaking to the very root of who we are, the ground of our collective subconscious mind, which drives our every cell and all the autonomous aspects of our bodies. All of our dreams and emotions arise from these mystical dark waters. The dark side of the moon is where all the mystery happens. When we sit on the dark side of the moon, we can gaze into the universe without distraction, without the phantom of light in our eyes. And so, the whole album invites us to enter the unknown, to dig into the dark side of our minds, and lives.

●

Beyond Pink Floyd's earlier fascination with space, as depicted in song titles like "Interstellar Overdrive" and "Set the Controls for the Heart of the Sun," *Dark Side of the Moon*—despite Waters' occasional protestations—was an obvious metaphor for the mental illness that viciously consumed Syd Barrett.

"Amid the chaos there is beauty and hope for mankind," David Gilmour expressed. "The *Dark Side of the Moon* itself is an allusion to the moon and lunacy...what goes on inside people's heads—the subconscious and the unknown."

The "unknown" of "Brain Damage" then morphs into the album's glorious but all-too-brief coda, "Eclipse." Built on a simple, repeating theme, the song carries a unifying message that continues to speak to people on a grand scale, fifty years on.

The seeds to "Eclipse" were originally planted three years earlier, with "Give Birth to a Smile," the warmhearted finale to *The Body*, written and performed by Ron Geesin and Roger Waters. The track not only features a clutch of dynamic women soul singers, similar to the choir on *Dark Side of the Moon*, but also has Ron Geesin playing piano alongside Waters' bandmates, Gilmour, Wright, and Mason, on a rare non-Floyd track.

"It's amazing how Roger Waters made so much out of so little," Brian Ritchie muses. "Waters' contribution to rock was using very simple modular improvisational and compositional elements and reshuffling them successfully for decades. In the process he created a distinctive approach that was accessible up to a stadium level. Not much avant-garde music has ever made it to the stadium.* Perhaps those design ideas were inspired by his architectural studies."

In need of a climactic ending to the album, Roger Waters wrote the lyrics to "End" (as "Eclipse" was first known) on a sheet of notebook paper and first shared it with the band before a gig at Bristol's Colston Hall. But while he composed the music and lyrics and sings the lead vocal on the track, "Eclipse" remained a band effort. Rick Wright's organ glissando lifts the song into a higher realm, a triumphant finale inclusive of all humanity. Like Beethoven's "Ode to Joy," "Eclipse" is an ecstatic anthem, a planetary hymn that reverberates to the upper realms of the heavens—designed, as Beethoven described "Ode to Joy," to "melt the clouds" and "drive the dark of doubt away."

"One day I'll write music that people will pray to," a young Brian Wilson proclaimed, as he battled the demands and ignorance of his band, family, and record company while composing "Good Vibrations," which peaked at No. 1 on the *Billboard* charts in December 1966.

As implied by its title, "Our Prayer," which opened the Beach Boys' lost 1967 opus, *Smile*, radiates a divine quality, like a sparkling incantation intoned by a transcendental barbershop choir of sun-bleached angels with sand between their toes. It's strange (yet not uncommon) that a band so discordant in their interpersonal relationships could create such harmonious music. (The Beatles would also manage to come together while in the thick of discord to coo the mesmerizing "Because" on their farewell album, *Abbey Road*.)

---

* With the possible exception of David Bowie, who shared many of the same influences.

In an interview with *Floydian Slip*, Aubrey Powell waxed poetic about a series of photographs of Pink Floyd taken by Storm Thorgerson in London's Belsize Park that revealed moments of warmth and camaraderie that would eventually dissolve into bitterness following the band's enormous success:

> They're all sitting on a bench or they're camping around, or they got their hands in front of their face or they're eating sandwiches and drinking cups of tea. You see a band in their absolute heyday. It was just before they left to go on their first tour for *Dark Side of the Moon*. Before the album came out, and you see a band with a chemistry so locked together, they are absolutely best friends, best buddies, they're on a roll, they know they've made a great album, and it's all about fun. You never ever saw Pink Floyd like that. There was this enigmatic band that hid behind their spacey music and hid behind their light shows.

As Roger Waters recalled, the sessions for *Dark Side* "were very relaxed." He described the group as being "jolly keen" about making what they believed would become a hit record. Never again would Pink Floyd achieve this level of camaraderie, cooperation, and collaboration.

Band dynamics are complicated. Allegiances continually shift and breakdown, whether fueled by ego, jealousy, or battles over credit and songwriting royalties. "There's no mystery involved. The music often depends on how the band is getting along together," John Frankovic stresses. "When everyone is best friends getting along together, the music thrives. But when they're feuding, there's nothing!"

Pink Floyd flourished best as a unit when each member freely contributed to the project at hand. The result of a group effort, their unique brand of enchantment, built on simple melodies and a mysterious sonic atmosphere that transports the listener beyond the drudgery and ugliness of everyday life to an uncharted, phantasmagoric universe.

For Nick Mason, *Dark Side* represents Pink Floyd's pinnacle, their "last willing collaboration. After that, everything with the band was like drawing teeth; ten years of hanging on to a married name and not having the courage to get divorced."

"Eclipse" offers a hand of kindness, an invitation to participate in a greater sense of humanity beyond our limited individual vision. The song stands in contrast to "Brain Damage," where the echoing maniacal laughter raging inside the lunatic's skull starts to consume our tortured protagonist, who finds himself painted into a corner by the rantings of his raging mind.

Roger Waters is at his most humane on "Eclipse." Lasting just barely over two minutes, the song is Pink Floyd's fleeting "Kumbaya" moment. Lacking all traces of their renowned cynicism, they earnestly beckon the world to come together and unite, despite the hippie dream having recently been beaten to a pulp by the one-two punch of the Manson clan and the Rolling Stones' calamitous Altamont Speedway concert in December 1969.

Like "I'll Be Seeing You" or Vera Lynn's "We'll Meet Again"—songs that conveyed a ray of hope for mankind in the face of the gloom-filled turbulent years of World War II—"Eclipse" offers a promise of better days on the horizon, beyond life's misery and the dreaded mystery of death's veil.

●

Over the years, *Dark Side of the Moon* has become a universal symbol, resonating with human beings across the planet, reaching beyond all borders of country, culture, politics, and religion. But Waters would quickly dispose of such egalitarian sentiments in future projects, his music growing increasingly bleak with "Welcome to the Machine," the Orwellian gloom of *Animals*, and the nightmare vision of *The Wall*.

While Roger wrestled with Syd's whimsical verse, he eventually found his voice in straightforward symbolism and social commentary. *Dark Side of the Moon* "uses the sun and moon as symbols," Waters explained. "The light and the dark, the good and the bad … the life force as opposed to the death force. I think it's a very simple statement, saying all the good things life can offer are there for us to grasp, but that the influence of some dark force in our natures prevents us from seeing them."

Not to count bolts on a battleship, but the words "all," "everyone," and "everything" appear repeatedly throughout the song as the foundation of Waters' mantra. They are found in nearly every line. "Eclipse" reprises earlier sentiments in "Money," as he sings, "And all that you buy, beg, borrow, or steal." A nod to "Us and Them" also reappears, with "all that you fight" and "everyone you slight." No one can deny Waters' economy and craftsmanship in composing this enduring song cycle.

"The word 'all' was derived from the name of God in the Sphere of Jupiter on the Tree of Life, which is known as 'AL,'" Robbi Robb imparts. "AL represents all manifestations of God—abundance majesty, glory et cetera. It is in this sphere where life takes on form. All things come from God (or god, with a small *g*, if you prefer). So here is Roger Waters addressing the great mystery! Whether All or AL. 'ALL that you touch and ALL that you see is ALL that your life will ever be.' There is no place that God is not, right?"

Once more, Waters grappled with the ephemeral nature of "Time" within the lines: "And all that is now / And all that is gone." Then comes the all-inclusive "everything under the sun is in tune," followed by the album's closing twist, which reminds us that the sun is sometimes eclipsed by the moon. Employing universal symbols of the sun and moon, Waters conveys the age-old paradox— forces of light versus dark, the good and bad inherent in human nature, life versus death. This allegory, while quite simple, communicates clearly without extraneous imagery. Much like the Who's tender prayer of "See Me, Feel Me" within the otherwise rocking "We're Not Gonna Take It," "Eclipse" reaches out in a sincere attempt to connect to the greater whole of humanity.

"If you, the listener, are affected by [dark forces], and if that force is a worry to you, well, I feel exactly the same too," Waters reassured his fans.

●

Rick Wright's billowing keyboards seamlessly linked "Brain Damage" and "Eclipse" together as one. Both pieces are capable of standing on their own, but radio stations often played the two together. Of "Eclipse," Gilmour later told *Rolling Stone*, "There's nothing to [the song]. There's no chorus, there's no middle eight; there's just a straight list." So, every four lines, we'll do something different."

Gilmour's vocal harmonies are enhanced by the crew of sultry sirens—Lesley Duncan, Doris Troy, Barry St. John, and Liza Strike (whose vocals previously illuminated Elton John's "Tiny Dancer," from his 1971 album *Madman Across the Water*)—who lend a continuity to the album.

According to Strike, Gilmour directed the vocal session for "Eclipse" knowing "exactly what he wanted, directing the choir, even when they improvised."

As the song ends, the track continues to run for another forty seconds, returning to the pulse that initially ignited the album. It now fades away, leading us back to where we started, but transformed somehow ... a bit wiser, weary, yet hopeful ... perhaps ...

In a live setting, the Floyd often stretched the song out further, as Durga McBroom recalls:

> On the Australian shows, my sister sang the ad-libs at the end of the song and just slaughtered it. We both share the same plus four-octave range, but I have about seven notes below her, and she has seven notes above me. So, she was better suited for it. But that part of the song is where you can really let your hair down. The greatest part of being a musician is that you are paid to be nuts! I let myself get really crazy. The biggest gift that losing my husband [Mark Hudson, who died in July 2015] gave me was to reach another, deeper level of emotion in my songs and music.
>
> In the musical interlude before "Eclipse" starts, there's some crazy laughter on the album [courtesy of the band's roadie, Roger "The Hat" Manifold]. I always did that part live but took it a step further. I'd start giggling and then laugh until I'm belly laughing, guffawing. Then I'd start to cry, and then laugh and cry at the same time and people would just lose it when I did that. It was very cathartic.

Waters claimed to harbor little nostalgia for the band's early days, when they played "Interstellar Overdrive" "for hours and hours." But Pink Floyd's inclination toward excessive jamming cannot be blamed on Barrett alone. While "Echoes" comprised the entire second side of *Meddle*, early versions of "Eclipse" were known to last nearly forty-five minutes when performed during Pink Floyd's 1972 world tour.

While the band became the favorite whipping boys of rock critics on both sides of the pond, *Sounds* magazine proclaimed their October '72 show at the

Wembley Empire Pool (a joint benefit concert for War on Want and Save the Children) embodied "what psychedelic music is all about," with dry ice, flashing strobe effects, and Roger Waters setting his gong ablaze during "Set the Controls for the Heart of the Sun."

●

It wasn't until *Dark Side* was nearly finished that Waters conceived of the idea of recording spoken-word segments that are peppered throughout the album, creating a sonic montage that gives the record a stronger sense of continuity. Writing out a series of questions on index cards, Roger recorded the answers of various people around Abbey Road, from roadies and crewmembers to Paul and Linda McCartney, who were recording *Red Rose Speedway* at the time. Waters was unamused by the McCartneys' coy replies; he had little patience for anyone (not even a former Beatle) "trying to be funny." On the other hand, he found Wings guitarist Henry McCulloch refreshingly honest when justifying his past acts of drunken violence, while Floyd roadie Chris Adamson astounded everyone when he confessed to having been "mad for fucking years." But it was Gerry O'Driscoll's everyman wisdom that dovetailed perfectly with the zeitgeist of *Dark Side of the Moon*.

In his thick Irish accent, Abbey Road's indomitable doorman proclaims, "There is no dark side of the moon, really. As a matter of fact, it's all dark." Upon first hearing this quip, the band unanimously agreed they had to "finish the album off with that!" Alan Parsons later pointed out that Gerry had originally added, "The only thing that makes it look alight is the sun." But, finding his afterthought "anticlimactic," they decided to leave it on the cutting room floor.

While finishing *Dark Side*, Waters and Gilmour apparently had "massive rows," over the album's mix. The guitarist later told *Mojo* magazine he wanted the album to sound "big and swampy," with the spoken-word segments confined to the background. Mason sided with Waters' esthetic choice of a dry mix; Chris Thomas (who'd worked on *The White Album* and John Cale's *1919*, and would later helm definitive platters by the Pretenders and Sex Pistols) was ushered in as "referee" (as David Gilmour dubbed him) to make a few adjustments and help settle the dispute. Not surprisingly, Parsons felt slighted by Thomas' tweaks, claiming his choices did little to change the album's original sound.

Much to his dismay, Thomas recalled Gilmour and Waters separately sneaking into the studio in hopes of manipulating the final mix to their liking. Ask any recording engineer and they will say a sense of diplomacy and detachment are integral to their job. Thankfully, Thomas "didn't see a problem" and found a middle ground. But, in the end, David's atmospheric esthetic won out over Roger's desire for a more stripped-down mix.

Although he didn't get his way, Roger took it as a good sign that his then-wife, Judy, burst into tears after hearing the completed album.

"My God, we'd done something fantastic here," David is said to have murmured the first hearing the glorious coda of "Eclipse" dissolve into silence.

It's also interesting to note that George Martin's orchestral arrangement of the Beatles' "Ticket to Ride" from the *Help!* soundtrack album could be heard playing under O'Driscoll's comments on early pressings of the record. Whether it was eventually edited out due to an artistic choice or a bean counter's demand remains uncertain.

Despite the album's overall grim message of madness, fear, and death, Roger Waters, in an interview with *Classic Albums*, urged fans to follow "the path toward the light, rather than walk into the darkness."

9

OFF THE WALL: THE STRANGE WORLD OF TRIBUTE ALBUMS

While there are over fifty "official" Pink Floyd covers bands operating in America alone, only a few of them reveal a trace of originality in their name choice (making one wonder about the creativity of their presentation). Perhaps the most interesting monikers among the slew of Floyd imitators across the globe are Pink Fraud in the UK and Pink Froyd from San Diego. Not surprisingly, there are three groups performing under the name of Us and Them (in the US, Chile, and UK); Us Not Them, from New York, manages a bit of pluck.

The flood of recorded tributes to Pink Floyd's eighth album is both surprising and predictable. Surprising in that the musicians involved were clearly obsessed with replicating and interpreting music that so many hold as "untouchable." Whether using the original recording as a catalyst for their concepts or as a blueprint to strictly adhere to, there have been quite a few worthy of a listen.

While some might scream sacrilege before even hearing it, the Austin Lounge Lizards' high-gear bluegrass version of "Brain Damage" must be experienced to be believed. Famous for their offbeat humor on tunes like "Jesus Loves Me (But He Can't Stand You)" as well as a cover of Devo's "Kool Whip," these swingin' Lizards handle Pink Floyd's classic with just the right balance of respect and irreverence. The lead-off song on their 1991 album *Lizard Vision*, "Brain Damage" was recorded live, with tight, high-lonesome harmonies, driving banjo, and slippery mandolin leads. The Lizards reinvent Waters' plodding dirge as they whip through the song in two and a half minutes, to the delight of the crowd.

While Roger Waters' "Money" was a cynical celebration of all that pounds and dollars can buy, the Mothers of Invention's *We're Only in It for the Money* was a scathing denouncement of everything hippie, particularly the Beatles' Summer of Love masterpiece, *Sgt. Pepper's Lonely Hearts Club Band*. Nobody was safe from Frank Zappa's stinging sarcasm. He was an equal-opportunity satirist who enjoyed exposing the buffoonery of every stripe of phony and ignoramus, whether right wing or left. Despite his long, scraggly hair, motley band, and virtuosic, often self-indulgent guitar solos, Frank mercilessly skewered the hippies comprising his audience, while having zero tolerance for the commercialism that drove the counterculture or the self-destructive drug lifestyle it extolled. "Flower power sucks!" Frank shouts in a shrill, sped-up voice on *Money*'s "Absolutely Free," while his old-timey "Concentration Moon" offers a "final solution" to the hordes of runaways that flooded Haight-Ashbury in the spring of 1967. "Cop kill a creep—Pow! Pow! Pow!" the band maniacally chants, making you wonder whether Zappa was joking or not.*

If Zappa ever set his sights on desecrating *Dark Side of the Moon*, his musical mockery of the seventies classic would have undoubtedly resembled the Squirrels' *The Not So Bright Side of the Moon*. Released in 2000 by the Seattle indie label Popllama Records, Rob Morgan's brainchild was recorded and mixed in a ten-day whirlwind. Like all the best parody, it is wickedly smart, technically sharp, and worthy (while rarely reverential) of the subject it is lampooning.

Rather kicking the album off with a heartbeat, *The Not So Bright Side* begins with a series of rhythmic hiccups, echoed by laughter, while an obnoxious Cabbage Patch doll voice loosely paraphrases the interviews interspersed throughout the original album. A cheesy, Steely Dan–inspired version of "Breathe" features a

---

* Perhaps the most hilarious/offensive aspect of *Money* was its parody of the famous *Sgt. Pepper* album cover by Cal Schenkel. Beyond spelling their name out in a mess of watermelon and carrots, the Mothers (along with Jimi Hendrix) are pictured with the likes of Rasputin, Soupy Sales, Lee Harvey Oswald, and Pope Paul III.

Originally set for an October 1967 release date, Frank and the Mothers suddenly found themselves facing a potential lawsuit. Despite Zappa personally calling Paul McCartney to let the Fabs in on his prank, *We're Only in It for the Money* was delayed by five months until March 1968, thanks to the suits at Capitol Records, who forced Zappa to reverse the album jacket art and put the photo of his motley band, posed in dresses before a very familiar bright yellow background, on the front, while the original cover was designated to the album's gatefold.

jazzy pedal-steel guitar played by Don Pawlak that conjures the image of Chic Corea playing Texas swing in a dimly lit Waco cocktail lounge. The Squirrels' version of "On the Run" blends a hole-in-the-muffler sequencer with the sounds of someone blowing bubbles, more hiccups, a bit of gargling, a twangy Jew's harp, a nuclear explosion, and a horse whinnying.

The sonic collage leading into "Time" is filled with hilarious touches. While drummer John Hollis plays pots and pans, Morgan adds a variety of tick-tocks and chimes, along with a cuckoo and the electric insect buzz of an alarm clock, topped off with the incessant whooping of a car alarm. "Our neighbor came running down the street to see if his car was getting broken into. Then looked at us weird and walked off," Rob laughed.

Kurt Boloch (of Fastbacks fame) cuts loose with a spaghetti-western lead guitar, laden with gobs of dirty sauce before the band suddenly turns left into a reggae groove on the chorus (three years before the Easy Star All-Stars came along and reworked the entire album into a Jamaican jam).

"I would call us the great rock 'n' roll equalizers," Morgan told journalist Dennis R. White. "We take really shitty songs and we elevate them. Then we take really great songs, and we grind them through the skewer, and we pound it all together into a dough. Basically, we take the entire history of pop music, smash it together into a ball and throw it back in your face. Some people understand it, and some people don't. There's not a lot of middle ground."

There was absolutely no attempt at creating "a middle ground" in the Squirrels' version of "The Great Gig in the Sky," as Joey Klein substitutes Clare Torry's voluptuous gush with his own's psychotic warbling before handing the microphone over to a whining dog appropriately named Ella. Guitarist Jimmy "J. T." Thomas busts a sizzling, snarling lead while Morgan and company quote Frank Zappa's dark ballad from *Zoot Allures,* chanting, "The torture, the torture, the torture never stops!"

The mashup (or, as Rob calls it, "mudley—a muddled medley") of Roger Waters' and Barrett Strong's "Money" is brilliant. Morgan spills and splatters the song's lyrics like beer down his shirt in a performance that no one else except perhaps Jim Morrison could have delivered, had he lived to become an over-the-hill lounge-singer. Enter Skerik, saxophonist with the Seattle tribal jazz/funk band Critters Buggin, who rips the tune apart with some nasty, raspy reed work, before giving way to Jimmy Thomas' lead guitar, which leaves the song a smoldering slag heap.

"When I got the Roger Waters gig in 2000, I had to learn the 'Money' solo note for note," Skerik recalls.

It's a great solo. Dick Parry has a perfect sound for this song. But listening closely, it sounds like it was cobbled together from multiple takes and assembled as one, which made it more challenging to learn. Also, counting rests in 7/4 time signature is much harder than playing the notes. At the sound check at the Gorge [Amphitheater in George, Washington], we played the song and the band stopped after my solo and started clapping. At first, I thought they were clapping for this guy who was walking down the aisle. Then I turned to Roger and realized it was for me. He said, "Congrats, you got the gig." I didn't know the sound check was an audition!

Afterward, the keyboard player told me if I'd made a mistake, they would've used samples to play the solo. They said they had terrible luck with saxophonists on that tour. I played two shows with them and flew on the private jet. It was awesome.

We'd start the second set with "Set the Controls for the Heart of the Sun." The stage was dark, but the audience could tell we were there. I was standing right next to Roger. He leaned over and asked, "Fancy coming to Denver with us?" And I said "No, sorry, I can't, I have a studio session." He looked at me like I was crazy ... like, *Why the fuck are you here in the first place? No gig on earth is gonna be better than this!* And of course, that makes sense now. Also, the record I turned the rest of the tour down for didn't come out for twenty years!

Kevin Crosby's funky popping bass transforms the Squirrel's version of "Us and Them" into a badass space groove with an arrangement that is almost too cool to satirize. "I told Kevin to play it like Bowie's *Let's Dance* ... but at its worst," Morgan laughed. But true to the original, the Squirrels' version employs a full scope of dynamics, until at last unleashing a tsunami of sound, catapulting Skerik's Albert Ayler–inspired sax, sputtering, stuttering, and scorching all the way.

Tom Morrison, whose "internal combustion synthesizer" and various keyboards pour like sonic butterscotch from the speakers, threads fugue-like phrases throughout "Any Colour You Like," while vocals poke holes in the nearly straight-faced arrangement, with chicken clucks and a variety of absurdist vocalese.

Reminiscent of the Bonzo Dog Doo-Dah Band's lunatic brand of nouveau vaudeville, the Squirrels' version of "Brain Damage" is so thoroughly demented and irreverent it could be used in a court of law, should anyone still needed evidence to prove Morgan and company are certifiably insane.

Built on an "oompah" waltz from a pumping fuzz synth tuba and an off-kilter calliope, the Squirrels' "Eclipse" captures the surreal atmosphere of the Beatles' "Being for the Benefit of Mr. Kite." The hiccups and mad laughter return us back to the album's opening.

●

On February 18, 2003 (barely a month shy of the thirtieth anniversary of the release of *Dark Side*), the Easy Star All-Stars released *Dub Side of the Moon*, a fun and refreshingly original take on the Pink Floyd classic. A sense of humor and adventure drives these tracks. While the band clearly loves and respects the original album, they fearlessly interpret and embellish it with some very clever and creative touches. Breathing new life into a time-worn classic with irresistible reggae rhythms accented by funky clavinet riffs and plenty of reverb-drenched rimshots, Easy Star's reimagining of "Money" is cool and brilliant (employing the sound of a bong hit in lieu of coins as the song's downbeat), while their take on "Us and Them" lays down a sexy groove suggestive of early '70s Marvin Gaye. If you had always wished Pink Floyd would kick the groove a little harder so you could dance to their music rather than space out to it, here's your chance!

Two years later, Vocomotion released *Dark Side of the Moon A Cappella*, which spotlights the strength and beauty of Pink Floyd's melodies with a small choir of eight celestial voices. The flexibility and range of their vocalese stretches from the Beach Boys' vanilla "ahh" to the jazzy scat of Lambert, Hendricks, and Ross. You must keep reminding yourself that all of these sounds are being generated by human voices, as they easily replicate everything from sequencers to tick-tocking clocks. Grooves are chanted with beatboxing/vocal percussion by the album's producer, Freddie Feldman, while Wright's hypnotic piano intro to "Great Gig" is brilliantly arranged for voice by Jon Krivitsky, and Gilmour's slide guitar is transformed into a series of sensual "oooh's" and "ahh's."

"I was trying to honor the original recording as much as possible," Krivitsky stresses. "Their harmonies were gorgeous and simple. But when you listen to it repeatedly, like I did in order to write the arrangements, you realize there are some super-complicated passages that you might need a degree just to understand."

"Money" begins with a series of vocal warm-up exercises, until the singers break into a rhythm comprised of "mmm's," coughs, and "hmm's," driven by beatbox rhythm from Feldman, who also growls a bluesy scat solo in lieu of Dick Parry's sax. "Us and Them" seems tailormade for an a cappella arrangement, as milk/honey-pure tonalities pour from a human calliope. "We rehearsed and performed the music together, we recorded each voice independently, in order to isolate all the parts," Jon says. While it's a serious tribute, the members of Vocomotion never seem to lose their sense of fun and wonder. Just hope they show up outside your window on Christmas Eve.

Comprised of two violins, a viola, and a bass, LA's Vitamin String Quartet also added a cello and guitar to a few of the tracks on their *Dark Side* tribute, broadening the album's dynamic. Building off a hypnotic pulse, the VSQ transform "The Great Gig in the Sky" into a melancholy meditation worthy of Chopin, without a showy display of bravura.

Like the loonies sitting on the lawn in a gentle medicated haze, the strings of VSQ flutter and float like white butterflies on a spring day, building toward the chorus of "Brain Damage." A few of the strings whirr and veer off into the ether, evoking a multicolored dragonfly buzzing on the coda of "Grantchester Meadows."

In 2009, the San Francisco "jam-grass" band Poor Man's Whiskey recorded their downhome tribute to Pink Floyd, dubbed *Darkside of the Moonshine*. Kicking off with a round of drunken laughter, the band falls into a percolating take of "Breathe," complete with high-lonesome vocals, flat-picked guitar and mandolin, weeping fiddle, and dobro. To the sound of moonshine dripping from a still, with hound dogs howling in the distance, a bouncy banjo drives their hillbilly version of "On the Run." Clucking chickens and bleating nanny goats add to the atmosphere, until a clutch of rude roosters rouses the band into a mad rambling take of "Time." The feathery tremolo of Jason Beard's mandolin opens the door for Nate Leath's fiddle, which soars to the former heights of Clare Torry's vocal on "The Great Gig in the Sky," a smart interpretation of the piece.

A rhythm track comprised of hiccups and puke sounds lays the foundation to PMW's reimagining of "Money" as "Whiskey." The rewritten lyrics recount the pleasure and pain intrinsic to the "root of all evil," while the arrangement is both tight and driving and will punch you in the head like a gulp of white lightnin':

> *Whiskey, use it as gas*
> *I'm alright Jack,*
> *keep your hands of my glass*

What is striking, once again, is how these songs can transcend any genre they are cast into. They don't just endure these various interpretations, they become infused with new life and energy.

With Josh Brough's banjo clip-clopping like horses' hooves into a prairie sunset, "Us and Them" suddenly resembles a stoned campfire song being howled at the moon by a band of lonesome cowpokes. The album unexpectedly shifts gear with an old-timey, medicine-show feel on "Brain Damage," before bursting open into "Eclipse," Nate Leath's fiddle flying freely over the coda while the band sings "eclipsed by the moon" and the album fades into silence.

Poor Man's Whiskey's take on the classic Hipgnosis album cover is another brilliant bit of parody, with the prism replaced by an empty glass jug, illuminated by a beam of white light that splinters into a rainbow. The image is a perfect metaphor for how a sip of white lightnin' illuminates the brain, while causing one to ponder the dark side of alcoholism and its power to eclipse our lives in a similar way as mental illness.

While Wayne Coyne and his band the Flaming Lips are notorious for their wild ideas, their 2010 release *The Flaming Lips and Stardeath and White Dwarfs with*

Henry Rollins and Peaches Doing Dark Side of the Moon is surprisingly tame. Coyne's track-by-track remake allegedly began after he gave a snarky reply to a meddling iTunes rep who suggested the Lips should record a cover version of *Dark Side of the Moon*. Certain the answer would be "maybe not," Coyne and the Lips took the task seriously.

Kicking off the 2013 tribute album *The Many Faces of Pink Floyd: A Journey Through the Inner World of Pink Floyd* with guitar wizard Adrian Belew's cover of "Speak to Me / Breathe" was a smart move. Not only is his evocative vocal well suited for the song's ethereal melody, but Belew—best-known for his inspired fretwork with Zappa, Bowie, Talking Heads, King Crimson, along with a handful of inventive solo albums—is one of the few guitarists who can do justice to Gilmour's playing and is capable of stretching the boundaries of a venerated classic.

While tribute records are all too often a losing proposition, Adrian's interpretation adds a new dimension to the music's legacy. But the standout on the album is Edgar Winter's version of "Money." His organ brings a slinky groove to the song, while his "white trash" vocal adds an edgy, sleaze factor missing from the original. Even better is Edgar's greased-lightning alto sax solo, reminiscent of the late, great Phil Woods. The Winter remake of "Money" also features the impeccable rhythm section of Tony Levin and Bill Bruford, integral to King Crimson's 1981 milestone album *Discipline*.

10

OF WIZARDS, SHARKS, AND HOUSEHOLD OBJECTS

"The '60s were gone, and the early '70s went through a very fallow period," producer Shel Talmy grumbles. "Everything started getting corporate in a very short period of time. It was not the same. The music scene was pretty much all over as we knew it."

While the enormous success of *Dark Side* catapulted the members of Pink Floyd into the upper echelon of fame and fortune, they continued (briefly) to shun the trappings of the ever-growing corporate rock machine. When EMI organized an album release party for *Dark Side* at the London Planetarium, Rick Wright, always the gentleman, was the only bandmember who made an appearance.

Despite Waters claiming "the space thing was a joke" in a 1987 *Rolling Stone* interview, the choice of a planetarium for the album's launch ironically set a precedent for Pink Floyd's music as the go-to soundtrack to a thousand and one laser shows to come.

As Waters pointed out, *Dark Side* was "simply how I was feeling in 1972." He considered it "a well-structured album [that still] holds up very well." Notwithstanding its "meandering passages," he believed the record's tight editing gave the album a crucial continuity, which is "very easy to digest ... easy listening despite being serious." He also found it "interesting that people are still buying it."

So, what is behind the enduring allure of Pink Floyd's enduring masterpiece? Roger Waters himself has insinuated that the album, which mysteriously appeals to one generation after the next, is nothing more than "easy listening" music.

"It may sell on sheer aural sensationalism," Robert Christgau mused in his *Village Voice* review, "but the studio effects do transmute David Gilmour's guitar solos into something more than they were when he played them."

Gary Lucas jokes (sort of):

> The overall "immaculate" and flossed sound of David Gilmour's guitar is the ultimate ear candy that sucks the masses in when he solos, or rather the masses suck in like Gilmour gummy drops. Let's face it, your standard issue acidhead is *not* going to have the dreaded "bad trip" listening to *Dark Side of the Moon*. Unlike *Piper at the Gates of Dawn*, which is sometimes frightening stuff— courtesy of Syd, who dusted off the cobwebs in his lysergically lit cranium to take you down to the far shores of madness on a track like "Bike." Or, even more poignantly, "Jugband Blues," which leaves you staring into the abyss while the abyss stares back at you, and wondering, as Syd sang in the lyrics, "What exactly is a joke?"

◑

Having achieved unfathomable success with *Dark Side of the Moon*, the members of Pink Floyd unsurprisingly gobbled up every thrill and grabbed every bauble their newfound wealth could buy. But in the process of ascending to such previously unimaginable heights, they soon found themselves floundering about in the lukewarm jacuzzi of fame.

For Roger Waters, the picnic ended abruptly with his divorce from his first wife, Judy. And then there was a bit of flak over the band's corporate sponsorship deal with Gini, the French bitter-lemon soft drink company. Many devoted Pink Floyd fans felt bewildered after discovering their counterculture heroes had posed for soda advertisements. The band members were quickly castigated as "sellouts" by idealists who still naively struggled to create a new society whose values were based on something beyond "The Machine" that Pink Floyd raged against.

Attempting to justify their decision to cuddle up to the Establishment, Nick Mason claimed Gini's dubious patronage was meant "to help lower the price of tickets for their fans." While attempting to keep whatever vestiges of their rock 'n' roll bad-boy image alive, he added, "We thought we'd rip them off for loads of cash." But ultimately, Mason confessed, "Neither of those [things] happened."

Waters, not surprisingly, was indifferent to the whole ordeal; he wrote a song called "Bitter Love" that has remained unreleased.

◐

Pink Floyd's choice of projected images to illustrate their live shows also revealed their nouveau-riche status. Filmmaker Anthony Stern contacted the band with the idea of synching clips from his experimental film *Wheel* (a.k.a. *The Rose-Tinted Monocle*), which contained lost footage of Syd and the band performing at the UFO, to their stage presentation of *Dark Side*.

Not surprisingly, the film's poetic subtitle "was an observation of Syd's," Stern explained. "He was looking at my camera, which had a rose-coloured Ratten 85 filter on the lens . . . which makes the film suitable for filming outdoors. We were talking about seeing the world through rose-tinted spectacles. He pointed to the camera and said, 'Well that's a rose-tinted monocle.' That was a typical Syd-type quip."

Wheel "was a diary film that had this romantic, slightly LSD inspired view of the world," Stern added. The subtitle was particularly fitting as it was a perfect metaphor his "rose-tinted approach" to making movies.

Discovering it years later in his "cave of forgotten dreams," Stern felt *Wheel* was a perfect fit for the Floyd's latest project. After showing the band the recently unearthed clips while using *Dark Side* as its soundtrack, the director recalled Waters' response as "incredibly friendly, warm and enthusiastic," while the band responded with unanimous thumbs-up.

But, in the end, the Floyd's manager Steve O'Rourke chose a rapid-fire montage comprised of Lear Jets, New York skyscrapers, piles of cash, and writhing female bodies in various states of undress as the accompanying eye candy to "Money." Validating nearly every cliché of Western capitalism and sexism, the video enticed the Floyd's adolescent fans to believe they could have it all. But the trappings of the rock 'n' roll dream had already begun to overwhelm Rick Wright, who, despite all the glamour and gear, exclaimed, "Christ, all I'm doing is playing an organ!"

One look at Storm Thorgerson's photo on the back cover of *Ummagumma*, with the band's roadies Alan Stiles and Peter Watts (whose lunatic laughter can be heard echoing throughout *Dark Side*) posed with all their gear laid out on a runway at London's Biggin Hill Airport, inspired critic Joel Vance, in the August '73 issue of *Stereo Review*, to liken Pink Floyd's display of auditory artillery to that of the "incidental impedimenta of a panzer division."

"As a kid," Greg Lisher recalls, "I remember seeing that photo on the back of *Ummagumma* with all of their instruments laid out all over the ground, in front of their mobile van and thinking wow, what a statement! Pink Floyd was really such a pioneering art rock band. Trying different approaches and looking at composition from all angles. Stripping things down and building things back up. Breaking the norms just to see where things would go. They really used everything available to them to explore the boundaries of the sonic canvas and take the music to another place."

While the mass of Pink Floyd's equipment (which included a pair of timpani and Roger's giant gong) seemed mind-boggling at the time, it was a mere pittance of what the band's touring arsenal would become.

◖

Searching for a spark of inspiration to catapult themselves out of the carefully constructed niche they now found themselves trapped in, David Gilmour suggested the best strategy would be for the band to do "something weird [and] far out, that nobody could possibly understand." But as guitarist Steve Howe of Yes would later impart, "If you try to look at inspiration too closely, it disappears. It's like that . . . intangible."

One idea everyone agreed on was to record an entire album comprised of various found objects in lieu of employing the standard rock toolkit of guitars, keyboards, bass, and drums.

The seeds for Pink Floyd's ninth album, tentatively titled *Household Objects*, were planted four years earlier, on "Grantchester Meadows." Beginning with the sound of chirping birds over a hypnotic, fingerpicked guitar, Roger Waters' folksy, bucolic ballad eulogizing his Cambridge childhood field of dreams gently fades out as an irritating insect loudly buzzes from speaker to speaker before finally meeting its fate under the quick, hard smack of a flyswatter.

One year later, on their 1970 album *Atom Heart Mother*, the band recorded the evocative instrumental track "Alan's Psychedelic Breakfast." Bookended by the sound of a dripping faucet, the oddly fascinating "Psychedelic Breakfast," is a three-part suite weaving a keyboard fugue from Rick Wright with recordings of glasses clinking and eggs and bacon frying on the stove, before morphing into a lightly fingerpicked tune that David Glimour sweetened with a series of gentle slide riffs. Bits of muttered monologue from Alan Stiles follow, until the entire band falls in, building toward a lovely crescendo before fading out once more with the plink-plonk of a leaky tap.

While Mason considered "Alan's Psychedelic Breakfast" "a fantastic idea," he ultimately felt disappointed in the finished piece "because of the rush" in which it was assembled.

Despite moments of great innovation, Gilmour considered *Atom Heart Mother* the band's least creative effort, most likely due to his lack of interest in and involvement with the project. Although the album went to No. 1 in Britain, Waters dismissed it as "really awful and embarrassing." *Atom Heart Mother*'s flaws began to reveal themselves with its extensive overdubbing process. Noticeable timing issues arose between Nick Mason's trademark plodding drums and Ron Geesin's epic (and excessive) arrangements, which include ten-piece brass fanfares, a twenty-person choir, and a solo cello interlude. Geesin was none too happy with the final outcome, referring to the six-part suite as "Floyd vs. Geesin," or, better yet, "An Argument in E Minor for Soloist and Orchestra."

Stanley Kubrick and a million-plus Pink Floyd fans didn't agree. Initially, the visionary director was so intrigued with the album that he considered using it as the soundtrack to his latest film, an ultraviolent portrait of Britain's societal disintegration called *A Clockwork Orange*. But Waters objected after learning Kubrick intended on editing their music to fit his film. Oddly, *Atom Heart Mother* (particularly the volcanic vocal and bloated brass passages) might have made a better soundtrack to an earlier Kubrick film, 1960's *Spartacus* with Kirk Douglas.

○

One of Pink Floyd's most far-reaching experiments, *Household Objects* was constructed from the recorded sounds of reverberating wine glasses, whooshing brooms, clinking beer bottles, thumping rubber bands, and tapping rulers.

"I've always felt the differentiation between a sound effect and music is a load of shit," Roger Waters expounded in *ZigZag* magazine. Whether generated by a dripping faucet or a guitar, Waters knew that the most basic sound (thanks to a healthy curiosity and multitrack tape recorders) could be used to create new compositions—sometimes with a surprising outcome. He recalled recording a series of tracks without tempered instruments. Instead, the Floyd employed bottles, silverware, and a variety of tools to construct what Waters described to *ZigZag*, as "a really nice piece."

On the surface, the project seemed like a clever prank whose inspiration lay somewhere between cartoonist/inventor Rube Goldberg and avant-garde composer John Cage.

Inspired by the constant flood of new gadgetry on the market intended to make modern life easier, Goldberg employed everyday objects to construct whimsical contraptions that accomplished the simplest of tasks by the most complicated means possible. While people were amazed that Goldberg's grand gizmos actually worked, his prime motivation was to provoke laughter.

A musical pioneer and prankster of the highest order, John Cage created a series of controversial compositions, whether by employing silence (which was inevitably interrupted by the audience coughing or restlessly shifting about in their seats) or preparing pianos with paperclips, rubber erasers, screws, and bolts placed on or between the strings, altering the sound of the instrument. Inviting an element of chance, Cage often employed the ancient Chinese oracle the *I Ching* as the basis for many of his compositions, as Syd Barrett would for the lyrics to his song "Chapter 24."

Cage and Goldberg's avant-garde pranks eventually reached mainstream America on the night of March 3, 1963, when a young, skinny Frank Zappa, in a suit and an even skinnier tie, appeared on *The Steve Allen Show* to teach the hipster host how to "play a bicycle."

"How long have you been playing bike, Frank?" Allen asked the slightly nervous twenty-three-year-old.

"About two weeks," the self-described "composer" replied.

Given a generous fifteen minutes of fame, Frank proceeded to demonstrate "all the different types of sounds you can get from a bicycle," including plucking the spokes of the front wheel, which Allen likened to the tone of a koto (a

Japanese zither). Frank then proceeded to beat the wheels with drumsticks, while Allen claimed to hear "steel drums from Trinidad." Frank also made a series of harsh tones by sawing the spokes with a bass bow and blowing into a hole in the handlebars.

Zappa then invited Allen to join him to perform "a composition" for two bikes and a prerecorded tape comprised of somebody struggling to play clarinet and "a woman singing" recorded off the radio. Zappa suggested the house band join in by making "any noise" as inspiration struck. To their credit, the host and musicians gleefully participated, creating a high-spirited bit of musique concrète. Late-night viewers from coast to coast watched, bemused, as the trombone player held his horn backward and blew into the bell, while the clarinetist removed his mouthpiece to fashion strange bird calls.

Afterward, Allen congratulated Zappa on his "far-sightedness," while adding, in an obvious imitation of Groucho Marx, "And as for your music, don't ever do it around here again!"

Occasional random sounds (when not too overbearing in the mix) can loan an intriguing, unexpected, poetic atmosphere to a song—as was the case with the infamous "Typewriter Tape," recorded with a Sony TC-100 mono tape recorder on June 25, 1964, in Santa Clara, California, while the Jefferson Airplane's Jorma Kaukonen was still a senior in college, when the recent Texas transplant Janis Joplin sang a handful of blues standards accompanied by Jorma's slippery solo guitar riffs and steady foot stomp. In the background, Kaukonen's then-wife, Margareta, can be heard typing a letter. At times, the rhythmic pounding and clatter from her typewriter seems to punctuate their jam, creating a synchronicity that, years later, spurred some fans to interpret the intermittent tapping as some sort of Dadaist drumkit.

According to John Leckie, engineer at George Martin's Air Studios, *Household Objects* was originally the brainstorm of Nick Mason, but constructing an entire album from sound effects apparently became a daunting chore, and the project was sadly shelved. While fragments of the recordings found their way onto *Wish You Were Here*, Alan Parsons claimed he was "disappointed [it] never came to anything."

☾

While an "anything can happen" approach to performing and recording music is an often messy, sometimes thrilling and rewarding prospect, it is routinely frowned upon by managers and record label marketing departments, who ultimately want a product they can sell. The element of chance is just too risky and bad for business.

But there is a kind of kismet that occurs when audio sound and visual imagery are randomly mashed up, as on any given *Monday Night Football* or World Series broadcast. Tired of incessant commentary, you might switch off the sound and cue up some music, when suddenly you notice all the players on the field moving in time to the music, perfectly synchronized like dancers in a cosmic ballet.

At some point, someone—no one knows exactly who—dropped the needle on *Dark Side of the Moon* following Leo the famous MGM lion's third fearsome roar at the start of *The Wizard of Oz*, and two masterpieces of contemporary culture were suddenly, perfectly synchronized. Then, on August 1, 1995, journalist Charles Savage alerted the public to this strange phenomenon with an article in the Indiana newspaper the *Fort Wayne Journal Gazette* titled "The Dark Side of the Rainbow."

The famous film's opening credits roll over a feathery bank of sepia-toned clouds that drift by, from right to left, as "Breathe" begins with David Gilmour's sweeping slide guitar. Dorothy (Judy Garland) and her dog Toto appear, dancing down the long dusty road slicing through the wide-open Kansas prairie. Ignored by her fretful Aunt Em (Clara Blandick) and absentminded Uncle Henry (Charlie Grapewin), Dorothy balances briefly on a rustic fence rail until she comes tumbling down into the pig pen, as "Breathe" morphs into the ominously minor-keyed electronica of "On the Run." As Dorothy is fished out by Zeke, the friendly farmhand (Bert Lahr), the music seems to reflect her frustration and inner turmoil as dark clouds gather on the distant horizon. She looks longingly to the great expanse of the Midwestern sky, as if a UFO is hovering above, coming to rescue her from the overwhelming doldrums of farm life, as she silently mouths the words to "Over the Rainbow."

As the otherworldly "On the Run" winds down, the clouds part and the sun beams down again on the bucolic Kansas plains. A moment later (approximately at the nine-minute mark), the clocks of "Time" begin to chime and clang, alarming the viewer to the arrival of that nasty prig Miss Almira Gulch (as played by Margaret Hamilton). The wheels of her bicycle seem to spin in perfect synchronicity with the mechanical cacophony of the clocks. Gilmour's reverb-drenched guitar sets the dark emotional tone of the unfolding scene as the dreaded Miss Gulch, heartless in a black hat, has come to take away Dorothy's beloved dog, Toto. If *The Wizard of Oz* had been a silent film, the director could not have chosen a more fitting soundtrack.

There's more . . . the tornado churns in a dark and foreboding spiral to the eerie "The Great Gig in the Sky." And the black-and-white film suddenly bursts into color as a bewildered Dorothy tries to acclimate to the bizarre surroundings of "Munchkinland," while "Money" kicks off side two.

While *The Wizard of Oz* dazzled the public in 1939 with its sweeping transformation, contrasting the mundane (black-and-white) life on the Kansas prairie to the colorful wondrous dreamscape of Oz, filmmakers had already experimented with the new technology of color film as early as 1902. The process called Kinemacolor was used on two short films, *A Visit to the Seaside* in 1908 and *Rive Del Nilo* (*Banks of the Nile*) in 1911. But Kinemacolor was extremely costly, utilizing film originally shot in black-and-white and needing two projectors, each equipped with a red and green filter, along with . . . a prism, needed to blend the two light sources together onto a single screen to create the first color movies.

Another curious moment in *The Dark Side of the Rainbow* occurs when the Wicked Witch of the West, clad in black, faces off with Glenda, the Good Witch of the North, dressed in blue and white, as Gilmour sings, "Black and blue . . . and who knows which is which and who is who," from "Us and Them."

A further strange coincidence occurs as Ray Bolger's weak-in-the-knee Scarecrow goes dancing down the Yellow Brick Road, reeling and collapsing as he mouths the words to another of the film's classic songs, "If I Only Had a Brain." Meanwhile, Roger Waters delivers "Brain Damage," which contains the line, "Got to keep the loonies on the path." The album ends with the return of the primordial pulse as Dorothy leans her ear against the Tinman's chest straining to hear his absent heartbeat.

To imagine the members of Pink Floyd intentionally programming *Dark Side of the Moon* to match the action of *The Wizard of Oz* is total lunacy, and perhaps the greatest example of fan culture gone mad since the "Paul Is Dead" hoax exploded in October 1969 and Beatles fans became convinced the Fabs had dropped a variety of clues that Paul McCartney had "blown his mind out in a car" and *Sgt. Pepper's* emcee—"the one and only Billy Shears"—had secretly replaced Paul, so as not to cause any mass suicides or rash action on the part of their devoted followers. And then there are those who believe Elvis is still alive, claiming they saw him last week, driving a Mr. Softee truck, giving away free ice cream to all the girls and boys.

"It's absolute nonsense," Nick Mason told MTV in 1997. "It has nothing to do with *The Wizard of Oz*. It was all based on *The Sound of Music*," he added dryly. While David Gilmour dismissed the odd synchronicities as the machinations of "a guy with too much time on his hands," Alan Parsons was flat-out "disappointed" when he finally watched it. "If you play any record with the sound turned down on the TV, you will find things that work," he told *Rolling Stone* in 2003.

"I would say anybody who's willing to listen to *Dark Side of the Moon* and watch *The Wizard of Oz* is already a very sensitive, creative person," Flaming Lips' front man Wayne Coyne told *Mother Jones* in April 2010. "If you're willing to do that, you're going to see possibilities in things. So, it does actually work. But I think anything probably would."

While having earned a reputation for being "far out," Coyne claimed he's never been a stoner. "I believe it probably has to do with how stoned you are as to how well you think that [connection] works," he surmised. "For me it never really worked that well, because *Dark Side of the Moon* ends and there's still forty-five minutes left of *The Wizard of Oz*."

According to obsessed "Floydies," this catalog of cosmic coincidences also includes "Echoes." Clocking in at twenty-three minutes, the gorgeous, side-length tone-poem from *Meddle* is said to synch perfectly with the fourth segment of Stanley Kubrick's *2001: A Space Odyssey*, which also happens to be exactly twenty-three minutes long.

Not surprisingly, Roger Waters finds all of this ridiculous. Known for having little patience for flakey fans, Waters blew his top on July 6, 1988, when the madhouse atmosphere of Montreal's Olympic Stadium drove him to the point of distraction. In a moment of mounting frustration, he spit on a rowdy stage jumper while struggling to deliver the gentle intro to "Pigs on the Wing." In defense of what many consider an unconscionable act, Waters asserted, "We wanted the audience to actually listen … I used to get terribly annoyed when they didn't." For better or worse, this sad incident was said to have inspired *The Wall*.

On a brighter note, another link between *Dark Side of the Moon* and *The Wizard of Oz* is the presence and power of rainbows, whether as the symbol of Judy Garland's heart-wrenching plea for escape in "Over the Rainbow" or the stream of color exploding from the prism on the album's pristine cover. In both circumstances, they represent a gateway to another dimension where all mankind will one day be free of heartache and suffering.

Years before *The Dark Side of the Rainbow* dazzled stoners worldwide, Mort Garson had already reimagined the Hollywood classic with his wacky, whimsical 1968 album *The Wozard of IZ (An Electronic Odyssey)*, recounting the adventures of a beatnik chic named Dorothy with heavy New York accent, enhanced with gobs of mascara and Moog synthesizer.

Garson, a Julliard-trained pianist and arranger, boasts one of the strangest discographies in modern music, ranging from sessions with Doris Day and Mel Tormé, to orchestrating corny easy-listening LPs, to helping to forge hits by Paul Revere and the Raiders and Bill Withers. Having met Robert Moog in 1968, Garson immediately understood the synthesizer's capacity as a new "means of expression," employing its mesmerizing effects for incidental music for the July 25, 1969, television broadcast of Armstrong, Aldrin, and Collins landing on the moon. He later recalled conjuring "a big, symphonic sound for the blastoff, some jazzy riffs for the zero [gravity] game of catch, psychedelic music for a section that used negative and diffuse colors on shots taken inside the ship, and a pretty melody for the moon. After all, it's still a lovely moon," he added.

O

One of the most curious examples of how *Dark Side of the Moon* has permeated Western culture is a serious scientific study recently conducted by David H. Evans, PhD, Professor Emeritus of Biology, and his crew at the University of Florida, in Gainesville. Published in December 2021, *Shark Side of the Moon: Are Shark Attacks Related to Lunar Phase?* presents the first global survey investigating the effect of lunar illumination on sharks' predatorial behavior. Dating back to incidents that took place in the 1500s, the study is mainly focused on unprovoked shark attacks from 1970 to 2016 (the years covering the greatest known number of shark-human interactions).

Dr. Evans and his crew didn't mess around. Matching the date and location of attacks with lunar phase data, they created the International Shark Attack File (ISAF) to present their findings. While noting that "lunar light alone is not enough of a mechanism to explain the observed biological changes" in sharks, the study nonetheless "finds statistical evidence for greater-than-expected numbers of shark attacks during lunar phases closer to the full moon." Or, to put it more succinctly, "The results here strongly support the idea that moon phase does play a role in overall risk of shark attack."

So, next time you go skinny dipping on a full moon, splashing about in the glistening waves with your sweetheart, just remember those screams you hear might not belong to Clare Torry on "The Great Gig in the Sky" but rather to yourself or someone you love!

While we're on the subject of screaming, some clever prankster recently created a brilliant mashup/parody by combining a clip of Yoko Ono vocalizing before a small crowd gathered at the Museum of Modern Art with an instrumental track of "The Great Gig in the Sky" mixed beneath her intense cries and screams and posted it on YouTube. No matter how the diminutive Japanese conceptual artist shredded her vocal cords, she never possessed Torry's pipes and vocal control. Yet it's surprising just how well her Kabuki-inspired shrieks work with the classic Pink Floyd track (despite the flood of hateful comments it inspired from the YouTube peanut gallery).

11

SHINE ON, AND ON

While *Dark Side of the Moon* probed the shadowy corridors of inner space, Pink Floyd's 1975 follow-up, *Wish You Were Here*, confronts the "comfortably numb" routine of our daily lives. "Have a Cigar" throws a left hook at the greed and superficiality of the record business, while "Welcome to the Machine" presents a dystopian vision of the future like those found in books by George Orwell and Anthony Burgess. Waters would continue exploring many of these same themes on *Animals* and *The Wall* and into his solo career.

According to David Gilmour, the albatross of success weighed heavily on the band and "trapped us creatively."

"We cracked it. We'd won the pools. What are you supposed to do after that?" Nick Mason asked, pondering the dark side of success. While their sold-out stadium concerts thrilled millions around the globe, the droll drummer likened such events to "Tupperware parties with 50,000 people."

If Pink Floyd were guilty of sacrificing spirit for the sake of form while recording *Dark Side of the Moon*, they made up for it two weeks into their North American tour when they played a legendary midnight show at Radio City Music Hall in New York on Sunday, March 17, 1973. As *Sounds* magazine pointed out, Radio City, which seats just 6,200 people, was one of the few venues the Floyd performed at that was specifically built for live music. (Famous for its annual Christmas pageants and dance reviews by the high-kicking Rockettes, Radio City remains a favorite venue of New Yorkers for attending new film premieres.)

The crowd that night ranged from blissful to the uptight. While some were anxious about getting good seats at a general-admission show, others were already a bit drunk, in keeping with the tradition of St. Patrick's Day, and everybody else was either stoned or tripping for the occasion. No matter what state they were in, the audience had stood in line for hours in near-freezing temperatures. The show ran late, and it was 1:30 in the morning by the time the band appeared, bathed in pink fog, standing on a riser that lifted them above the hallowed stage, as a glowing orb they'd nicknamed "Mr. Screen" flashed a steady stream of colors and images behind them. In the controlled, cushy environs of Radio City Music Hall, the Floyd's lights and quadraphonic sound were never better.

Having forged their reputation on unpredictability and improvisation, Pink Floyd now served up the same well-oiled set every night. And the Radio City gig was no different in that regard. Beginning with a set of "older stuff," Rick Wright heralded "Obscured by Clouds" like an electronic pied piper on his synthesizer, and the band kicked into their first space jam of the night, before shifting gears into the hard groove of "When You're In." The exotic, hypnotic "Set the Controls for the Heart of the Sun" featured a mesmerizing interlude into Rick Wright's synthesized wonderland, propelled by Nick Mason's majestic mallets, about which Danny Frankel points out:

> There was a time in the mid-'60s when some drummers became aware of playing with mallets. They were probably influenced by classical or jazz musicians.* Beyond Nick Mason, whose playing is so expansive you can't tell where it starts or finishes, there was Mick Fleetwood [whose gentle rumble propels Peter Green's lovely "Albatross"]. Other standouts are Mitch Mitchell on Jimi Hendrix's "May This Be Love" [a.k.a. "Waterfall"] and Charlie Watts on the Stones' "Moonlight Mile." These are mostly British drummers, but Maureen Tucker of the Velvet Underground used mallets on "Ocean," "Heroin," and "Venus in Furs." Mo is known for holding a mallet in the right hand [with] a stick turned around in her left. She was influenced by Olatunji, who played in the African split style, using one stick and one hand on his drums.†

---

* Mason claimed to have been inspired by Chico Hamilton after seeing the film *Jazz on a Summer's Day*.

† The Nigerian drummer Michael Babatunde Olatunji's 1959 album *Drums of Passion* was the record that introduced most Americans to world music.

Following "Heart of the Sun" came what was, according to many Floyd connoisseurs, the best live version of the disquieting "Careful with that Axe, Eugene" to ever grace a bootleg cassette. Waters' howl was never more feral and fearsome. Whether inspired by the majestic music hall or the presence of celebrities rumored to have been among the crowd that night, including Andy Warhol, Truman Capote, and members of the Grateful Dead, the band was clearly on fire. "Echoes" sparkled with wonder, as if discovering a ring of moonlit fairies dancing to a funk groove while walking in the deep woods ... or was that just the effect of Rick Wright's synth evoking a school of screaming whales in the deepest indigo of the ocean?

Taking a brief intermission, the band let the fragments of their audience's blown minds settle for a few minutes before returning with the entirety of *Dark Side of the Moon*. Then, leaving the audience slack-jawed and too dazed to respond, they waved goodbye and slipped away with a flippant "Cheers! See ya again!"

A moment later, they returned with a pulverizing encore of "One of These Days." While the mechanical spin-cycle rhythm from Wright's sequencer sent the audience hurtling headfirst through the void, Gilmour's searing guitar tore at the edges of the stratosphere. As if this wasn't enough, Waters bashed a gong (treated with an extra dollop of phase), demolishing whatever was left of the crowd's hearing and brains. Masters of dynamics, Pink Floyd smartly shifted gears once more, playing one last gentle instrumental to help reacquaint their crowd with what they once knew as reality before sending them into the cold spring morning.

While most of the audience would have first heard the new tracks from *Dark Side* played on FM radio stations around New York, the album had been out for only two weeks in the States, yet it was apparent to those assembled on that March night that Pink Floyd's new "masterpiece" was an altogether different beast when witnessed live.

This was certainly the case for *New York Times* critic John Rockwell, who managed to stay up past his usual bedtime to review the band's "sci-fi rock" for the March 19 edition of the paper. While moved by Pink Floyd's "long, brooding instrumentals" and their "clever 360-degree sound system," Rockwell found the concert's visual aspects "pretty spectacular," particularly "the ball [that] emitted steam in a way that suggested photographs of the sun and its corona, cast[ing] dappled mirror-dots throughout the hall." (Hmm ... sounds like our steadfast critic might've caught a contact high from the proliferation of joints being passed around the theater that night.)

Walking out into the early hours of the morning, the exhilarated but exhausted crowd was greeted by one of Mother Nature's best special effects: it was snowing.

○

No matter what heights Pink Floyd scaled, they were certain to meet with the unvarnished vitriol of the press. *Melody Maker* slammed *Dark Side* as "diabolically uninteresting," while John Roundtree's review in *Records and Recording* likened the album to "classical muzak." According to Robert Christgau in the *Village Voice*, Pink Floyd had created "a kitsch masterpiece, taken too seriously by definition, but not without its charm."

Given the task of reviewing the album for *Rolling Stone* in May of 1973, journalist, sometime punk-rocker, and future museum commissioner Loyd Grossman described David Gilmour's voice as "weak and lackluster," while complaining that "The Great Gig in the Sky" "probably could have been shortened or dispensed with." Yet, in his next breath, Grossman praised the album for its "textural and conceptual richness" and "a certain grandeur that exceeds the mere musical melodramatics rarely attempted in rock."

While some were justified in their critiques of the band, who publicly admitted to having become "bored" with the routine of recording and performing, the insults often reached a point of absurdity, as illustrated by Nick Kent in the November 23, 1974, issue of the *NME*. "Infuriated" by the band's "most uninspired" concert at Wembley Empire Pool, Kent let his vendetta against Pink Floyd explode into a bitter tirade. Perturbed by the length of their interminable jams, he pronounced Mason and Waters "the dullest [rhythm section to fill] a large auditorium," while dissing Wright as "merely an adequate keyboard player." Turning his sights on David Gilmour, Kent allowed that he was "an adequate guitarist [who] projects little personality in his playing." But it was the "filthy" hair that hung below his shoulders, "with a spectacular festooning of split ends," that most incensed the critic.

The band's approach, he observed, "seemed to be, better bloody get this over with," before comparing them to "workmen" hired "to dig up the road."

"I cannot think of another rock group who live a more desperately bourgeois existence," he groused. While Kent described the entire affair as a vision of "hell" second only to Dante or Bosch, he returned the following night, whether due to a masochistic streak or an inability to say no to a free ticket. But while Mr. Kent found the sound had improved, the band's attitude evidently had not.

Rude as Kent's comments were, Rick Wright later publicly thanked the cantankerous critic for the much-needed wake-up call. Not surprisingly, Waters wrote off all future criticism from the press as "so much neurotic wailing."

Not everyone felt the need to diss Pink Floyd. As Robert Lindsay wrote in the *Sunday Telegraph* on August 25, 1991, "Pink Floyd had literally wrenched *Dark Side of the Moon* from their audience's imagination." Later in the piece, he compared Pink Floyd's 1975 concert before a crowd of 75,000 at Knebworth House to "a religious event."

In Tibet, large groups of meditators have been known to witness similar emanations of spirits, whether those of benevolent bodhisattvas or of the fierce and terrifying Mahakala, who is known to scare Death to death. In a similar circumstance, critic Joel Vance, in the August 1973 issue of *Stereo Review*, felt the reaper's presence in the strains of an "ARP synthesizer ... and something that sounds like a man suddenly waking up and remembering he has tied a pillowcase over his head," along with Pink Floyd's "comatose vocals. ... The whole thing, and this is not a knock, [hmmm ... really?] would make an excellent score for a horror movie, in black-and-white, like *Night of the Living Dead*."

Not everyone begrudged the Floyd their massive success. As John Peel later wrote, after learning of Gilmour and Mason purchasing matching Ferraris at the astronomical sum of over £160,000 each: "Jealous? Of course, I am! But perhaps they deserve the pleasures such an exotic purchase can bring."

○

While the media played hardball with Pink Floyd, fellow musicians have tended to be a bit more forgiving.

"The album was an absolute piece of perfection!" counters Plasticland's John Frankovic. "It was perfectly played and perfectly produced and mastered. After listening closely to Gilmour's guitar nuances played in the studio, you have to wonder how those parts would sound live, in the moment, when it wasn't quite so controlled. 'Brain Damage' always appealed to me most because it seems to have a looseness the other songs lack."

In the wake of *Dark Side*'s unprecedented success, Roger Waters believed he had some artistic capital to spend, and no one—either in the band or their management—could or was willing to stand up to his stringent personality or concepts.

While on the verge of breaking up, Pink Floyd soldiered on with recording their new album, *Wish You Were Here*. Exhausted by the rancorous atmosphere permeating the sessions, Waters began referring to the project as "Wish You Weren't Here." Nick Mason admitted to DJ Nicky Horne, "I really wish I wasn't there." Gilmour complained that the band were just "floundering around," while claiming Roger's lyrics began to "overshadow the music."

In his 1974 documentary *Pink Floyd Live at Pompeii*, French film director Adrian Maben captured a telling moment when he interviewed Rick Wright at the Abbey Road canteen. Wright subtlety laid bare the roiling emotions that eventually lead to his ejection from the group by Waters in 1985 when he claimed, "We're very tolerant of each other ... there are a lot of things unsaid."

Maben was less subtle when he likened working with Pink Floyd to having to cooperate with the Cambodian dictator and mass murderer Pol Pot. Waters later dismissed the interview scene shot in EMI's canteen, claiming the band was "fucking stoned."*

○

While factions and feuds continued to simmer, the members of Pink Floyd found other ways to spend their time. Having fallen from a second-story window and now permanently confined to a wheelchair, Soft Machine's Robert Wyatt needed serious help. Wyatt had already written the bulk of the songs that would comprise his milestone album *Rock Bottom* when Nick Mason stepped in, loaning his drums, fame, and production skills to the project. Wyatt then appeared on *Top of the Pops* in September 1974, singing his great cover of the

---

* Despite creating the classic stoner album of its day, or perhaps of all time, Pink Floyd, following the tragedy of Syd Barrett, tried to keep their drug intake on the downlow. They admitted to the occasional toke of a joint or slug of Southern Comfort, though, and cocaine was said to be a constant vitamin during tours throughout seventies.

Monkees' "I'm a Believer" with his eyes closed, rocking in his wheelchair with Mason behind him, laying down the beat in a big black hat and handlebar moustache. Helping to transform Neil Diamond's pop valentine into a psychedelic joyride were Matching Mole pianist Dave MacCrae, Fred Frith on lead guitar, and rhythm guitarist Andy Summers (soon to join the Police). When the show's producers tried to convince the recently paralyzed singer to appear in a large wicker basket (after all, it was a family program, and no one should have to suffer the disturbing sight of an entertainer in a wheelchair), Wyatt resolutely told the stuck-up arbitrators of sensitivity and taste to "fuck off!"

In the meantime, Gilmour also pursued a few projects of his own. While playing at a friend's wedding in 1973, he discovered Unicorn, who had been kicking around for the past ten years under various names and formations. Joining the group onstage to jam on Neil Young's "Heart of Gold," Floyd's guitarist was impressed by both their chops and their "spot-on harmonies." After cutting some demos at his home studio, David spirited the band to Olympic Studios, where he produced and played steel guitar on their debut album, *Blue Pine Trees*.

In 1975, a friend passed on a homemade demo tape of a sixteen-year-old singer/songwriter named Kate Bush to David, who was immediately gobsmacked by the young girl's striking originality. Gilmour immediately bankrolled the needed studio time for Kate to cut something more professional sounding, hoping to catch the ears of EMI's tastemakers. Signing Kate soon after, the record company proved absolutely clueless as how to handle her career. Although Bush had already written over two hundred songs and formed a band to play in London pubs, EMI stalled the release of her first album, *The Kick Inside*, until 1978, certain the young, "unexperienced" artist would be crushed either by disappointment or success. In the event, Kate's debut was the first album in the UK by a woman who'd written all of her own songs. It sold over a million copies, while the single "Wuthering Heights" climbed to No. 1 on the British singles charts, where it took up residency for most of March 1978. Once again, the engineers driving "the gravy train" proved they had no sense of direction.

○

Although it remains a blur in the collective memory of all involved, the date generally agreed on is August 21, 1975 (a full moon), when John Lydon first auditioned for Malcolm McLaren, owner of SEX, an "anti-fashion" boutique that sold rubber fetish-wear and provocative punk designs by Vivienne Westwood. McLaren was searching for a lead singer for a new band he was forming. Just nineteen at the time, Lydon, a gnarly street urchin, would soon become the world-renowned "Johnny Rotten." McLaren had spotted him busking for spare change with a violin on the Kings Road. Hunched and ragged, with green hair, the epitome of punk appeared in the doorway of his shop, wearing a Pink Floyd T-shirt held together with safety pins. He'd scrawled the words "I Hate" above a photo of the band and gouged out their eyes. For his audition, Johnny mimed to a jukebox playing Alice Cooper's "I'm Eighteen," grasping a showerhead like a microphone in his white-knuckled fingers. McLaren and the rest of the band—comprised of Steve Jones, Paul Cook, and Glen Matlock—fell over in hysterical laughter. Allegedly, Lydon, whom McLaren described as "an arrogant little shit," only got the gig as the Sex Pistols' front man after threatening to bash Matlock's skull in with a hammer if they said no.

Years later, John Lydon found himself deeply conflicted after Roger Waters invited him to perform some songs from *Dark Side of the Moon* at an LA concert in 2008. Although he claimed to be "thrilled," Lydon hemmed and hawed, "wary of the jam-session end of things. . . . I wanted to do it," the former Mr. Rotten claimed, "just not when twenty thousand people were there."

Two years later, in 2010, Lydon recalled the missed opportunity for the *Guardian*. "You'd have to be daft as a brush to say you didn't like Pink Floyd, they've done great stuff." But then, unable to stop himself from taking a shot at the Establishment the band had come to represent to so many rock fans, the eternal punk added, "They've done rubbish too." Despite slagging off Pink Floyd as pretentious and "holier than thou," Lydon, upon meeting Dave Gilmour, considered him "an alright bloke."

Ever the gentleman, David Gilmour told *Q Magazine* in June 1999, "I thought the Sex Pistols were rather good." After meeting Lydon, Gilmour recalled, in his typically dry manner, "He said he never really hated Pink Floyd and actually he was a bit of a fan. I confess to not having entirely believed it in the first place. I mean, who could hate us?"

THE DARK SIDE OF THE MOON PLAYLIST

FOREWORD

"Lucifer Sam," Pink Floyd

"Interstellar Overdrive," Pink Floyd

"Astronomy Domine," Pink Floyd

"Brain Damage," Pink Floyd

PROLOGUE

"Echoes," Pink Floyd

"Good Vibrations," the Beach Boys

"Strawberry Fields Forever," the Beatles

"American Pie, Pt. 1," Don McLean

1 A LOOSE AND HALLUCINATING CANNON

"Music in the Air," Lou Rawls

"Surfin' Safari," the Beach Boys

"Charmaine," the Bachelors

"Sunshine of Your Love," Cream

"White Room," Cream

"Wreck of the Hesperus," George Harrison

"You Turn Me On," Ian Whitcomb

"Apache," Hank Marvin

"Road Runner," Bo Diddley

"Rock Island Line," Lonnie Donegan / Lead Belly

"Lucy Leave," Syd Barrett / the Tea Set

"King Bee," the Rolling Stones / Slim Harpo

"Papa's About to Get Mad," Pink Anderson

"Every Day in the Week Blues," Pink Anderson

"I'm Gonna Fight for You J. B.," John Mayall

"I'm So Glad," Cream / Skip James

"Smokestack Lightnin'," the Yardbirds / Howlin' Wolf

"House of the Rising Sun," the Animals / Lead Belly

"Eyesight to the Blind," the Who / Sonny Boy Williamson

"Hound Dog," Elvis Presley / Big Mama Thornton

"Ball and Chain," Janis Joplin / Big Mama Thornton

"To Sir with Love," Lulu

"Dedicated Follower of Fashion," the Kinks

"Fire," the Crazy World of Arthur Brown

"Dance the Night Away," Cream

"Granny Takes a Trip," the Purple Gang

"Jugband Blues," Pink Floyd

"Strangely Strange but Oddly Normal," Dr. Strangely Strange

"Arnold Layne," Pink Floyd

"Frosty Morning," Dr. Strangely Strange

"Have You Seen Your Mother, Baby, Standing in the Shadows," the Rolling Stones

"Madam George," Van Morrison

"Walk on the Wild Side," Lou Reed

"See Emily Play," Pink Floyd

"Eleanor Rigby," the Beatles

"Penny Lane," the Beatles

"Johnny B. Goode," Chuck Berry

"Bad Karma," the Holy Modal Rounders

"2,000 Light Years from Home," the Rolling Stones

"Apples and Oranges," Pink Floyd

"Fat Old Sun," Pink Floyd

"My Little Red Book," Love / Manfred Mann

"Raindrops Keep Falling on My Head," B. J. Thomas

"Do You Know the Way to San Jose," Dionne Warwick

"In the Midnight Hour," Wilson Pickett

"My White Bicycle," Tomorrow

"Have a Cigar," Pink Floyd
"Vegetable Man," Syd Barrett
"Dark Globe," Syd Barrett
"Say You Don't Mind," Denny Laine
"Waterloo Sunset," the Kinks
"Shine On You Crazy Diamond," Pink Floyd

THE PLASTIC PAISLEY PIPER INTERLUDE
"Careful with That Axe, Eugene," Pink Floyd
"Eight Miles High," the Byrds
"East-West," the Paul Butterfield Blues Band

2 LET THERE BE MORE LIGHT
"(I Can't Get No) Satisfaction," Devo / the Rolling Stones
"Lucy in the Sky with Diamonds," the Beatles
"They're Coming to Take Me Away Ha-Haaa," Napoleon XIV
"Suzanne," Leonard Cohen
"19th Nervous Breakdown," the Rolling Stones
"Visions of Johanna," Bob Dylan
"The End," the Doors
"Lather," Jefferson Airplane
"From a Prison," Richie Havens
"Comfortably Numb," Pink Floyd
"Alice's Restaurant," Arlo Guthrie
"For What It's Worth," Buffalo Springfield
"21st Century Schizoid Man," King Crimson
"Paranoid," Black Sabbath
"Acute Paranoia Blues," the Kinks
"Merry Go Round," Wild Man Fischer
"Parade at the Funny Farm," Crazy People
"The Rubber Room," Porter Wagoner
"Sorrow on the Rocks," Porter Wagoner
"The Cold Hard Facts of Life," Porter Wagoner
"Time," Pink Floyd

"All Day and All of the Night," the Kinks
"You Really Got Me," the Kinks
"Well Respected Man," the Kinks
"David Watts," the Kinks
"Welcome to the Machine," Pink Floyd
"Another Brick in the Wall," Pink Floyd

A BRIEF CULTURAL HISTORY OF THE MOON
"Cinnamon Girl," Neil Young
"After the Gold Rush," Neil Young
"Harvest Moon," Neil Young
"Helpless," Neil Young
"Rocket 88," Ike Turner and Jackie Brenston
"Space Is the Place," Sun Ra
"Mr. Spaceman," the Byrds
"Space Odyssey," the Byrds
"Moonhead," Pink Floyd
"The Laughing Gnome," David Bowie
"Space Oddity," David Bowie
"Fly Me to the Moon," Frank Sinatra
"People," Barbra Streisand
"Spinning Wheel," Blood, Sweat, and Tears
"Everyday People," Peggy Lee
"Everybody's Gone to the Moon," Jonathan King
"Lunar Rhapsody," Les Baxter
"Set the Controls for the Heart of the Sun," Pink Floyd
"Back to the Wall," Medicine Head
"One and One Is One," Medicine Head
"Eclipse," Pink Floyd

3 SPEAK TO ME / BREATHE
"Speak to Me," Pink Floyd
"Breathe," Pink Floyd
"Air," the Incredible String Band

"Give Birth to a Smile," Ron Geesin and Roger Waters
"She's Not There," the Zombies
"And I Love Her," the Beatles
"Down by the River," Neil Young
"40,000 Headmen," Traffic
"The Sound of Silence," Simon and Garfunkel
"It's Only Love," the Beatles
"You're So Good to Me," the Beach Boys
"Badge," Cream

4 ON THE RUN
"On the Run," Pink Floyd
"The Great Gig in the Sky," Pink Floyd
"Money," Pink Floyd
"Tomorrow Never Knows," the Beatles
"Us and Them," Pink Floyd
"Season of the Witch," Donovan
"Free Four," Pink Floyd
"Spirit in the Sky," Norman Greenbaum
"Wot's ... Uh the Deal," Pink Floyd
"Burning Bridges," Pink Floyd
"Your Saving Grace," Steve Miller Band
"Childhood's End," Pink Floyd

A QUICK HISTORY OF ELECTRONIC SOUND BEFORE PINK FLOYD
"Point Me at the Sky," Pink Floyd
"I Am the Walrus," the Beatles
"Pow R. Toc. H," Pink Floyd
"Dear Prudence," the Beatles
"I Want You," the Beatles
"Across the Universe," the Beatles
"Loup, the First Indian on the Moon," Paul McCartney
"Cybernaut," Tonto's Expanding Head Band
"Tama," Tonto's Expanding Head Band

5 TIME / THE GREAT GIG IN THE SKY

"Big Black Smoke," the Kinks

"Mother," John Lennon

"If I Were a Bell," Miles Davis

"Time Has Come Today," the Chambers Brothers

"Sirius," the Alan Parsons Project

"Vocalise," Anna Moffo

"Bad Trip," 50 Foot Hose

A BRIEF HISTORY OF THE CONCEPT ALBUM FROM 1940 TO 1973

"You're Probably Wondering Why I'm Here," the Mothers of Invention

"Her Majesty," the Beatles

"Whole Lotta Love," Led Zeppelin

"You Need Love," Willie Dixon

"I Ain't Got No Home in This World Anymore," Woody Guthrie

"Lost Highway," Hank Williams

"The Great Atomic Power," the Louvin Brothers

"When I'm Sixty-Four," the Beatles

"Lovely Rita," the Beatles

"She's Leaving Home," the Beatles

"A Day in the Life," the Beatles

"Lucy in the Sky with Diamonds," the Beatles

"Within You Without You," the Beatles

"Cabinessence," the Beach Boys

"In Another Land," the Rolling Stones

"She's a Rainbow," the Rolling Stones

"2000 Light Years from Home," the Rolling Stones

"Crimson and Clover," Tommy James and the Shondells

"Sing This All Together—See What Happens," the Rolling Stones

"The Lantern," the Rolling Stones

"Gomper," the Rolling Stones

"Norwegian Wood," the Beatles

"First There Is a Mountain," Donovan

"Happiness Stan," Small Faces

"HappyDaysToyTown," Small Faces

"Number Three," the Pretty Things

"Misery Factory," the Pretty Things

"She Says Good Morning," the Pretty Things

"Private Sorrow," the Pretty Things

"Amerik," the Pretty Things

"Windenberg," the Pretty Things

"Balloon Burning," the Pretty Things

"Death," the Pretty Things

"Baron Saturday," the Pretty Things

"The Journey," the Pretty Things

"The Amazing Journey," the Who

"Good Morning, Good Morning," the Beatles

"I Can See for Miles," the Who

"A Quick One, While He's Away," the Who

"Yes Sir, No Sir," the Kinks

"Mr. Churchill Says," the Kinks

"Tin Soldier Man," the Kinks

"Victoria," the Kinks

"Pinball Wizard," the Who

"You've Got to Hide Your Love Away," the Beatles

"California Dreamin'," the Mamas and the Papas

"Cross-Eyed Mary," Jethro Tull

"My God," Jethro Tull

"Hymn 43," Jethro Tull

"Wind-Up," Jethro Tull

"Space Oddity," David Bowie

"Life on Mars?," David Bowie

"Hang on to Yourself," David Bowie

"Five Years," David Bowie

"Stone Love," David Bowie

"Suffragette City," David Bowie

"Moonage Daydream," David Bowie

"Starman," David Bowie

"Heroin," the Velvet Underground
"Satellite of Love," Lou Reed
"Berlin," Lou Reed
"Stephanie Says," the Velvet Underground
"Superstition," Stevie Wonder
"You Are the Sunshine of My Life," Stevie Wonder
"Living for the City," Stevie Wonder
"Higher Ground," Stevie Wonder

6 MONEY / US AND THEM
"How Many More Times," Led Zeppelin
"Pigs (Three Different Ones)," Pink Floyd
"Sheep," Pink Floyd
"Hey You," Pink Floyd
"Green Onions," Booker T. and the MG's
"Do Re Mi," Woody Guthrie
"Greenback Dollar," the Kingston Trio
"Money," Barret Strong
"Twist and Shout," the Beatles / the Isley Brothers
"Won't Get Fooled Again," the Who
"Children of the Revolution," T. Rex
"It's Alright Ma, I'm Only Bleeding," Bob Dylan
"Which Side Are You On?," the Almanac Singers / Billy Bragg
"Lay the Lily Low," Baptist hymn
"Jack Munro," traditional folk song
"Working Class Hero," John Lennon
"Just One Look," Doris Troy
"Brown Eyed-Girl," Van Morrison
"Burning of the Midnight Lamp," Jimi Hendrix
"You Can't Always Get What You Want," the Rolling Stones
"When You're In," Pink Floyd

THE STRANGE SAGA OF "LOUIE LOUIE" AND THE MOTHERS OF PREVENTION

"Louie Louie," the Kingsmen / Richard Berry
"I Want to Hold Your Hand," the Beatles
"Lawyers, Guns, and Money," Warren Zevon
"Jet Liner," Steve Miller
"Life in the Fast Lane," the Eagles
"Who Are You," the Who
"The Devil Went Down to Georgia," Charlie Daniels
"Rocky Mountain High," John Denver
"Porn Wars," Frank Zappa

7 ANY COLOUR YOU LIKE

"Any Colour You Like," Pink Floyd
"Funky Dung," Pink Floyd

8 BRAIN DAMAGE / ECLIPSE

"Only a Northern Song," the Beatles
"Have You Got It Yet?," Syd Barrett / Pink Floyd
"Marrakech Express," Crosby, Stills, and Nash
"Ode to Joy," Ludwig van Beethoven
"Our Prayer," the Beach Boys
"Because," the Beatles
"I'll Be Seeing You," Jimmy Durante / Billie Holiday / Big Crosby
"We'll Meet Again," Vera Lynn
"See Me, Feel Me," the Who
"We're Not Gonna Take Take It," the Who
"Ticket to Ride," George Martin's orchestral arrangement from the soundtrack to *Help!*

9 OFF THE WALL

"Brain Damage," the Austin Lounge Lizards
"Jesus Loves Me (But He Can't Stand You)," the Austin Lounge Lizards
"Kool Whip," the Austin Lounge Lizards / Devo

"Nine Types of Industrial Pollution," the Mothers of Invention

"Money," Barrett Strong

"Being for the Benefit of Mr. Kite," the Beatles

10 OF WIZARDS, SHARKS, AND HOUSEHOLD OBJECTS

"Bike," Pink Floyd

"Alan's Psychedelic Breakfast," Pink Floyd

"If I Only Had a Brain," from the soundtrack to *The Wizard of Oz*

"Pigs on the Wing," Pink Floyd

The Hebrides, Opus 26 "Fingal's Cave," Felix Mendelssohn

"Paranoid Android," Radiohead

11 SHINE ON, AND ON

"Albatross," Fleetwood Mac

"May This Be Love" (a.k.a. "Waterfall"), Jimi Hendrix

"Moonlight Mile," Rolling Stones

"Ocean," Velvet Underground

"Heroin," Velvet Underground

"Venus in Furs," Velvet Underground

"I'm a Believer," Robert Wyatt / The Monkees

"Heart of Gold," Neil Young

"Wuthering Heights," Kate Bush

"I'm Eighteen," Alice Cooper

BIBLIOGRAPHY

BOOKS

Acharya, Pundit. *Breath Is Life* (Nyack, NY: Prana Press, 1951)

Beard, Chris Joe. *Taking the Purple: The Extraordinary Story of the Purple Gang—Granny Takes a Trip ... And All That!* (Chris Joe Beard, Kindle edition, 2014)

Blake, Mark. *Comfortably Numb: The Inside Story of Pink Floyd* (Cambridge, MA: Da Capo Press, 2008)

Boyd, Joe. *White Bicycles: Making Music in the 1960s* (London, England: Serpent's Tail, 2006)

Farren, Mick. *Give the Anarchist a Cigarette* (London, England: Jonathan Cape Ltd., 2001)

Gillet, Charlie. *The Sound of the City: The Rise and Fall of Rock and Roll* (New York: Outerbridge and Dienstfrey, 1970)

Gilmore, Mikal. *Stories Done: Writings on the 1960s and Its Discontents* (New York: Free Press, 2008)

Gleason, Ralph J. *The Jefferson Airplane and the San Francisco Sound* (New York: Ballantine Books, 1969)

Goodman, Matthew. *The Sun and the Moon: The Remarkable True Account of Hoaxers, Showmen, Dueling Journalists, and Lunar Man-Bats in Nineteenth Century New York* (New York: Basic Books, 2008)

Hepworth, David. *Never a Dull Moment: 1971, the Year that Rock Exploded* (New York: St. Martin's Griffin, 2016)

Houghton, Mick. *Becoming Elektra: the True Story of Jac Holzman's Visionary Record Label* (London, England: Jawbone, 2016)

Leech, Jeanette. *Seasons They Change: The Story of Acid and Psychedelic Folk* (London, England: Jawbone, 2010)

MacDonald, Bruno. *Pink Floyd—Through the Eyes of the Band, Its Fans, Friends, and Foes* (New York: DaCapo, 1997)

Mason, Nick. *Inside Out: A Personal History of Pink Floyd* (San Francisco: Chronicle Books, 2005)

Miles, Barry. *The British Invasion* (New York: Sterling Publishing Co., 2009)

Miles, Barry. *Hippie* (New York: Sterling Publishing Co., 2009)

Morton, Richard. *Psychedelia 1966–1970* (New York: Jack Sterling Books, 2017)

Oldham, Andrew Loog. *Stoned* (London, England: Vintage, 2001)

Oliver, Paul. *The Story of the Blues* (Radnor, PA: Chilton Book Company, 1975)

Palmer, Robert. *Rock 'n' Roll* (New York: Harmony Books, 1995)

Povey, Glenn, and Russell, Ian. *Pink Floyd: In the Flesh* (New York: St. Martin's Griffin, 1997)

Rogan, Johnny. *Timeless Flight: The Definitive Biography of the Byrds* (Brentwood, England: Square One Books, 1990)

Savage, Jon. *England's Dreaming: Anarchy, Sex Pistols, Punk Rock, and Beyond* (New York: Saint Martin's Press, 1992)

Schaffner, Nicholas. *The British Invasion* (New York: McGraw-Hill Book Company, 1983)

Schaffner, Nicholas. *Saucerful of Secrets: The Pink Floyd Odyssey* (New York: Dell Publishing, 1991)

Shea, Stuart. *Pink Floyd FAQ: Everything Left to Know . . . and More!* (New York: Backbeat Books, 2009)

Smith, Joe. *Off the Record: An Oral History of Popular Music* (New York: Warner Books, 1988)

Townshend, Pete. *Who I Am* (New York: Harper Collins Publishers, 2012)

Unterberger, Richie. *Urban Spacemen and Wayfaring Strangers: Overlooked Innovators and Eccentric Visionaries of '60s Rock* (San Francisco: Backbeat Books, 2000)

Whitcomb, Ian. *Rock Odyssey: A Chronicle of the Sixties* (New York: Limelight Editions, 1994)

Young, Rob. *Electric Eden: Unearthing Britain's Visionary Music* (New York: Faber and Faber, 2010)

Zappa, Frank, with Occhiogrosso, Peter. *The Real Frank Zappa Book* (New York: Poseidon Press, 1989)

ARTICLES

Boyd, Joe. "The Madcap Laughs No More," *Prospect*, August 27, 2006.

Cabo, Ricardo Matos, and Ramos, Manuel. "A Conversation with Anthony Stern," *Lux*, September 10, 2014.

French, Lindsay A, Midway, Stephen R., Evans, David H., and Burgess, George H. "Shark Side of the Moon: Are Shark Attacks Related to Lunar Phase," *Frontiers in Marine Science*, December 1, 2021.

Gloudeman, Nikki. "15 Minutes with Flaming Lips' Wayne Coyne," *Mother Jones*, April 12, 2010.

"Making of Pink Floyd's *Dark Side of the Moon*, The," *Classic Rock*, March 1, 2022.

Matthews, Austin. "The Reluctant Spacerockers," *Shindig!*, January 2014.

McKnight, Connor. "Roger Waters and Nick Mason Zigzag Interview," *ZigZag* no. 32, winter 1973.

Piepenbring, Dan. "A New Machine," *Paris Review*, September 19, 2016.

Roberts, Andy. "A Little Upstate Folk Festival—Woodstock and the ISB," *Be Glad for the Song Has No Ending*, winter 1994.

Satchell-Baeza, Sophia. "Transparent Materials Through Which Light Passes. An Interview with Anthony Stern," *La Furia Umana* No. 21, 2011.

Warburton, Dan. "Keith Rowe," *Paris Transatlantic*, January 2001.

Whittle, Nathan. "S. F. Sorrow—The First Concept Album of Its Kind," *Louder Than War*, August 30, 2018.

WEBSITES

www.braindamage.co.uk

www.floydianslip.com

www.joeboyd.co.uk/writing

www.the-paulmccartney-project.com/song/loup-1st-indian-on-the-moon/

www.youtube.com/watch?v=MVA0PMlhAQo (Norman "Hurricane" Smith Talks About His Recording Sessions with Pink Floyd)

ACKNOWLEDGMENTS

Great thanks to the Assorted Lunatics who generously gave of their time and thoughts to be interviewed for this book! They include:

WILLIE ARON keyboardist and guitarist with Thee Holy Brothers, Syd Straw, and Leonard Cohen

MICHAEL BLAIR percussionist and drummer with Elvis Costello, Lou Reed, Tom Waits

DR. MATTHEW BOBROWSKY astrophysicist and science educator, Delaware State University

ROY BOOK BINDER folk/blues singer/songwriter and guitarist

DARREN BROWN Violent Femmes' road manager

PETE BROWN poet, percussionist, and lyricist with Jack Bruce, for hit songs by Cream and Mountain

CINDY CASHDOLLAR dobro picker and steel guitarist

"TRIXIE DANE" surgery nurse

JONATHAN ELIAS composer and producer with Yes, Grace Jones, and Duran Duran

DANNY FRANKEL drummer with Lou Reed, k.d. lang

JOHN FRANKOVIC bassist with Plasticland

JEFF HAMILTON multi-instrumentalist and producer with Violent Femmes and Beatallica

NORMAN HATHAWAY graphic artist and author

RICHIE HAVENS singer/songwriter and guitarist

BRIAN KEHEW author, producer and engineer, and keyboardist with the Who and the Moog Cookbook

MARIJKE KOGER-DUNHAM artist and clothing designer who, with partner Simon Posthuma, comprised the 1960s Dutch design collective the Fool

JON KRIVITSKY vocalist and arranger for a cappella group Vocomotion

VICTOR KRUMMENACHER bassist and singer/songwriter with Camper van Beethoven and Monks of Doom

CAROL LIPNIK New York singer/songwriter and chanteuse

GREG LISHER guitarist with Camper van Beethoven and Monks of Doom

GARY LUCAS guitarist with Captain Beefheart, guitarist and co-songwriter with Jeff Buckley

CORK MARCHESCHI electronic shaman with the Fifty Foot Hose and neon sculptor. A detail of his piece *L'influenza delle Stelle* (*Influence of the Stars*) can be seen on the book's cover.

ARIF MARDIN producer and arranger

KENNY MARGOLIS keyboardist with Mink DeVille, Smithereens, Cracker

DURGA McBROOM vocalist with Pink Floyd (post–Roger Waters era)

LES McCANN jazz pianist, vocalist, and electronic explorer

ROB MORGAN musical arranger, vocalist, and concept artist with the Squirrels

ROBERT MUSSO guitarist and recording engineer (Bill Laswell / Axiom Records)

IVAN PETER PAWLE bassist and keyboardist with Dr. Strangely Strange

MATT PIUCCI singer/songwriter and guitarist with Rain Parade and Crazy Horse

FERNANDO PERDOMO multi-instrumentalist and producer

GLENN REHSE singer/songwriter, guitarist, and keyboardist with Plasticland

GRANT RICHTER electronics wizard with F/i

BRIAN RITCHIE bassist with Violent Femmes

ROBBI ROBB singer and guitarist with the psychedelic space-rock band the 3rd Ear Experience

STAN SCHNEIR bassist, lap steel player, pedal steel guitarist, and producer with the Incredible String Band

DEREK SEE guitarist with Rain Parade

ELLIOTT SHARP multi-instrumentalist and avant-garde composer

JUDI SILVANO jazz vocalist

SKERIK saxophonist with the Seattle tribal jazz/funk band Critters Buggin'

LARRY "RATSO" SLOMAN author and journalist

PETER STAMPFEL singer, banjoist, fiddler, and guitarist with the Holy
  Modal Rounders

"SUZANNE" mother

SHEL TALMY producer of the Kinks, the Who, Small Faces, Manfred Mann

MICHAEL TEARSON late night DJ on WMMR 93.3, Philadelphia

JOSHUA WHITE Joshua Light Show, Fillmore East, March 8, 1968–June 27,
  1971

HAL WILLNER producer and conceptual artist

ROBIN WILLIAMSON bard and multi-instrumentalist, formerly of the
  Incredible String Band

STEVE WYNN guitarist and singer/songwriter, the Dream Syndicate

●

Grazie to John Cerullo for inspiring me to take the great leap.

Tom Seabrook for his razor-sharp editing.

And to the lovely Marilyn Cvitanic, whose love shines brighter than a July Supermoon.

INDEX

OTHER BOOKS AND ALBUMS BY JOHN KRUTH

BOOKS

Bright Moments: The Life and Legacy of Rahsaan Roland Kirk (Jackalope Press second edition, 2022)

Hold On World: The Lasting Impact of John Lennon and Yoko Ono's Plastic Ono Band, Fifty Years On (Backbeat Books, 2021)

A Friend of the Devil: The Glorification of the Outlaw in Song, from Robin Hood to Rap (Backbeat Books, 2017)

This Bird Has Flown: The Enduring Beauty of Rubber Soul, Fifty Years On (Backbeat Books, 2015)

Rhapsody in Black: The Life and Music of Roy Orbison (Backbeat Books, 2013)

To Live's to Fly: The Ballad of the Late Great Townes Van Zandt (Da Capo Press, 2007)

Bright Moments: The Life and Legacy of Rahsaan Roland Kirk (Welcome Rain Books, 2000)

ALBUMS

Love Letters from the Lazaretto (Smiling Fez Records, 2020)

Forever Ago (ARS Spoletium, 2018)

The Drunken Wind of Life: The Song/Poems of Tin Ujevic (Smiling Fez Records, 2015)

Splitsville (Smiling Fez Records, 2008)

Eva Destruction (Crustacean Records, 2007)

Songs from the Windy Attic (Smiling Fez Records, 2004)

Everywhere You've Never Been (Label M, 2000)

Last Year Was a Great Day (Gadfly Records, 1998)

The Cherry Electric (Weasel Disc, 1995)

Banshee Mandolin (Flying Fish Records, 1992)

Greasy Kid Stuff (Chameleon Records, 1989)

Midnight Snack (Hopewell Records, 1987)

AWARDS

The ASCAP/Deems Taylor Award for "Best Musical Biography" for *To Live's to Fly*, 2008

PERIODICALS

The ASCAP/Deems Taylor Award for "Best Timely Article": "Ceremonies Against the Virus: Bachir Attar of the Master Musicians of Jajouka," published by *Please Kill Me*, 2020

Runner up, "Best Music Articles of 2005," Da Capo Press, 2005